HUSSERL'S PHENOMENOLOGY

Cultural Memory
in
the
Present

Mieke Bal and Hent de Vries, Editors

HUSSERL'S PHENOMENOLOGY

Dan Zahavi

STANFORD UNIVERSITY PRESS

STANFORD, CALIFORNIA

Stanford University Press
Stanford, California

Printed in the United States of America
on acid-free, archival-quality paper.

Library of Congress Cataloging-in-Publication Data
Zahavi, Dan.
  [Husserl's fænomenologi. English]
  Husserl's phenomenology / Dan Zahavi.
      p.   cm. — (Cultural memory in the present)
  Translated by the author.
  Includes bibliographical references and index.
      ISBN 0-8047-4545-5 (cloth) — ISBN 0-8047-4546-3 (paper)
      1. Husserl, Edmund, 1859–1938—Contributions in phenomenology.   2.
  Phenomenology. I. Title. II. Series.
      B3279.H94 Z3513 2003
      193—dc21   2002007738

Original Printing 2003

Typeset by Classic Typography in 11/13.5 Adobe Garamond.

Contents

Preface to the English Edition

A few years ago I was urged to have *Husserls Fænomenologi* (originally published in Danish in 1997) translated and published in English. In the spring of 2000, I started to translate the book myself, and at the same time I used the opportunity to rework the text completely, making numerous improvements, clarifications, and additions to the manuscript. I am grateful to John Drummond (Fordham University) and Eduard Marbach (Universität Bern) for their comments on an early version of the translation.

I am grateful to the director of the Husserl-Archives in Leuven, Professor Rudolf Bernet, for permission to consult and quote from Husserl's unpublished research manuscripts.

Finally, I would like to thank Ryan Gable for having gone through the text and suggested numerous grammatical and linguistic improvements.

Introduction

Edmund Husserl was born into a Jewish family on April 8, 1859, in Proßnitz, Moravia (then part of the Austrian Empire). Between 1876 and 1882 he studied physics, mathematics, astronomy, and philosophy, first in Leipzig, and then in Berlin and Vienna. He defended his doctoral dissertation in mathematics in Vienna in 1882, where, in the years immediately following, he attended lectures by the prominent psychologist and philosopher Franz Brentano. In 1886, Husserl converted to Protestantism, and in 1887 he defended his *Habilitation* on the concept of number at the university in Halle, where he was employed for the next fourteen years as *Privatdozent*. During this period he was particularly interested in a series of foundational problems in epistemology and theory of science. His reflections on these themes resulted in his first major work, *Logische Untersuchungen*, which was published in 1900–1901. As a result of this work, Husserl was invited to the university in Göttingen, where he taught from 1901 to 1916, first as an *Extraordinarius Professor*, and from 1906 as an *Ordinarius Professor*. His next major work, which marked his turn to transcendental philosophy, was published in 1913 under the title *Ideen zu einer reinen Phänomenologie und phänomenologischen Philosophie I* (volumes II and III were published posthumously). In 1916 Husserl moved to Freiburg im Breisgau, where he took the chair in philosophy, succeeding the neo-Kantian Heinrich Rickert. It was during these years that both Edith Stein and Martin Heidegger worked as his assistants. Because of their editorial work, Husserl's famous lectures, the *Vorlesungen zur Phänomenologie des inneren Zeitbewußtseins*, were published in 1928. When Husserl retired in the same year, it was Heidegger who took over his position. During the following years two books were published: *Formale und Transzendentale Logik* (1929) and *Méditations cartésiennes* (1931).[1] In the last five years of his life, Husserl was a victim of the anti-Semitic legislation passed by the Nazis following their assumption of power in Germany in 1933. In that year he was eliminated from the list of university professors and was also—partly as a result of Heidegger's complicity—denied access to the university library. Although Husserl was isolated from the German university milieu during the 1930s, he was invited to give papers in Vienna and Prague in 1935, and it was these lectures that constituted the core of his last major work, *Die Krisis der europäischen Wissenschaften und die transzendentale Phänomenologie*, the first part of which was published in a Yugoslav periodical in 1936.[2]

The books that Husserl himself published were by and large programmatic introductions to phenomenology, making up only a very small part of his enormous production. Husserl had the habit of writing down his reflections each day, and when he died on April 27, 1938, these so-called research manuscripts (together with his lectures manuscripts and still unpublished books) amounted to some 45,000 pages. All of these manuscripts were, for evident reasons, not safe in Germany. (Almost the entire first edition of the posthumously published work *Erfahrung und Urteil*, published in Prague in 1939, was destroyed by the Germans.) But shortly after Husserl's death, a young Franciscan, Hermann Leo Van Breda, succeeded in smuggling all of Husserl's papers out of Germany to a monastery in Belgium. Thus, before the onset of the Second World War, the Husserl-Archives were founded at the Institute of Philosophy in Leuven, where the original manuscripts remain to this day. At the time of the founding of the archives, the critical edition of Husserl's works—*Husserliana*—was begun. The critical edition, which so far contains thirty-four volumes, consists not only of new editions of the works that were published during Husserl's life, but also, and more important, of his previously unpublished works, articles, lectures, papers, and research manuscripts.[3]

*

Husserl's output was enormous, making it unlikely that any one person has ever read everything he wrote. This fact not only makes Husserl research a relatively open affair—one never knows whether a manuscript will suddenly appear that undermines one's interpretation—it also complicates the attempt to write an exhaustive systematic account of his philosophy. Thus, no single work, and particularly not an introduction of this size, could possibly treat all aspects of Husserl's philosophy in full. To put it differently, I have been forced to make choices. Let me say a few words about the perspective I have chosen.

The title of the book is *Husserl's Phenomenology*, and it is exactly the development of his *phenomenology* that I wish to describe, rather than some other more traditional aspects of his philosophy, such as, for example, his formal ontology or his essentialism.

My presentation is divided into three main parts, combining, to a large extent, systematic and chronological perspectives. It roughly follows the development in Husserl's philosophy from the early analyses of logic and intentionality, through his mature transcendental philosophical analyses of reduction and constitution, to his late analyses of intersubjectivity and lifeworld.

The first part focuses on Husserl's early theory of intentionality. On the one hand this is a natural choice, since Husserl's description of the object-directedness of consciousness is among his most important and influential analyses. On the other hand, the analysis of intentionality is particularly suitable as a key to Husserl's thinking in general. A good part of his later analyses, whether it be his detailed analyses of different concrete phenomena or his more fundamental transcendental philosophical reflections, can be seen as attempts to radicalize and develop the insights contained in his initial investigation of the intentionality of consciousness.

In the second part, I account for the main elements in Husserl's transcendental philosophy. Why does Husserl claim that phenomenology is a kind of idealism, and how should one understand his repeated assertion that subjectivity is world-constituting? It is in this context that I will present Husserl's concepts of epoché, reduction, and constitution.

After having described the motives for, the road toward, and the development of the more formal and fundamental core concepts in Husserl's phenomenology, I will, in the third and longest part, turn toward a number of Husserl's more concrete phenomenological analyses. These (by and large) late investigations of body, time, and intersubjectivity should not simply be understood as analyses where Husserl just applies already established phenomenological principles. As will become clear from my presentation, Husserl's analyses of these concrete topics led to a continual revision of the fundamental principles of phenomenology.

*

My presentation will be based on the works that Husserl himself published, on the texts that have subsequently been published in Husserliana, as well as on a number of still unpublished manuscripts. Although this book is intended as an introduction to Husserl's phenomenology, it is more than merely a presentation of the standard reading of Husserl's philosophy. It will also draw upon my own research.

The decision to make use of Husserl's research manuscripts where necessary requires a defense against a common methodological objection. Some (critical) Husserl scholars, for instance Paul Ricoeur, have defended the view that an interpretation should be based almost exclusively on the writings published by Husserl himself.[4] They have argued that it is problematic to make use of unpublished book manuscripts or research manuscripts that Husserl kept back from publication, and that he might even have written for his own eyes only. Texts that he wrote in order to obtain an insight through the very process of writing (Hua 13/xviii–xix) might have been rejected for publication exactly because he was dissatisfied with them.[5] If we look at the account of Husserl's working method and publication plans, which Iso Kern provides in his introduction to the three volumes on intersubjectivity (cf. Hua 14/xx), it is obvious however that the relation between the research manuscripts and the published works is more complex.

First, Husserl worked on many of the late research manuscripts in an attempt to write a definitive systematic presentation of his philosophy, a presentation that never found its final form. But this was not because Husserl was dissatisfied with the content of these manuscripts, but rather because he kept losing himself in minute analyses (Hua 15/xvi, lxi).

Second, and even more importantly, because of his recurrent problems with completing a systematic and comprehensive account, Husserl at times worked quite explicitly for his *Nachlaß* (cf. Hua 14/xix, 15/lxii, lxvii–iii). Thus he frequently remarked that the most important part of his writings were to be found in his manuscripts. For instance, in a letter to Adolf Grimme on April 5, 1931, Husserl remarks: 'Indeed, the largest and, as I actually believe, most important part of my life's work still lies in my manuscripts, scarcely manageable because of their volume' (Hua 15/lxvi; cf. 14/xix).

Last but not least it is also possible to adopt a systematic perspective. If a number of Husserl's unpublished analyses are better worked out and more convincing than the analyses that we find in his published works, there seems to be no philosophical (but only philological) reasons to restrict oneself to the latter.

1

The Early Husserl: Logic, Epistemology, and Intentionality

Logische Untersuchungen (1900–1901) was not Husserl's first published work, but he considered it to constitute his 'breakthrough' to phenomenology (Hua 18/8). It stands out as not only one of Husserl's most important works, but also as a key text in twentieth-century philosophy. It is in *Logische Untersuchungen*, for instance, that one finds Husserl's first treatment of a whole range of key phenomenological concepts, including a detailed analysis of *intentionality*. It is precisely intentionality that has so often been emphasized as a central theme in Husserl's thinking (cf. Hua 3/187), and it will serve well as a guideline for a presentation of his philosophy.

Before I discuss Husserl's early notion of intentionality, however, it will be necessary to give a brief presentation of the contribution that originally made Husserl famous, namely his criticism of what is known as *psychologism*. It was against this critical background that the concept of intentionality was originally introduced.

Husserl's Criticism of Psychologism

Logische Untersuchungen consists of two main parts: the *Prolegomena zur reinen Logik* (which by and large contains the criticism of psychologism) and the six *Untersuchungen zur Phänomenologie und Theorie der Erkenntnis* (which culminates in the analysis of intentionality). In the preface to the work, Husserl briefly describes the aim he has set himself, characterizing

Logische Untersuchungen as providing a new foundation for pure logic and epistemology (Hua 18/6). The status of logic and the conditions for the possibility of scientific knowledge and theory are his particular interests. The concept of epistemology used by Husserl in *Logische Untersuchungen*, however, is slightly different from the one currently in use. According to Husserl, the cardinal question facing a theory of knowledge is to establish how knowledge is possible. The task is not to examine whether (and how) consciousness can attain knowledge of a mind-independent reality. These very types of question, as well as all questions as to whether or not there is an external reality, are rejected by Husserl as being *metaphysical questions*, which have no place in epistemology (Hua 19/26). More generally (and this is very crucial when it comes to an understanding of his early concept of phenomenology), Husserl does not want to commit himself to a specific metaphysics, be it a realism or an idealism. Instead, he wants to address formal questions of a more Kantian flavor, particularly questions concerning the condition of possibility for knowledge (Hua 18/23, 208, 19/12, 26).

Husserl's answer to these questions in the *Prolegomena* proceeds along two tracks. On the one hand, he is engaged in a critical project which seeks to show that a popular position at that time was in fact incapable of accounting for the possibility of knowledge. On the other hand, he tries in a more positive move to spell out some of the conditions that have to be fulfilled if knowledge is to be possible.

The view criticized by Husserl is known as *psychologism*. Its main line of argumentation is as follows: Epistemology is concerned with the cognitive nature of perceiving, believing, judging, and knowing. All of these phenomena, however, are psychical phenomena, and it is therefore obvious that it must be up to psychology to investigate and explore their structure. This also holds true for our scientific and logical reasoning, and ultimately logic must therefore be regarded as a part of psychology and the laws of logic as psycho-logical regularities, whose nature and validity must be empirically investigated (Hua 18/64, 18/89). Thus psychology provides the theoretical foundation for logic.

According to Husserl, this position commits the error of ignoring the fundamental difference that exists between the domain of *logic* and *psychology*. Logic (as well as, for instance, mathematics and formal ontology) is not an empirical science and is not at all concerned with factually existing objects. On the contrary, it investigates ideal structures and laws, and its investigations are characterized by their certainty and exactness. In contrast, psychology is an empirical science that investigates the factual nature of consciousness, and its results are therefore characterized by the same vagueness and mere probability that marks the results of all the other empirical sciences (Hua 18/181). To reduce logic to psychology is consequently a regular category mistake that completely ignores the ideality, apodicticity (indubitable certainty), and aprioricity (nonempirical validity) characterizing the laws of logic (Hua 18/79–80).[1] These features can never be founded in or explained by reference to the factual-empirical nature of the psyche.

The fundamental mistake of psychologism is that it does not distinguish correctly between the *object* of knowledge and the *act* of knowing. Whereas the act is a psychical process that elapses in time and that has a beginning and an end, this does not hold true for the logical principles or mathematical truths that are known (Hua 24/141). When one speaks of a law of logic or refers to mathematical truths, to theories, principles, sentences, and proofs, one does not refer to a subjective experience with a temporal duration, but to something atemporal, objective, and eternally valid. Although the principles of logic are grasped and known by consciousness, we remain conscious of something *ideal* that is irreducible to and utterly different from the *real* psychical acts of knowing.

This distinction between the ideal and real is so fundamental and urgent to Husserl, that in his criticism of psychologism he occasionally approaches a kind of (logical) Platonism: The validity of the ideal principles are independent of anything actually existing.[2]

No truth is a fact, i.e. something determined as to time. A truth can indeed have as its meaning that something is, that a state exists, that a change is going on etc. The truth itself is, however, raised above time: i.e. it makes no sense to attribute temporal being to it, nor to say that it arises or perishes (Hua 18/87 [109–110]).

The truth that 2 + 3 = 5 stands all by itself as a pure truth whether there is a world, and this world with these actual things, or not (Hua 9/23).

In the First Investigation, which carries the title 'Ausdruck und Bedeutung,' Husserl continues his argument for a distinction between the temporal act of knowing and the atemporal nature of ideality, but this time in a meaning-theoretical context. As Husserl points out, when we speak of 'meaning' we can refer to that which we mean, for instance 'that Copenhagen is the capital of Denmark,' but we can also refer to the very act or process of meaning something, and these two uses must be resolutely kept apart. After all, it is possible for different people to entertain the same meaning, to mean the same again and again, although the concrete process of meaning is new in each case. Regardless of how frequently one repeats the theorem of Pythagoras, regardless of whom it is that thinks it, or where and when it happens, it will remain identically the same, although the concrete act of meaning will change in each case (Hua 19/49, 97–98).

Obviously, Husserl is not denying that the meaning of an assertion can be context-dependent, and that the meaning of the assertion might therefore change if the circumstances are different. His point is merely that a formal variation in place, time, and person does not lead to a change in meaning. The truth value of the claim 'In January 2000, the Danish prime minister was a man' will remain the same regardless of whether it is being asserted today or tomorrow, by me or by a friend, in Copenhagen or in Tokyo. (Exceptions to this are occasional or indexical expressions like 'I,' 'here,' and 'now' [Hua 19/85–91].)

The very possibility of *repeating* the same meaning in numerically different acts is in itself a sufficient argument to refute psychologism as a confusion of ideality and reality. If ideality were really reducible to or susceptible to the influence of the temporal, real, and subjective nature of the psychical act, it would be impossible to repeat or share meaning, just as it is impossible to repeat a concrete psychical act the moment it has occurred, not to speak of sharing it with others. (We can of course perform a *similar* act, but similarity is not identity.) But if this really were the case, scientific knowledge as well as ordinary communication and understanding would be impossible (Hua 18/194). Thus, Husserl can argue that psychologism entails a self-refuting skepticism. To attempt a naturalistic and empiristic reduction of ideality to reality is to undermine the very possibility of any theory, including psychologism itself.

As already mentioned, along with his rejection of psychologism Husserl also tries to specify the conditions that have to be fulfilled if knowledge is to be possible, and he distinguishes between two types of ideal and a priori conditions of possibility: the *objective* (logical) and the *subjective* (noetic) (Hua 18/240). The objective conditions are the fundamental principles, structures, and laws that constitute the a priori foundation for any possible theory and that cannot be violated without violating the very concept of theory. Husserl here mentions the demand for consistency and noncontradiction (Hua 18/119). More surprisingly, however, Husserl also calls attention to the so-called *noetic* conditions of possibility. These are the conditions that have to be fulfilled if we are to speak of realized knowledge in the subjective sense. If the knowing subject did not possess an ability to distinguish between truth and falsity, between validity and nonvalidity, fact and essence, evidence and absurdity, then objective and scientific knowledge would not have been possible either (Hua 18/240, 3/127). It might be tempting to ask if this does not lead Husserl back into a kind of psychologism, but obviously consciousness can be investigated by disciplines other than empirical psychology, and as Husserl emphasizes, he is not interested in real or causal conditions of possibility, but in ideal ones. That is, his aim is not to discover the factual psychological or neurological conditions that have to be fulfilled if members of Homo sapiens sapiens are actually and in fact to attain knowledge, but to explore the abilities that any subject (regardless of its empirical or material constitution) has to be in possession of if it is to be capable of knowledge (Hua 18/119, 240).

This opening toward subjectivity becomes even more manifest if one takes the step from the *Prolegomena* to the second part of *Logische Untersuchungen*. The central and positive task of the *Prolegomena* was to show that objectivity and scientific knowledge presuppose ideality. Even if it is impossible to reconcile scientific objectivity with a psychological foundation of logic, one is however still confronted with the apparent paradox that objective truths are known in subjective acts of knowing. And, as Husserl points out, this relation between the objective ideality and the subjective act has to be investigated and clarified if we wish to attain a more substantial understanding of the possibility of knowledge. We need to determine how the idealities are justified and validated by an epistemic agent.

Husserl's distinction between the ideal and the real is in many ways similar to Gottlob Frege's distinction. But the very important difference between the phenomenological and the Fregean criticism of psychologism is that Husserl believed it to be necessary to follow up on this criticism by way of an analysis of intentionality, and this interest in subjectivity and the first-person perspective is not shared by Frege.[3]

According to Husserl, psychologism can be radically overcome only if it is possible to present an alternative account of the status of logic and objectivity. But in order to do so, it is necessary to pay direct attention to the ideal objects themselves, and not merely make do with empty and speculative hypotheses. This requires a return to the things themselves, to base our considerations only on that which is actually *given*. To phrase it differently, if we are to examine in a nonprejudicial manner what ideality or reality is, we need to pay attention to its experiential givenness. But in order to do so it will also be necessary to undertake an investigation of consciousness, since it is only in, or rather for, consciousness that something can appear. Thus, if we wish to clarify the true status of ideal logical principles or real physical objects we have to turn toward the subjectivity that experiences these principles and objects, for it is only there that they show themselves as what they are (Hua 19/9–13, 3/III, 3/53). Consequently, the answers to the fundamental questions that we find in epistemology and in the theory of science call for an 'unnatural' change of interest. Instead of paying attention to the objects, we must reflect on, thematize, and analyze the acts of consciousness. It is only in this way that we will be able to reach an understanding of the relation between the act of knowing and the object of knowledge (Hua 19/14).

Despite Husserl's strong criticism of psychologism, his interest in the fundamental problems of epistemology made it necessary for him to return to consciousness. Occasionally, *Logische Untersuchungen* has been described as a deeply divided work: *Prolegomena zur reinen Logik* is characterized by the criticism of psychologism, whereas *Untersuchungen zur Phänomenologie und Theorie der Erkenntnis* culminates in a descriptive analysis of consciousness—but as Husserl writes in the new preface to the second edition of *Logische Untersuchungen*, the opposition is more apparent than real. We are dealing with a work consisting of a series of systematically related investigations that approach an increasingly complex level of reflection. And only a superficial reading could lead to the misunderstanding that the work should commit itself to a new type of psychologism (Hua 18/11, 19/535, 24/201). Although Husserl himself in the first edition had been so imprudent to characterize phenomenology as a *descriptive psychology*, he soon realized that this was a serious mistake (Hua 22/206–208), for he was interested neither in an analysis of the psycho-physical constitution of man, nor in an investigation of empirical consciousness, but in an understanding of that which intrinsically and in principle characterizes perceptions, judgments, feelings, and so forth (Hua 19/23, 357, 22/206–208).

Let me briefly summarize the account given so far. Husserl criticizes the psychologistic attempt to reduce ideality to psychical processes. A proper analysis shows the irreducible difference between the act of knowing and the object of knowledge (in this case, the laws of logic). This difference must be maintained, although there remains a connection between the two, a connection that an adequate analysis has to explore if it is not to make do with empty postulates. If one wants to understand ideality, one ultimately has to return to the conscious acts in which it is given. This return to subjectivity is not a relapse back into psychologism, however. First of all, there is no attempt to *reduce* the object to the acts, but only an attempt to understand the object in *relation* or *correlation* to the acts. Secondly, Husserl wants to *understand* and *describe* the a priori structure of these acts. He is not interested in a naturalistic *explanation* that seeks to uncover their biological genesis or neurological basis.

The Concept of Intentionality

Let us now proceed to the second part of the *Logische Untersuchungen*, to the part entitled *Untersuchungen zur Phänomenologie und Theorie der Erkenntnis*. In the Fifth and Sixth Investigation Husserl is occupied with the question of what it means to be conscious. As already mentioned, this does not refer to an analysis of the empirical conditions that have to be fulfilled in order for Homo sapiens sapiens to be conscious—for instance the possession of a sufficiently developed brain, an intact sensory apparatus, and so on—but in an analysis of what consciousness as such implies, regardless of whether it belongs to humans, animals, or extraterrestrials (cf. Hua 24/118). Husserl is not interested in sensory physiology or neurology, but in epistemology, and he is claiming that an answer to questions like 'what does it mean to imagine a unicorn,' 'to anticipate the coming harvest,' or 'to think of the square root of 4' can take place in abstraction from the physical and causal elements that empirically and factually might be involved. This is the case not only because Husserl is interested precisely in the strictly invariant and essential nature of consciousness—and not in the nature of the neurological processes that might accompany it empirically—but also because he is interested in the cognitive dimension of consciousness, and not in its biological substratum.[4] Husserl wants to describe our experiences as they are given from a *first-person perspective*, and it is no part of my experience of, say, a withering oak tree, that something is occurring in my brain.[5] Thus, already early on Husserl stresses the (metaphysical) *presuppositionlessness* of phenomenology. Phenomenology is supposed to be neither more nor less than a faithful description of that which appears (be it subjective acts or worldly objects), and should, as a consequence, avoid metaphysical and scientific postulates or speculations (Hua 19/27–28).

In his analysis of the structure of experience, Husserl pays particular attention to a group of experiences that are all characterized by being conscious *of* something, that is, which all possess an object-*directedness*. This attribute is also called *intentionality*. One does not merely love, fear, see, or judge, one loves a beloved, fears something fearful, sees an object, and judges a state of affairs. Regardless of whether we are talking of a perception, thought, judgment, fantasy, doubt, expectation, or recollection, all of these diverse forms of consciousness are characterized by intending objects and cannot be analyzed properly without a look at their objective correlate, that is, the perceived, doubted, expected object.

In a moment I will present some aspects of Husserl's detailed analysis of intentionality, but in order to illustrate why this analysis is so significant, it might be useful to mention some alternative and still prevalent views.

1. A widespread position has been that consciousness can be likened to a container. In itself it has no relation to the world, but if it is influenced causally by an external object, that is, if information (so to speak) enters into it, such a relation can be established. More precisely, a conscious state can be said to be directed at an object if and only if it is influenced causally by the object in question. According to this view, intentionality is a relation between two objects in the world. Thus, there is no fundamental difference between feeling (that is, being conscious of) the heat of the sun, and being heated by the sun. That this *objectivistic* interpretation of intentionality is wrong is relatively easy to show. The real existing spatial objects in my immediate physical surrounding only constitute a very small part of what I can be conscious of. When I am sitting at my desk, I cannot only think about the backside of the moon, I can also think about square circles, unicorns, next Christmas or the principle of noncontradiction. When I am thinking about *absent* objects, *impossible* objects, *nonexisting* objects, *future* objects, or *ideal* objects, my directedness toward these objects is obviously not brought about because I am causally influenced by the objects in question.

When I am thinking about a unicorn, I am not thinking about nothing, but about something, and an analysis of our fantasies and hallucinations quickly reveals that they are also intentional. That it is possible to intend objects that do not exist is a decisive argument against a theory that claims that an object must influence me causally if I am to be conscious of it. To put it differently, my intention does not cease being intentional if it turns out that its object does not exist.

11. If it turns out that the objectivistic interpretation of intentionality is wrong, one could be tempted to argue for a *subjectivistic* interpretation instead. Intentionality is a relation between consciousness and its object. This relation can only obtain if both relata exist. However, since the object does not always exist in reality, intentionality must first and foremost be understood as a relation to an intramental object, that is, to an object immanent to consciousness. But this interpretation is also wrong. As Husserl points out, to assume that the intentional object is act-immanent, that is actually contained in the intention and therefore in possession of the same mode of being as the experience itself, leads to a rejection of the categorial distinction between act and object. That such a distinction does exist is easy to illustrate (Hua 19/385).

First of all, one can point to the identity of the object. We can be directed toward the same object in different mental acts (two numerical different perceptions can perceive a numerical identical tree), and for that reason, the identity of the object cannot depend on the identity of the act. If the object of my intention were really act-immanent, it would imply that I would never be able to experience the same object more than once. Every time I tried to perceive the object anew it would be by means of a new perception and therefore be a new object. For the very same reason it would also be impossible for several subjects to experience the same object. This second misinterpretation of intentionality is simply another version of the same fallacy that we already encountered in *Prolegomena*. Psychologism ignored the difference between the temporal act of knowledge and the ideal object of knowledge and sought to reduce the latter to the first. In a related manner subjectivism (subjective idealism) seeks to reduce the intentional object to mental content.

Second, Husserl ceaselessly emphasizes the difference between the mode of givenness of our acts and the mode of givenness of our objects. If we take a physical object, such as my pen, it is characterized by its *perspectival appearance* (Hua 3/86–89). When we perceive an object we have to distinguish between that which appears and the very appearance, since the object never appears in its totality, but always from a certain limited perspective. (Something similar is the case when we *think* of an object, since we will then always think of it under a certain description or conception.) No single appearance can consequently capture the entire object; the object is never exhausted in a single givenness, but always *transcends* it. Not in the sense that the object somehow hides behind the appearances—as an unknowable Kantian thing in itself—nor in the sense that it is simply the sum of all the appearances, but in the sense that it is an identity connecting all of the different appearances.

Whereas it is always possible to experience the object from other perspectives than the one from which it is currently given, the situation is different when it comes to the givenness of consciousness itself. If I attempt to thematize my visual perception in reflection, then this perception will not be given perspectivally. It does, so to speak, not have a hidden backside. (It is true that the act is temporally extended and in that sense never given to reflection in its temporal totality, but as Husserl points out, this kind of incompleteness is quite different from the one that characterizes the perspectival givenness of physical objects [Hua 3/94].) But if the object were really intramental, if it were really contained in consciousness and part of the stream of consciousness, it would have to share the nonperspectival givenness of the act, but this is not the case. This not only holds true for our directedness toward real objects, but also for our directedness toward 'unreal' objects, which likewise can be characterized as a directedness toward *transcendent* objects.

If in January 2000 I promise to bring a bottle of Beaujolais vintage 2002 as a present to my father's 80th birthday in 2003, then this promise will be fulfilled if, in 2003, I give a real, physical, bottle of wine as a present. If the object of my promise, which when the promise was made didn't exist, had been a mental object, I would not have been able to fulfill the promise in the said way. A promise that concerns a mental object cannot be fulfilled by presenting an extramental object; if I at first identify the object of my intention with an immanent mental object, it cannot later change and become identical with a transcendent, extramental, object.

If I think about a flute-playing faun, we are confronted with an intentional act with a definite structure that intends a faun. But this faun is not contained immanently in the act. No matter how careful we analyze the act, we will not be able to discover the faun as a part of it. Not only does the faun possess a number of qualities that my consciousness lacks, for instance the ability to jump around and play flute, but in contrast to the act the fantasied faun also appears perspectivally. Moreover, to claim that the objects of hallucinations and fantasies exist psychically would have absurd consequences. It would imply that those pink elephants or golden mountains and so forth which I imagine or hallucinate exist just as truly and actually as the act of imagination itself, for which reason a universal claim like 'there are no golden mountains' would be false (Hua 22/310, 3/49).

If it is accepted that the so-called 'unreal' objects exist neither intramentally nor extramentally, and for that reason do not exist at all, is the consequence then that hallucinations, fantasies, misperceptions, and the like are not intentional? The answer is no. The point Husserl is trying to make is exactly that the acts in question are intentional regardless of whether or not their object exists, and that it, for that very reason, is unnecessary to ascribe the 'unreal' objects a kind of mental existence (or 'intentional inexistence' to use Brentano's terminology) in order to save the intentionality of the acts.

iii. I have frequently talked about the *intentional object*. This is not to be identified with some mental construction, but is simply the object of my intention. If I look at my fountain pen, then it is this real pen, which is my intentional object, and not some mental picture, copy, or representation of the pen (Hua 3/207–208, 22/305). Indeed, Husserl would claim that in the case of perception we have a direct and unmediated acquaintance with the object in question. By making this claim Husserl is defending a form of direct perceptual realism and is thereby colliding with a still very popular theory known as the *representative theory of perception*. This theory starts out with the innocent question of how to establish a relation between the object and the subject of perception. Let us assume that I am looking at a red rose. In this case, I have an experience of the rose, but of course, this cannot mean that the rose qua physical object is present in my consciousness. The representative theory of perception therefore claims that the rose affects my sensory apparatus, and that this causes a mental representation of the rose to arise in my consciousness. According to this theory, then, every perception implies two different entities, the extramental object and the intramental representation.

In contrast, Husserl claims that it is an error to believe that one has clarified the intentional relation between consciousness and object by claiming that the object is outside consciousness and the representation of it is inside (Hua 19/436). The crucial problem for such a theory remains—that is, to explain why the mental representation, which by definition is different from the object, should nevertheless lead us to the object. Husserl's criticism is mainly based on this difficulty, but already the assumption that there are two different entities must be rejected as being unfaithful to experience. When I perceive a rose, then it is this rose, and nothing else which is the object of my perception. To claim that there is also an immanent rose, namely an intramental picture or representation of the rose, is a pure postulate that does not explain anything, as Husserl rightly emphasizes (Hua 3/207–208).

Husserl's main argument against the representative theory of perception consists in an intentional analysis of representations and representational consciousness. Although his criticism is mainly directed against the image version of the representative theory of perception, that is the version that claims that the mental representation refers to the real object by way of similarity (by looking like it), his arguments are more fundamental in nature. Ultimately they strike against all models that claim that our perception is indirect and that it is mediated by something different from the perceptual object itself.

That something represents something different (that X represents Y) is according to Husserl not a natural property of the object in question. An object is not representative in the same way that it is red, extended, or metallic. Regardless of how much two things look alike, it does not make one into a picture or image of the other. Two copies of the same book may look alike, but that does not make one into a representation of the other; and whereas resemblance is a reciprocal relation, this is not the case for representation.[6] On the contrary, if X is to represent Y, X needs to be interpreted as being a representation of Y. It is exactly the interpretation, that is, a particular form of intentionality, that confers X with its representative function. If one takes Dürer's portrait of Emperor Maximilian, then this painting is first and foremost a physical object with a particular appearance. A blue frame, with a canvas, and some layers of paint. It is because of an interpretation that it first becomes a portrait *of* Maximilian, and it is only by means of this interpretation that the painting refers to and represents Maximilian. As Husserl writes,

A painting is only a likeness for a likeness-constituting consciousness, whose imaginative apperception, basing itself on a perception, first gives to its primary, perceptually apparent object the status and meaning of an image. Since the interpretation of anything as an image presupposes an object intentionally given to consciousness, we should plainly have a *regressus in infinitum* were we again to let this latter object be itself constituted through an image, or to speak seriously of a 'perceptual image' immanent in a simple perception, *by way of which* it refers to the 'thing itself' (Hua 19/437 [594, transl. modified]. Cf. Hua 19/398.).

Husserl's analysis shows that the representative reference is parasitic. The object which is interpreted *as* a representation must first be perceived. But in this case, the representative theory of perception must obviously be rejected, since the claim of this theory was that perception itself is made possible through representation. If representation presupposes perception, and more generally, intentionality, it cannot explain it.[7]

According to Husserl, we are 'zunächst und zumeist' directed at real objects in the world. This directedness is direct, that is, unmediated by any mental representations. So, rather than saying that we experience *representations*, one could say that our experiences are *presentational*, and that they *present* the world as having certain features.

*

Given the presentation so far, it should be clear 1) that Husserl claims that intentionality is not merely a feature of our consciousness of actually existing objects, but also something that characterizes our fantasies, our predictions, our recollections, and so forth; and 2) that Husserl argues that the intended object is not itself a part of or contained in consciousness (Hua 19/385).

If we compare a perception of a withering oak tree with a fantasy of a flute-playing faun, it would be 1) false to say that we in the first case are intentionally referring to an object, whereas this is not the case for the fantasy. It would also be wrong to claim 2) that in both cases we are intentionally referring to an existing intramental object. Nor is it the case 3) that in the perception we are intending an extramental or transcendent object, whereas in fantasy we are intending an intramental or immanent object. Finally, it would also be wrong to say 4) that in the first case we are intending an object that exists both immanently and transcendently, whereas we in the second case are intending an object that only exists immanently. No, the correct description must be 5) that in both cases we are intending or referring to a transcendent, extramental object. The difference is that whereas the referent exists in the first case, it does not exist in the second. Schematically viewed:

TABLE I

Different theories of intentionality

	Perception	Fantasy
1. Theory	The act intends an object	The act does not intend an object
2. Theory	The act intends an object which exists immanently	The act intends an object which exists immanently
3. Theory	The act intends an object which exists transcendently	The act intends an object which exists immanently
4. Theory	The act intends an object which exists immanently as well as transcendently	The act intends an object which exists immanently
5. Theory	The act intends a transcendent object, which exists	The act intends a transcendent object, which does not exist, that is, the act contains a reference, but no referent

Against this background it can be claimed that the intentions that are directed toward 'unreal' objects are just as much characterized by their *reference* to or *directedness* toward a transcendent object as are ordinary perceptions. In contrast to normal perceptions, however, the referent does not exist, neither intramentally or extramentally. In the case of a hallucination, the pink elephant exists neither inside nor outside of consciousness, but the act of hallucination still contains a reference to a transcendent, extramental, object (Hua 19/206). As Husserl writes:

If I represent God to myself, or an angel, or an intelligible thing-in-itself, or a physical thing or a round square etc., I mean the transcendent object named in each case, in other words my intentional object: it makes no difference whether this object exists or is imaginary or absurd. 'The object is merely intentional' does not, of course, mean that it exists, but only in an intention, of which it is a real (*reelles*) part, or that some shadow of it exists. It means rather that the intention, the reference to an object so qualified, exists, but not that the object does. If the intentional object exists, the intention, the reference, does not exist alone, but the thing referred to exists also (Hua 19/439 [596]).

In contrast to the so-called natural relations, intentionality is characterized by the fact that it does not presuppose the existence of both relata (for which reason it might be better to stop calling intentionality a relation). If A influences B causally, both A and B must exist; if A intends B, only A must exist. If it is true that I am sitting on a horse, both the horse and I must exist. If it is true that I intend a horse, the horse does not need to exist. Thus, an important aspect of intentionality is exactly its *existence-independency*. It is never the existence of the intentional object that makes the act, be it a perception or a hallucination, intentional. Our mind does not become intentional through an external influence, and it does not lose its intentionality if its object ceases to exist. Intentionality is not an external relation that is brought about when consciousness is influenced by an object, but is, on the contrary, an intrinsic feature of consciousness. The intentional openness of consciousness is an integral part of its being, not something that has to be added from without. Thus, intentionality does not presuppose the existence of two different entities—consciousness and the object. All that is needed for intentionality to occur is the existence of an experience with the appropriate internal structure of object-directedness (Hua 19/386, 427):

That a presentation refers to a certain object in a certain manner, is not due to its acting on some external, independent object, 'directing' itself to it in some literal sense, or doing something to it or with it, as a hand writes with a pen. It is due to nothing that stays outside of the presentation, but to its own inner peculiarity alone (Hua 19/451 [603]).

Against this background it should be obvious that one cannot take Husserl's analysis of intentionality in support of a metaphysical realism, as if Husserl should claim that we can only speak of a mind if there is also something mind-independent toward which it can be directed.[8] The analysis of intentionality 'merely' shows that there are conscious acts that because of their own nature are directed toward transcendent objects. This demonstration is sufficient, however, when it comes to an overcoming of a traditional epistemological problem, namely, the problem of how to make the subject and the object meet. It is not a problem for the subject to reach the object, since the subject is per se self-transcending, per se directed toward something different from itself. In the case of perception, this something is exactly the object itself, and not some image or copy of it.

Thus one of the decisive differences between Husserl's theory of intentionality and the theories that he was influenced by (for instance, Brentano's and Kasimierz Twardowski's theories of intentionality) is that Husserl stubbornly denies that the intentional object should be understood as an intramental content that in the best of cases serves as mediator for our access to the real, mind-transcendent object. As Husserl emphasizes, one can only intend an object if it is the object of our intention, that is, if it is the intentional object:

It need only be said to be acknowledged *that the intentional object of a presentation is the same as its actual object, and on occasion as its external object, and that it is absurd to distinguish between them.* The transcendent object would not be the object of *this* presentation, if it was not *its* intentional object. This is plainly a merely analytic proposition. The object of the presentation, of the 'intention', *is* and *means* what is presented, the intentional object (Hua 19/439 [595–596]).[9]

Thus, Husserl would claim that it is senseless to distinguish between the intentional and the real object. Not in the sense that all intentional objects are real, but in the sense that if the intended object really exists, then it is this real object, and no other, which is our intentional object.

The crucial question is now whether Husserl in *Logische Untersuchungen* is capable of giving a phenomenological account of the difference between the merely intended and the really existing object. When is it legitimate to call an object real? What does it mean that an object exists? In order to answer these questions, it is necessary to take a closer look at Husserl's own positive account, and not merely make do with his criticism of different misinterpretations of intentionality.

Act, Meaning, Object

According to Husserl, one can analyze every intentional experience from three different perspectives. One can focus on the psychical process, and analyse the *immanent* (reelle) *content* of the act. One can analyze the meaning of the experience, and thereby investigate its *intentional content.* Finally, one can focus on that which is intended, that is, on the *intentional object* that the act is conscious of (cf. Hua 19/129). I have just mentioned that the intentional object, far from being some mysterious quasi-real entity, is simply identical with the intended object—but what about the intentional content? As already mentioned, the intentionality of consciousness is not caused by an external influence, but is due to internal moments in the experience itself. Briefly put, it is the intentional content that makes consciousness intentional, furnishing the act with its directedness.

It is obvious that there are different types of consciousness. There is a difference between believing, wishing, or doubting that it is healthy to swim in the Dead Sea, just as there is a difference between watching the moon or a performance of *Swan Lake* (Hua 19/381). According to Husserl, it is possible to classify these differences more systematically, since every act is said to possess an intentional content with two different but inseparable moments.

Every intentional experience is an experience of a specific type, be it an experience of hoping, desiring, remembering, affirming, doubting, fearing, and the like. Husserl called this aspect of the experience the *intentional quality* of the experience. Every intentional experience is also directed at something, is also about something, be it an experience of a deer, a cat, or a mathematical state of affairs. Husserl called the component that specifies what the experience is about the *intentional matter* of the experience (Hua 19/425–426). Needless to say, the same quality can be combined with different matters, and the same matter can be combined with different qualities. It is possible to doubt that 'the inflation will continue,' doubt that 'the election was fair,' or doubt that 'one's next book will be an international bestseller,' just as it is possible to deny that 'the lily is white,' to judge that 'the lily is white,' or to question whether 'the lily is white.' Husserl's distinction between the intentional matter and the intentional quality consequently bears a certain resemblance to the contemporary distinction between propositional content and propositional attitudes (though it is important to emphasize that Husserl by no means took all intentional experiences to be propositional in nature).

Although the quality of the act and the matter of the act are abstract components that cannot exist independently of each other (Hua 19/430), Husserl nevertheless tends to give priority to the matter. According to him, it is the matter that provides the act with its directedness toward an object, whereas the quality merely qualifies this reference; it does not establish it (Hua 19/452).[10] Occasionally, Husserl also designates the matter of the act as the ideal *meaning* or *sense* of the act,[11] and his point is exactly that we intend an object by *meaning* something about it (Hua 19/54, 24/53, 150):

In meaning, a relation to an object is constituted. To use an expression significantly, and to refer expressively to an object (to form a presentation of it), are one and the same (Hua 19/59 [293]).

It is meaning or sense that provides consciousness with its object-directedness (and of course to speak of an object in this context does not necessarily designate an actually existing object, but just an intentional object, that is an intended object). More specifically, the matter does not only determine which object is intended, but also what the object is apprehended or conceived *as*. Thus, it is customary to speak of intentional 'relations' as being conception-dependent. One is not simply conscious of an object, one is always conscious of an object in a particular way, that is, to be intentionally directed at something is to intend something *as* something. One intends (perceives, judges, imagines) an object *as* something, that is, under a certain conception, description or from a certain perspective. To think about the capital of Denmark or about the native town of Niels Bohr, to think of Hillary Clinton's husband or of the last U.S. president in the twentieth century, to think about the sum of 2 + 4 or about the sum of 5 + 1, or to see a Swiss cottage from below or above—in each of these four cases one is thinking of the same object, but under different descriptions, conceptions, or perspectives, that is with different act-matters. Whereas one and the same act-matter can never intend (refer to) different objects, different act-matters can very well intend the same object (Hua 19/430).

Although we always intend the object by virtue of a meaning, it is important to maintain the difference between the *act*, the *meaning*, and the *object*. The object (be it an ideal object like the number 6, or a real object, like my antique watch) should neither be confused with the act (the very process of meaning something) nor with the ideal meaning that enable us to apprehend the object (Hua 19/211). In ordinary cases, we are not directed toward the meaning, but toward the object: 'Our interest, our intention, our thought—mere synonyms if taken in sufficiently wide senses—point exclusively to the thing meant in the sense-giving act' (Hua 19/47 [283]. Cf. Hua 19/108). That the meaning and the object should not be identified is perhaps especially clear from cases where different acts can have different act-matters but the same object.[12]

Although Husserl argues that meaning determines reference, it would be a mistake to think that his theory is only geared toward handling those types of reference that are normally expressed linguistically by the use of definite descriptions, that is, those cases where the matter of the act prescribes a certain object by detailing its properties descriptively. On the contrary, already early on Husserl was aware that 'this' refers directly rather than attributively, and even more important, he also realized to what extent perception involves a demonstrative component. When I perceive an object, I intend *this* object, and not just any object with similar properties (Hua 19/553–554).[13]

As already mentioned, Husserl also speaks of the immanent content of the act. What is this supposed to be? Let us assume that I am sitting and examining my pen. I look away for a moment, and then turn my gaze again toward the pen. In this case I have two distinct perceptions (and two distinct appearances) of the same pen (Hua 10/8). But where should we locate the difference? It is the same intentional object and the same intentional content, but we are dealing with two numerically distinct perceptions, two mental processes with their own separate immanent content. The perception is an experience, a temporal conscious process, and its immanent content are the moments or phases that together make up the concrete act qua psychical process (Hua 19/411). In contrast to the intentional object and the intentional content that transcend the act (after all the same object can be intended with the same ideal meaning in different acts, by me as well as by others) the immanent content is in a strict sense intramental and private. Thus, it makes no sense to speak of the same immanent content occurring in numerically different acts. But what exactly is this immanent content? All acts have an immanent content in the sense of an occurrent subjective intention. In addition, some acts include a further immanent element, namely a sensory component (Hua 19/362, 391, 527–528).

In a moment I will get back to these sensations (*Empfindungen*), but Husserl's description of the intention in terms of an immanent content calls for an explanation. The intention is nothing but the complex of matter and quality, but how can Husserl suddenly claim that this complex is immanent to the temporal flow of the act, when he earlier described it as an ideal intentional content? The solution is to be found in the theory of meaning defended by Husserl in *Logische Untersuchungen*. At that time Husserl understood the relation between the ideal meaning (that which can be repeated by me and shared with others without losing its identity) and the concrete act of meaning (the subjective process of intending something) as a relation between an ideality and a concrete instantiation thereof. As he says, the ideal meaning is the *essence* of the concrete intention: 'Meaning is related to varied acts of meaning . . . just as Redness *in specie* is to the slips of paper which lie here, and which all 'have' the same redness' (Hua 19/106 [330]).[14] The immanent content of an act is consequently an instantiation of an ideal intentional content that could equally well be tokened in other acts of the same type. Whereas the immanent content is literally contained in the act, since it makes up its constituent part, the ideal intentional content maintains a certain independence of the concrete act.

In order to clarify what Husserl understands by sensations, let me return to the example given above. I am sitting with the pen in my hand and turn it around in order to examine it carefully. In this process, I am always directed toward the same object and am constantly conscious of the pen. But this consciousness of one and the same object is so to speak established across a manifold. Not only because my perception qua temporal process is changing all the time, but also because I am constantly living through a changing manifold of visual and tactual sensations (Hua 19/396, 3/84).

These sensations are neither mental nor perceptual objects—Husserl is not suddenly defending a version of the representative theory of perception, he is not claiming that the direct object of our perception is an intramental sense-datum representing the external object. Rather, he is claiming that there are nonintentional experiential elements, moments of experiencing that make up part of the perceptual act. They are part of the experience, not part of that which is perceived. Since different sensory contents can be lived through although one and the same object is intended, that is, since the same object can be intended across different sensations, it is obvious that the two must be distinguished, and that the object cannot be reduced to a complexion of sensations.

Let me repeat: According to Husserl we are not directed toward this intramental content. The sensations constitute the act, but they are not that which is intended, they are not that which the act is conscious *of*. If I am looking at the Empire State Building, then it is this building, and not my visual act, that I perceive. The act and its immanent components are simply lived through (*erlebt*) unthematically and prereflectively (Hua 19/165, 387, 424). An interesting asymmetry is consequently revealed: That which is contained in the act is not that which we intend, and that which we intend is not contained in the act (Hua 10/89).

One crucial question is the following: What is it exactly that makes it possible to perceive an identical and stable object? It cannot be the mere presence of a manifold of sensations. Indeed, Husserl suggests that the sensations are interpreted and apprehended with a specific meaning, and that it is this objectifying apprehension that provides me with consciousness of an object (Hua 19/397). This meaning is, of course, the act-matter, and it is precisely by grasping and interpreting the sensations that the perceptual object is made to appear. It is because of this objectifying interpretation that we can transcend the experienced sensations (in the case of perception) and become directed toward an object. In other words, it is in the interplay between sensations and interpretation that the *appearance* of the object is constituted. To see a pen is to grasp a manifold of sensations with an objectifying and synthesizing interpretation. To hear a violin is to apprehend and classify the experienced manifold.

Apperception is our surplus, which is found in experience itself, in its descriptive content as opposed to the raw existence of sense: it is the act-character which as it were ensouls sense, and is in essence such as to make us perceive this or that object, see this tree, e.g., hear this ringing, smell this scent of flowers etc. etc. *Sensations*, and the acts 'interpreting' them or apperceiving them, are alike experienced, *but they do not appear as objects*: they are not seen, heard or *perceived* by any sense. *Objects* on the other hand, appear and are perceived, but they are not *experienced* (Hua 19/399 [567]).

It is only by being interpreted that the sensations win an intentional reference—only then do we have an object-directed perception. It is exactly because the sensations are in themselves nonintentional, that is, because they lack an intrinsic object-reference (Hua 10/89, 3/92), that they can be interpreted in different ways. In contrast to Brentano, Husserl would consequently *deny* that intentionality is an essential feature of our consciousness. Although the intentional acts constitute an absolutely central group of experiences (Hua 19/392), and although Husserl would later write that intentionality is of cardinal importance insofar as all experiences in some manner or other share in it (Hua 3/187), it is nevertheless the case that not every type of consciousness is an intentional consciousness. Apart from sensations, which are nonintentional, one could also point to a variety of other experiences that also lack an intentional object, for instance happiness, dizziness, nausea, anxiety, and so forth.

We have learned that the core of intentionality consists of the interpretation of something *as* something. As Husserl writes: '[T]he objects of which we are "conscious", are not simply *in* consciousness as in a box, so that they can merely be found in it and snatched at in it; . . . they are first *constituted* as being, what they are for us, and as what they count as for us, in varying forms of objective intention' (Hua 19/169 [385]. Cf. Hua 2/71–75.).

Signitive and Intuitive Givenness

According to Husserl, no intentional experience can lack the components of quality and matter. For that reason he calls this complex the *intentional essence* of the act. Although this intentional essence determines which object is intended, as what it is apprehended (with what properties), and in what way it is intended (as judged, questioned, doubted, and so on), we have, however, still not exhausted the different ways in which an object can be intended. As long as we only focus on our ability to intend or mean something, we can make do with the intentional essence, or as Husserl also calls it, with the *meaning-intention* (Hua 19/432). But the moment we wish to account for the *givenness* of the object, that is, for the object's different modes of appearance, we will have to go beyond the quality-matter dyad. Let me give a concrete example: If one compares the situation where, in the absence of my notebook, I judge 'it is blue' with the situation where the notebook is present, and where I see it and judge 'it is blue,' we are dealing with two acts of judging with the same quality and matter. But there remains an important difference between the two acts, a difference that must concern something beyond the intentional essence. In both cases I am making a judgment about one and the same object—namely the notebook— but whereas in the first situation I have an empty, or as Husserl writes, a merely *signitive* intention, in the second I have an *intuitive*, or, to be more specific, a perceptual intention where the notebook is bodily present (*leib-haftig*) and intuitively given *in propria persona* (Hua 19/434). When we wish to investigate the ways in which an act can intend an object, it is consequently not only possible to vary the quality and matter of the act, it is also possible to vary the *mode of givenness* of the intended object.

In this light, it proves necessary to distinguish the part of the act that makes possible the (qualified) directedness toward an object, that is, the intentional essence, and the part of the act that determines how the object is given. In *Logische Untersuchungen* Husserl mainly distinguishes between the *signitive*, the *imaginative* (*pictorial*), and the *perceptual* givenness (and I will focus on these three modes, but other important forms are fantasy and recollection):[15] I can talk about a withering oak I have never seen, but which I have heard is standing in the backyard, I can see a detailed drawing *of* the oak; or I can perceive the oak myself. Similarly, I can talk about how terrible it must be for homeless people to sleep on the streets; I can see a television program about it; or I can try it myself. These different ways to intend an object are not unrelated. On the contrary, according to Husserl, there is a strict hierarchical relation between them, in the sense that the modes can be ranked according to their ability to give us the object as directly, originally, and optimally as possible. The object can be given more or less directly, that is, it can be more or less *present*. We can also speak of different epistemic levels. The lowest and most empty way in which the object can appear is in the signitive acts. These (linguistic) acts certainly have a reference, but apart from that the object is not given in any fleshed-out manner. The imaginative (pictorial) acts have a certain intuitive content, but like the signitive acts, they intend the object *indirectly*. Whereas the signitive acts intend the object via a contingent representation (a linguistic sign), the pictorial acts intend the object via a representation (picture) that bears a certain similarity to the object. It is only the actual perception that gives us the object directly. This is the only type of intention that presents us with the object itself in its bodily presence (Hua 19/646, 3/90–91). As Husserl puts it, all types of *re*-presentation (*Vergegenwärtigung*) are derived acts that refer to a proper presentation (*Gegenwärtigung*) which is the mode of givenness where the object is given directly, originally, and optimally.

Given the above, it should be evident that Husserl takes linguistic intentions to be less original and fundamental than perceptual intentions. They are, to use a technical term, *founded* intentions. That X is founded on Y doesn't mean that X can simply be derived from or reduced to Y, but simply that X is conditioned by and cannot exist independently of Y (Hua 19/281–282).[16] Thus, Husserl would claim that linguistic meaning is rooted in a prelinguistic and prepredicative encounter with the world. To use the prefix pre- in this context does not only refer to the fact that the experiences in question are temporally prior to language (or language acquisition), but also to the fact that our perceptual acquaintance with the world is a permanent condition of and a source for linguistic meaning. Even though a person might know terms like 'crimson,' 'scarlet,' and 'vermilion,' the person would lack a proper knowledge of the involved concepts if he were blind, and therefore unable to see these colors.

Husserl's concept of prelinguistic experience entails a criticism of the linguistic-philosophical assumption that all meaning is linguistic in nature.[17] For Husserl (as for Maurice Merleau-Ponty) this conception is the outcome of an intellectualistic abstraction that makes it impossible to comprehend how the perceived could ever function as a guiding line for a linguistic description. To detach sense and the sensuous (*Sinn* and *Sinnlichkeit*) from each other, to deny the continuity between the perceptual givenness of an object and its predicative articulation, is to make the relation between conceptual thinking and perception incomprehensible and contingent.[18]

To deny the existence of prelinguistic cognitive competencies, of prelinguistic syntheses of identification, and to claim that every apprehension of something *as* something presupposes language use not only makes it impossible to comprehend how the language user should ever have been able to learn a language in the first place, it also flies in the face of results from contemporary developmental psychology.[19]

Husserl's interest in the dimension of prelinguistic experience (analyses that are worked out in later works such as *Analysen zur passiven Synthesis* and *Erfahrung und Urteil*), does not imply that he completely neglects the function of language. On the contrary, he readily acknowledges that it is impossible to understand the possibility of scientific knowledge without taking language into account (cf. Hua 19/7–8, and p. 136 below). But for Husserl the analysis of the contribution of language is an analysis of something founded.[20]

But let me return to the example with the notebook. If I am looking for my notebook and find it, then we are dealing with a situation where the found notebook, or to be more exact, the perceptually given notebook, satisfies or *fulfills* my intention. Whereas at first I had a mere signitive intention, it is now being fulfilled by a new intention, where the same object is given *intuitively*. That which was first thought is now also seen. The relation between the meaning-intention and its fulfillment in intuition can be compared to the classical relation between concept/thought and intuition (Hua 19/522, 538–539).

Instead of speaking of the emptiness or fullness of the intention, one could also speak of the absence or presence of the intended object (cf. Hua 19/567). So, when Husserl claims that the object is bodily present in perception, that the perception gives us the real object itself, he does not violate the principle of existence-independence that was earlier emphasized as a central feature of intentionality. When Husserl, in this context, speaks of the real object, he is not seeking to introduce another object than the intentional, but is simply speaking of the intentional object in a particular mode of givenness, namely as intuitively present. Husserl is, consequently, trying to avoid operating with a naive concept of being. Just like Kant, Husserl denies that the being of the object is an objective property like blue or heavy. Unlike Kant, however, Husserl does not identify the thing-in-itself (*das Ding an sich*) with the unknown cause of our experience, but simply with that which would fulfill our signitive intention. In short, being is interpreted phenomenologically as a particular mode of *givenness*. The perceptual givenness is identified with the self-presentation of the object (Hua 19/614, 646, 666). As Bernhard Rang writes:

In the relation of fulfillment two intentions directed at the same object coincide in such a fashion that a purely signitive, conceptual intention fulfills 'itself' in another intuitive intention which is directed at the same object. What was earlier 'merely' meant is now there as 'itself' in intuitive fullness. A difference between the merely intentional and the real object persists. But this difference is not a 'real' one, but one concerning the 'modes of givenness'. That is, the object in the *how of its givenness* differs between an 'empty' and an intuitively 'filled' conception. The object *which* is given in this intentional mode between empty and full, however, remains one and the same.[21]

To talk about my notebook, see a photograph of it, or write in it is not to be confronted with three different notebooks but with one and the same notebook given in three different ways. Even though the empty signitive intention and the intuition have the same intentional essence, the latter adds the intuitive fullness (*Fülle*) of the object. Apart from the quality and the matter of the act, the fullness is also an important part of intentionality. It is present in the intuitive acts, and absent in the signitive acts (Hua 19/600, 607–608).

Evidence

Husserl now attempts to understand knowledge, justification, and truth on the basis of this model of fulfillment. As long as we are making *signitive* claims, we are dealing with mere postulates. However these postulates can be confirmed only if our intentions are fulfilled: I cannot remember the color of my notebook, for instance, but think it is blue. I look for it, and when I find it, I realize that I was right. When I no longer merely think the notebook is blue, but intuit it, my belief is confirmed. When the object is intuitively given just as I intended it to be, my belief is justified and true; I am in possession of knowledge. More specifically, knowledge can be characterized as an identification or synthesis between that which is intended and that which is given (Hua 19/539, 566), and truth as an identity between the meant and the given (Hua 19/651–652). It must be emphasized, however, that we are talking of a synthesis of coincidence (*Deckung*) between that which is intended in two different acts, and not of a correspondence between consciousness and a mind-independent object. We are not talking about a classical correspondence theory of truth, since the coincidence in question is a coincidence between two intentions, and not between two separate ontological domains.

In the *Prolegomena*, Husserl claimed that mathematical truths are valid regardless of whether or not there exists a world with human beings. Now he seems to say the opposite, namely that truth is only present in a synthesis of coincidence, that truth is always known truth. This contrast is more apparent than real, however. It is correct that Husserl seeks to connect truth with knowledge, but he is not concerned with factual knowledge, but rather with the possibility of knowledge. A claim is true as long as it *can* be intuitively fulfilled, and not only when it is actually fulfilled.

It is in this context that Husserl introduces the concept of *evidence*. If I think that my notebook is blue and see it, then I realize in evidence that my belief is true. Is this evidence some specific but inexplicable and mysterious *feeling* of certainty that accompanies my belief? Is Husserl arguing that the criterion for truth is a private and infallible feeling? The answer is no. Husserl himself explicitly criticizes the so-called feelings of evidence for being psychological fictions (Hua 3/46, 334) and for leading straight to relativism. One can have feelings of certainty about virtually everything, and for that reason any reference to them is useless as a criterion or even definition of truth (Hua 24/156, 2/59, 18/183). On the contrary, for Husserl evidence in the strict sense of the term designates the ideal of a perfect synthesis of fulfillment where a signitive existence-positing intention (typically a claim) is adequately fulfilled by a corresponding perception, thus providing us with the very self-givenness of the object. Thus, when the object is no longer merely intended but also given intuitively (just as it is intended), it is given evidentially (Hua 19/651, 17/166). Husserl's concept of evidence is thus no attempt to absolutize or immunize the private opinions of the subject. There is nothing particularly private about evidence. Rather, Husserl's concept of evidence entails a claim about intersubjective validity (which I will return to later [cf. p. 116]), and is for that very reason open to criticism. Moreover, the possibility of error is part and parcel of experiential evidence (Hua 17/130), but this fact does not lead to skepticism, nor does it annul the performance of the evidence. For the only thing that can defeat a particular evidence is a new and stronger evidence (Hua 17/164). Thus,

Husserl's reflections on this issue have affinities with the current discussion of defeasibility.

In the work *Formale und Transzendentale Logik* (1929) Husserl makes use of a clarifying distinction between two different concepts of evidence. On the one hand, the term 'evidence' is used to designate the *originary*, that is original and optimal, givenness of the intended object. On the other hand, it is used to designate the existence of an actual synthesis of coincidence: A claim is evidently justified when it coincides with the first type of evidence (Hua 17/151–152). Husserl also speaks of truth as the correlate of evidence, and one can therefore also distinguish two different kinds of truth: Truth as disclosure vs. truth as correctness.[22] But although Husserl already operates with a type of truth on the prepredicative level—already the fact that the object shows itself as itself is a kind of (ontologically founded) truth—true knowledge cannot simply be identified with the mere presence of an intuition. Taken in isolation, the intuition is epistemologically irrelevant. It is only when the intuition serves the function of fulfilling a signitive intention that we acquire knowledge. The proper place for knowledge is the judgment.[23]

When a signitive intention is completely fulfilled by a corresponding intuition, the object is given exactly as it is intended—but this is very rarely the case. I have already mentioned that physical objects are given perspectivally. This fact has direct implications for the way in which they can be known. Our knowledge of physical objects are, as Husserl writes, characterized by a lack of coincidence between the intended and the given. We never perceive the object in its full totality, but always from a specific perspective (which obviously not only holds for three-dimensional objects, but for two-dimensional planes as well). But although, strictly speaking, we are presented with the profiles of the object, these are not what we intend. On the contrary, we intend the object itself. As Husserl says: 'Whether I look at this book from above or below, from inside or outside, I always see *this book*. It is always one and the same thing, and that not merely in some purely physical sense, but in the view of our perceptions themselves' (Hua 19/677 [789, transl. modified]). I intend the chair and not the perspectivally given surface of the front or the back, seat, and legs of the chair. Of course, I can choose to change my focus and instead intend the surface of the leg (instead of the whole chair), but that will be given in profiles as well. Our intentional directedness toward spatio-temporal objects are consequently characterized by the fact that we persistently transcend the given in order to grasp the object itself. Although perception is defined as the intentional act that aims at giving a full presentation of the intended object, that is, to let the object show itself fully as it is, this remains an ideal when it comes to physical objects. There will always remain profiles of the object that are not intuitively given. Our perceptual grasp of these objects will always remain *inadequate*. This is not to say, however, that there is no room for evidence when it comes to perception. Husserl makes a distinction between different types of evidence: *apodictic* (indubitable), *adequate* (exhaustive), and *inadequate* (partial) evidence. As he points out, it is unacceptable to transfer the demands we put on evidence in one domain to other domains where these demands are in principle incapable of being realized. Whereas our insight into certain mathematical relations (that 3 is greater than 2, for instance) might be considered exhaustive and indubitable, this does not hold true for our perception of physical objects, which remains tentative and corrigible. But this is only to be considered a fatal flaw if one makes the mistake of taking mathematics as the sole arbiter of what might count as evidence (Hua 3/321). To claim that physical objects are only given evidently if they appear in an exhaustive manner is to claim that physical objects can only appear in evidence the moment they cease to appear as physical objects, namely perspectivally. To put it differently, it is not possible to draw up absolute criteria for when an object is given in evidence, that is, appears optimally and originally. Depending on the type of object (for example, a physical object, a mathematical relation, and so forth) there are different originary modes of appearance. Thus, as Husserl insists, the perspectival givenness of physical objects does not merely reflect our finite intellect or the physical makeup of our sensory apparatus. It is, on the contrary, rooted in the things themselves. As Husserl writes, even God, as the ideal of absolute knowledge, would have to experience physical objects in the same perspectival manner. Otherwise it would no longer be physical objects that he was experiencing (Hua 3/351).

Let me just add, however, that there is obviously no reason to remain satisfied with that which a single perception can present us with. Although we can already speak of knowledge at this stage, that is, insofar as the intuitively given fulfills our signitive intention, our knowledge of the object will increase if more of its profiles are given intuitively. Knowledge is not merely a static relation between a signitive intention and an intuition, but a dynamical process that culminates when all of the profiles of the object are given intuitively. (It should be emphasized too that the profiles in question do not simply refer to the appearing surface of the object, but to the givenness of all of the properties of the object, be they properties that belong to the interiority of the object or properties such as solubility that only reveal themselves when the object interacts with other objects.)

The concept of fulfillment is consequently a concept with a large scope. It is not the case of an either-or. Either there is (absolute) fulfillment, or there is none. On the contrary, there can be various degrees of fulfillment. Its range can vary, but so can its clarity. If I see a withering oak from afar, then I am certainly confronted with the oak itself, the oak is intuitively present. But it is not as optimally given as if I stood closer by and could discern more details (Hua 19/614, 3/143–144). At the same time it should also be emphasized that Husserl does not define the optimal givenness by means of parameters like light and spatial presence. Stars are best seen when it is dark, and Husserl always understands optimal givenness as the kind of givenness that offers us the object with as much information and in as differentiated a manner as possible (Hua 11/205).

Categorial Objects and Wesensschau

So far my presentation has left out an important aspect of Husserl's theory. I have discussed only simple intentions and the fulfillment of these simple intentions. However, Husserl's concept of object is very broad (basically everything about which something can be predicated is an object), and fundamentally speaking he distinguishes between two different types of objects: real (perceptual) objects and ideal (categorial) objects. After all, it is not only possible to think about pear trees or the Empire State Building, but also about ideal notions like justice, the figure 3, the principle of noncontradiction, or about state of affairs (*Sachverhalte*) like 'the green book is lying beneath the papers on the desk.' In short, apart from simple intentions, there are also complex or categorial intentions that are founded on these simple intentions, and Husserl is not only thinking of our directedness toward the universal and essential (in contrast to the individual and contingent), but also of all forms of predication, conjugation or synthesizing, and the like. This step from simple intentions to complex intentions is a step from perception to intellection. I can see and touch a chair, and I can see the color blue, but although I can apprehend and understand that the chair *is* blue, it is not something that I can literally see or touch, since this is a state of affairs that doesn't occupy a position in physical space.

When we engage in categorial thinking we transcend the sphere of the sensuous, and in § 48 of the Sixth Investigation Husserl illustrates this move in the following way. Originally we are perceptually directed toward an object, say a chair. At this stage the object is simply given to us with all its determinations—its color, size, form, material composition, and so on—but none of these features are accentuated. Next, we pay attention to one of the properties of the chair focusing in on its color, for instance. Finally, and this is the stage where the categorial articulation is brought into play, we relate the two prior stages. We take the object *as* whole, and the part *as* part, and we intend the part *as* a part of the whole, and articulate it in a judgment: 'The chair is blue.' This predicative articulation is a categorial performance.

But now the question arises: How exactly are the categorial intentions *fulfilled*? If we take 'the green book is lying beneath the papers on the desk' as an example of a state of affairs, the formal or categorial elements of meaning like 'is,' 'beneath,' 'on' do not have perceptual correlates. One cannot see an 'is' or an 'on' (Hua 19/658). In other words, a large group of that which can be intended, including ideal objects such as 'justice,' 'the square root of 4,' and 'the law of gravity' can never be experienced perceptually. None of these objects can be seen, smelled, or heard. Nevertheless, according to Husserl, it is not only possible to intend a state of affairs signitively, it can also be given intuitively, and thereby be understood and experienced as true. It is possible to intuit *that* the green book is lying beneath the papers on the table, but only by means of a higher-order act which, although founded on the perceptions of the green book, papers, and table, nevertheless intends something that transcends these objects, namely their relationship and unity. The distinction between the signitive and the intuitive mode of givenness consequently remains relevant even when it comes to categorial objects, and Husserl therefore bites the bullet and enlarges the concept of intuition: We not only can speak of a *sensuous intuition*, but also of a *categorial intuition* (Hua 19/670–676). Formally speaking, the intuition is an act that brings us the object itself *in propria persona*, and this often calls for a complex intellectual performance. Even a theoretical argumentation or a conceptual analysis can be regarded as an intuition insofar as it brings us a state of affairs, an essential feature, or an abstract proof to originary givenness. The intuition is not necessarily sensuous, simple, or non-discursive, but merely non-signitive.

In the end, Husserl distinguishes between two different types of categorial acts. The *synthetic* and the *ideative*. Whereas the first type is characterized by remaining directed at the founding objects, the latter is not. To realize that 'the book is lying on the table' is to intend a higher-order object. But this synthetic object includes the founding elements 'book' and 'table,' and cannot be intended independently of these. In contrast, the ideative or eidetic acts seek to grasp the universal by abstracting from the individual or singular. In this process they will typically take their point of departure in a concrete and particular object—if the aim is to think of furniture as such, one might start out with considering the chair one is currently sitting in— but this object is simply the starting point and the ideative process does not remain fixed on it.

To summarize: Husserl's concept of experience is far more comprehensive than the one bequeathed to us from empiricism. We not only experience concrete and particular objects, but abstract or universal ones as well. As Husserl once put it in an article for the *Encyclopedia Britannica*, one of the tasks of phenomenology is precisely to overcome and replace the narrow empiristic concept of experience with an enlarged one, and to clarify all of its different forms, be they the intuition of essential structures, of apodictic evidence, and so forth (Hua 9/300, 3/44–45).

*

Let me finally mention an aspect of Husserl's philosophy that I have downplayed so far, namely Husserl's *essentialism*. As we have just seen, Husserl claims that we can experience ideal and categorial objects, and he even argues that it is possible to obtain essential or *eidetic* insights. At times this claim concerning the possibility of a *Wesensschau* has been taken to constitute one of the most important features of Husserlian phenomenology. But, although it is true that Husserl was more interested in insights into the essential structures of consciousness than in investigations of the factual and empirical composition of human consciousness, and although his phenomenology can in part be seen as an attempt to spell out the necessary and universal laws that govern and structure intentionality, this interest in essential structures is so widespread and common in the history of philosophy that it is nonsensical to take it as a defining feature of phenomenology.

Nevertheless, Husserl did in fact develop and employ some useful distinctions. One of these is the difference between *formal* and *material ontology* (Hua 3/37). Formal ontology is the name for the discipline that investigates what it means to be an object. It is considered a formal enterprise, for it abstracts from all considerations concerning content. It is not interested in the differences between siliceous stones, oak trees, and clarinets, that is to say, it is not concerned with the differences between various types of objects, but in that which is unconditionally true for any object whatsoever. The work of a formal ontology is consequently to be found in the elucidation of such categories as quality, property, relation, identity, whole, part, and so on. In contrast, the material (or regional) ontology examines the essential structures belonging to a given region or kind of object and seeks to determine that which holds true with necessity for any member of the region in question. For instance, what is it that characterizes mathematical entities as such, in contrast to psychical processes or physical objects? Each of the three would, according to Husserl, constitute a unique ontological region with its own proper features. The region of the physical can again be subdivided into a number of more specific regions, the domain of the chemical, the biological, and so forth.

Husserl not only claims that there are essential structures governing different ontological regions, he also claims that we can obtain knowledge about these structures. But how is that supposed to come about? To start with, Husserl points out that we are not only able to intend particular objects characterized by spatio-temporal position—for instance this 400-year-old tsuba that I am currently using as a paperweight, we can also intend that which characterizes physical objects qua physical objects, that is, that which invariantly holds true for all physical objects. To put it differently, there are not only mental acts that are directed toward singular objects, but also mental acts that intend the universal and ideal.

Whereas the investigation of the concrete features of the tsuba is an empirical investigation of a number of features that might very well have been different, this is not the case when it comes to the investigation of that which characterizes the tsuba qua physical object. According to Husserl, an insight into the latter can be acquired through a so-called *eidetic variation* or *eidetic reduction* (not to be confused with the *phenomenological* or *transcendental reduction*, which I will discuss in Part 2). This variation must be understood as a kind of conceptual analysis where we attempt to imagine the object as being different from how it currently is. Sooner or later this imaginative variation will lead us to certain properties that cannot be varied, that is, changed and transgressed, without making the object cease to be the kind of object it is. The variation consequently allows us to distinguish between the accidental properties of the object, that is, the properties that could have been different, and its essential properties, that is, the invariant structures that make the object into the type of object it is. According to Husserl, I can obtain an essential insight, a *Wesensschau*, if through an eidetic variation, I succeed in establishing the horizon within which the object can change without losing its identity as a thing of that type. In that case, I will have succeeded in disclosing the invariant structures that make up its essence (Hua 9/72–87, EU § 87).

Of course, Husserl would never claim that through some passive gaze we are able to obtain infallible insights into the essence of each and every object. On the contrary, the eidetic variation is a demanding conceptual analysis that in many cases is defeasible. Moreover, and this must be emphasized, Husserl's work does not consist of hairsplitting analyses of the difference between, say, dogs and cats. On the contrary, he is after far more fundamental distinctions, for instance, what distinguishes mathematical entities from works of art, physical objects, and mental acts.

Husserl's considerations concerning the possibility of an eidetic reduction and variation, his distinction between material and formal ontology, and his reflections on the relation between sensation and thought are all important philosophical investigations. Nevertheless, in my opinion, they all constitute part of the more traditional heritage in Husserl's philosophy and should consequently not be taken as the truly distinctive features of his phenomenology.

Phenomenology and Metaphysics

In order to understand the concept of phenomenology that is developed in *Logische Untersuchungen*, and, in particular, Husserl's later turn toward transcendental philosophy, it is important not to misunderstand Husserl's analysis of intentionality (as has occasionally happened) by claiming that his identification of the intentional object and the real object can be taken in support of a metaphysical realism. As I have already shown, Husserl's point is merely that the intentional object is the real object of the intention. Even more importantly: When he calls an object real, this characterization carries no metaphysical implications, nor does it imply that the object exists mind-independently. It is merely to be taken as a descriptive characterization: The object is intuitively given in its bodily presence.

In the beginning of my presentation, I mentioned that Husserl considered the question concerning the existence of an external reality as a metaphysical question that was of no relevance for phenomenology. Since throughout the text Husserl also repeatedly emphasizes the difference between the metaphysical and the phenomenological endeavor, it is not difficult to characterize Husserl's position in *Logische Untersuchungen*. It is metaphysically *neutral*. To be more specific, Husserl's early phenomenology is neither committed to a metaphysical realism nor to a metaphysical idealism.[24] (However, this neutrality does not prevent Husserl from criticizing certain metaphysical positions, such as a subjective idealism, which claims that the intentional object is a part of consciousness, or a naturalism, which claims that everything that exists—including intentionality itself—can and should be explained with the use of those principles and methods that are acknowledged by the natural sciences.)

It is exactly this metaphysical neutrality which is behind Husserl's repeated claim that the difference between a veridical perception and a misperception is irrelevant to phenomenology. As Husserl even says—with a formulation that has subsequently been much misunderstood and which I will return to later (cf. p. 61)—the very *existence* of the intentional object is phenomenologically irrelevant, since the intrinsic nature of the act is supposed to remain the same regardless of whether or not the object exists (Hua 19/59, 358, 360, 387, 396). Thus, according to Husserl's position in *Logische Untersuchungen*, there are no phenomenologically relevant differences between a perception and a hallucination of a blue book. In both cases we are dealing with a situation where the intentional object is *presented* in an intuitive mode of givenness. Whether or not this object also exists objectively is a question that is methodologically suspended.

Insofar as Husserl refrains from making any claims about whether or not the intentional object has any mind-independent reality, and insofar as he seems to think that this is a question that phenomenology is incapable of answering, his initial concept of phenomenology must be considered a very narrow one. The question is whether this restriction is legitimate, or whether it ultimately threatens to reduce phenomenology to some kind of descriptive psychology.[25] Basically, one can appraise Husserl's metaphysical neutrality in three different ways:

- One could say that the rejection of metaphysics and metaphysical issues is a liberating move, for the simple reason that these traditional questions are pseudo-problems that have already spellbound philosophers for far too long.

- One could claim that it becomes phenomenology to acknowledge that it is merely a descriptive enterprise and not the universal answer to all questions. In other words, there is a difference between phenomenology and metaphysics, and although the first might prepare the way for the latter, it does not in itself contain the resources to tackle metaphysical issues and should therefore keep silent about that which it cannot speak.

- In contrast to these first two reactions, which for quite different reasons welcome Husserl's metaphysical neutrality, the third option regrets it. It concedes that metaphysical problems are real problems, but since it also thinks that phenomenology has an important contribution to make in this area, it deplores Husserl's metaphysical neutrality as a self-imposed and unnecessary straitjacket.

Although I favor the third option, I actually have a certain sympathy for all three reactions. (In fact I think they are less incompatible than one should assume at first glance. Thus, it could very well be argued that there are a variety of different metaphysical questions, and that some might fall in the first category, some in the second and some in the third—that is, there are metaphysical pseudo-problems that phenomenology is wise to abandon, metaphysical questions that are beyond its reach, and metaphysical questions that it is capable of addressing.)

In Part 2 I will take up this issue again, claiming that Husserl's transcendental philosophical turn must be seen precisely as an attempt to overcome some of the ambiguities in *Logische Untersuchungen*. This interpretation is supported by the fact that Husserl himself was soon to complain about the shortcomings of his descriptive phenomenology.[26] As he points out in the lecture course *Einleitung in die Logik und Erkenntnistheorie* (1906–1907), if one really wishes to understand the relation between act, meaning, and intended object, one must leave descriptive phenomenology behind in favor of a transcendental phenomenology (Hua 24/425–427).[27]

I have already mentioned that Husserl took intentionality to imply a constitutive performance. To be conscious of something is not simply to be affected by the object in question. On the contrary, the object is only an object for us because of our own meaning-giving contribution. As Husserl remarks, it is our interpretation that enables the object to be for us (Hua 19/397). He also characterizes categorial objects as objects that can appear only as what they are in (or for) intentional acts (Hua 19/675). This characterization is repeated in lectures from 1907, where Husserl writes that the objects appear (are constituted) in intentional acts, and that it is only there that they can show themselves as what they are (Hua 2/72).

However, since Husserl fails to thematize the status of the phenomenon and refrains from clarifying the relation between appearance and reality, the metaphysical implications of his concept of constitution are left in the dark, making it impossible to decide whether Husserl's early concept of constitution implies a production or merely an epistemic reproduction of the object. When it concerns the early Husserl, there is therefore reason to accept the following statement by Robert Sokolowski:

> If subjectivity 'created' sense and objects when it constitutes them, then their contents should be explained by subjectivity. This is not the case; the contents are simply given as facticity, and not as something essentially deducible from subjectivity and its operations. Therefore, subjectivity does not cause or create senses and objects. It merely allows them to come about. It is their condition, and not their cause; consequently, Husserl's doctrine of constitution should not be interpreted in too idealistic a manner.[28]

Against this background, it should be evident that one cannot describe Husserl's transcendental philosophical turn as a fatal turn from a metaphysical realism to a metaphysical idealism. First, Husserl was not a metaphysical realist in *Logische Untersuchungen*, but understood phenomenology as a descriptive enterprise that remained metaphysically neutral. Second, Husserl's abandonment of this position cannot be called fatal, since this position is characterized by shortcomings and ambiguities; the very status of the phenomenon was never analyzed. Third, Husserl's own transcendental idealism is not a traditional idealism, but can, as we will soon see (cf. p. 72), be interpreted as an attempt to overcome both metaphysical realism and metaphysical idealism.[29]

2

Husserl's Turn to Transcendental Philosophy: Epoché, Reduction, and Transcendental Idealism

So far I have presented a number of central Husserlian analyses and distinctions. These seminal investigations of intentionality, evidence, and truth remained central to Husserl throughout his life, although he constantly sought to improve, refine, and deepen them. As I pointed out at the end of the first part, however, Husserl's very concept of phenomenology and his (anti)metaphysical position in *Logische Untersuchungen* were characterized by a number of unfortunate limitations and ambiguities. In the following the task will be to account for the change that occurred with Husserl's realization of the insufficiencies of a purely descriptive phenomenology and his corresponding turn toward transcendental phenomenology in *Ideen zu einer reinen Phänomenologie und phänomenologischen Philosophie I* (1913).[1]

Obviously, Husserl did not stop developing his analyses after 1913. Indeed to a certain extent his later writings can be seen as a series of meditations on the same fundamental themes. This implies that even an introductory examination of Husserl's transcendental philosophical position cannot restrict itself to *Ideen 1*, especially because Husserl's position in this very work belongs to the most criticized part of his writings, not only by later phenomenologists (Martin Heidegger, Maurice Merleau-Ponty, Paul Ricoeur), but also by Husserl himself. It would exceed the scope of this presentation if I were to account for all the different variations, but in the following I will focus both on Husserl's presentation in

Ideen 1 and on the account he offers in his last book, *Die Krisis der euro-päischen Wissenschaften und die transzendentale Phänomenologie* (1936).

Presuppositionlessness

One of the marked differences between *Logische Untersuchungen* and Husserl's later writings is his increasing belief in the foundational signifi-cance of phenomenology. Phenomenology is presented as a new, critical, and rigorous science, and Husserl takes its task to consist of a disclosure and examination of all the fundamental claims and assumptions that are presupposed by the positive (objective, dogmatic) sciences. Husserl's em-phasis on the scientific nature of phenomenology is not, however, an at-tempt to blur the difference between philosophy and positive science, but is merely an expression of his belief that phenomenology is committed to an ideal of fully justified knowledge, an ideal that the positive sciences fail to live up to since they fail to reflect on their own epistemological and metaphysical presuppositions in their exclusive orientation toward the ac-quisition of more and more results.[2]

The task of phenomenology is to thematize and elucidate the philo-sophical core questions concerning the being and nature of reality. Husserl, however, argues that it is impossible to carry out this investigation with the required radicality if one simply presupposes and accepts the metaphysical and epistemological assumptions that characterize our daily life, which is implicitly and unquestionably accepted by all of the positive sciences.

What kind of metaphysical assumptions is Husserl referring to? The most fundamental one is our implicit belief in the existence of a mind-, experience-, and theory-independent reality. This realistic assumption is so fundamental and deeply rooted that it is not only accepted by the positive sciences, it even permeates our daily pretheoretical life, for which reason Husserl calls it the *natural attitude*. Regardless of how obvious and natural this assumption might seem, Husserl insists that it is philosophically unac-ceptable to take its validity for granted. On the contrary, it must be tested thoroughly. Our investigation should be critical and undogmatic, shun-ning metaphysical and scientific prejudices. It should be guided by what is actually given, rather than by what we expect to find given our theoretical commitments. But the obvious question is how this investigation is to pro-ceed if it is to avoid prejudicing the results beforehand. Husserl's answer is deceptively simple: Our investigation should turn its attention toward the *givenness* or *appearance* of reality, that is, it should focus on the way in which reality is given to us in experience. We should, in other words, not let preconceived theories form our experience, but let our experience determine our theories. Thus, in § 24 of *Ideen 1*, Husserl describes the phenomenological *principle of principles* in the following manner. We should let the originary giving intuition be the source of all knowledge, a source that no authority (not even modern science) should be allowed to question.[3]

However, to turn toward the given is far easier said than done. It calls for a number of methodological preparations. In order to avoid presupposing commonsensical naiveté (as well as a number of different speculative hypotheses concerning the metaphysical status of reality), it is necessary to suspend our acceptance of the natural attitude. We keep the attitude (in order to be able to investigate it), but we bracket its validity. This procedure, which entails a suspension of our natural realistic inclination, is known by the name of *epoché*.

It is of crucial importance not to misunderstand the purpose of the epoché. We do not effect it in order to deny, doubt, neglect, abandon, or exclude reality from our research, but simply in order to suspend or neutralize a certain dogmatic *attitude* toward reality, that is, in order to be able to focus more narrowly and directly on the phenomenological given—the objects just as they appear. In short, the epoché entails a change of attitude toward reality, and not an exclusion of reality. It is only through such a suspension that we will be able to approach reality in a way that will allow for a disclosure of its true sense (Hua 8/457, 3/120, 8/465). To speak of the *sense* of reality in this context does not, as Husserl will continually emphasize, imply that the *being* of reality, that is, the really existing world, is somehow excluded from the phenomenological sphere of research:

The real actuality is not 'reinterpreted,' to say nothing of its being denied; it is rather that a countersensical interpretation of the real actuality, i.e., an interpretation which contradicts the latter's *own* sense as clarified by insight, is removed (Hua 3/120).

What must be shown in particular and above all is that through the epoché a new way of experiencing, of thinking, of theorizing, is opened to the philosopher; here, situated *above* his own natural being and *above* the natural world, he loses nothing of their being and their objective truths . . . (Hua 6/154–155 [152]).

First of all, it is better to avoid speaking of a phenomenological 'residuum,' and likewise of 'excluding the world.' Such language readily misleads us into thinking that, from now on, the world would no longer figure as a phenomenological theme, leaving only the 'subjective' acts, modes of appearance, etc., related to the world. In a certain way this is indeed correct. But when universal subjectivity is posited in legitimate validity—in its full universality, and of course, as transcendental—then what lies within it, on the correlate-side, is the world itself as legitimately existing, along with everything that it is in truth: thus the theme of a universal transcendental inquiry also includes the world itself, with all its true being (Hua 8/432).

'The' world has not been lost through the epoché—it is not at all an abstaining with respect to the being of the world and with respect to any judgment about it, but rather it is the way of uncovering judgments about correlation, of uncovering the reduction of all unities of sense to me myself and my sense-having and sense-bestowing subjectivity with all its capabilities (Hua 15/366).

Husserl also speaks of the *transcendental reduction* in this context, and even though the epoché and the reduction are closely linked and parts of one functional unity, Husserl occasionally speaks of the epoché as the condition of possibility for the reduction (Hua 6/154); consequently, it is necessary to distinguish the two: The epoché is the term for our abrupt suspension of a naive metaphysical attitude, and it can consequently be likened to a philosophical gate of entry (Hua 6/260). In contrast, the *reduction* is the term for our thematization of the correlation between subjectivity and world. This is a long and difficult analysis that *leads* from the natural sphere *back to* (*re-ducere*) its transcendental foundation (Hua 1/61). Both epoché and reduction can consequently be seen as elements of a transcendental reflection, the purpose of which is to liberate us from a natural(istic) dogmatism and to make us aware of our own constitutive (that is, cognitive, meaning-giving) contribution.

To perform the epoché and the reduction is not to abstain from an investigation of the real world in order to focus on mental content and representations, as it has occasionally been claimed (cf. p. 56 below). The epoché and the reduction do not involve an exclusive turn toward inwardness, and they do not imply any loss. On the contrary, the fundamental change of attitude makes possible a decisive discovery and should consequently be understood as an *expansion* of our field of research (Hua 6/154, 1/66). Husserl himself compares the performance of the epoché with the transition from a two-dimensional to a three-dimensional life (Hua 6/120). Suddenly, the perpetually functioning, but so far hidden, transcendental subjectivity is disclosed as the subjective condition of possibility for manifestation.

The Cartesian Way and the Ontological Way

But why should the suspension of our natural attitude lead us to transcendental subjectivity? In the course of his writings, Husserl attempts to justify this move in several different ways. Or, as it has become customary to say, in the course of his writings Husserl introduces several different *ways* to the transcendental reduction: the *Cartesian* way, the *psychological* way, and the *ontological* way.[4] In the following I will focus on the first way, which is present in *Ideen I*, and on the last way, which can be found in *Krisis*.

In *Ideen I*, Husserl points out that there is an obvious difference between the way in which spatio-temporal objects are given to consciousness, and the way in which consciousness is given to itself. Whereas objects appear perspectivally—never given in their totality, but always in a certain limited profile—this is not true for the self-appearance of consciousness. Whereas the object is given perspectivally, partially, and inadequately, and whereas it is necessary to run through an entire series of profiles in order to get an approximate presentation of the entire object, the experience itself appears immediately in its totality. For Husserl, this radical difference between the appearance of subjectivity and the appearance of an object proves that, phenomenologically speaking, there is a decisive difference between subjectivity and any object. He therefore argues that it is necessary to supplement a naturalistic investigation of consciousness, which simply sees it as yet another object in the world, with an investigation that seeks to investigate consciousness on it own terms, that is, from a first-person perspective. To put it differently, by distinguishing between the two modes of appearance, Husserl is basically calling attention to the difference between first-person and third-person phenomena.

This claim concerning the *difference* between subjectivity and objects is now complemented by a claim concerning the *priority* of subjectivity. As was already the case in *Logische Untersuchungen*, Husserl is not interested in the factual and empirical nature of subjectivity, but in its essential structure, purified and liberated from any contingent context. Inspired by Descartes' methodological doubt, Husserl claims that whereas it is possible to imagine the existence of a *worldless* subject, it is not possible to imagine the existence of a *subjectless* world. As it is formulated in the (in)famous paragraph 49 in *Ideen I*, an unprejudiced investigation of the intentional relation between consciousness and world must lead to the result that even an (imagined) nihilation of the world would leave consciousness intact. Whereas the objective world (understood as the coherent and rational organization of our intentional correlates) necessarily presupposes an intentional subject, the reverse is not the case.[5] Whereas the world can only appear for a subject, subjectivity does not need the world in order to be. The world, and more generally, every type of *transcendence*, is relative insofar as the condition for its appearance lies outside itself, namely, in the subject. In contrast the subject, the *immanence*, is absolute and autonomous since its manifestation only depends upon itself.

But what is the purpose of this thought-experiment? Husserl seeks to explain why a performance of the epoché and a thematization of the phenomenological given should lead to the discovery of transcendental subjectivity. By calling attention to the unique givenness and autonomy of subjectivity, Husserl claims that we are confronted with a dimension or aspect of the subject that in principle eludes a naturalistic and empirical investigation. If it is possible to imagine a worldless subject, the naturalistic account that consistently understands consciousness as a mere object in the world cannot be exhaustive. Through a Cartesian-inspired thought-experiment, our naturalistic understanding of consciousness is surmounted, and consciousness is revealed as an independent region of being and experience (Hua 3/105).

As already mentioned, the transcendental subject is the subject considered qua condition for appearance, phenomenality, manifestation. But what is the relation between the *transcendental* and the *empirical* (mundane or worldly) subject? As Husserl himself points out, it is quite a puzzle how consciousness can be something absolute that constitutes all transcendence, including the entire psycho-physical world, and simultaneously something that appears as a real part of the world (Hua 3/116). I will return to this problem later on, but already now it should be emphasized that Husserl (in contrast to Kant, and German Idealism for the most part) did not understand the transcendental subject as an abstract, ideal, general, or transpersonal subject. On the contrary, the transcendental subject, or to be more precise, *my* transcendental subjectivity is my concrete and individual subjectivity. But if the relation between the transcendental and the empirical ego is not a relation between a universal and a concrete subject, how should one then understand their relation? A relatively clear statement can be found in the following passage from Husserl's article in the *Encyclopedia Britannica*:

My transcendental ego is thus evidently 'different' from the natural ego, but by no means as a second, as one separated from it in the natural sense of the word, just as on the contrary it is by no means bound up with it or intertwined with it, in the usual sense of these words. It is just the field of transcendental self-experience (conceived in full concreteness) which can in every case, through mere alteration of attitude, be changed into psychological self-experience. In this transition, an identity of the I is necessarily brought about; in transcendental reflection on this transition the psychological Objectivation becomes visible as self-objectivation of the transcendental ego, and so it is as if in every moment of the natural attitude the I finds itself with an apperception imposed upon it (Hua 9/294).

The relation between the transcendental subject and the empirical subject is not a relation between two different subjects, but between two different self-apprehensions, a primary and a secondary.[6] The transcendental subject is the subject in its primary constitutive function. The empirical subject is the same subject, but now apprehended and interpreted as an object in the world, that is, as a constituted and mundanized entity.

It is in this context that Husserl calls attention to the fact that subjectivity can be thematized in two radically different ways, namely in a natural or psychological reflection on the one hand, and in a pure or transcendental reflection on the other (Hua 7/262, 1/72). When I perform a psychological reflection, I am interpreting the act reflected upon as a psychical process, that is, a process occurring in a psycho-physical entity that exists in the world. This type of self-consciousness—which Husserl occasionally calls a mundane self-consciousness—is just as worldly an experience as, say, the experience of physical objects, and if one asks whether it can provide us with an adequate understanding of subjectivity, the answer is no. Natural reflection presents us with a constituted, objectified, and naturalized subject, but it does not provide us with an access to the constituting, transcendental dimension of subjectivity (Hua 17/290, 8/71, 7/269, 6/255, 264). It is here that the pure or transcendental reflection is introduced, since its specific task is to thematize a subjectivity stripped from all contingent and transcendent relations and interpretations (Hua 3/117, 7/267). Husserl makes it clear, however, that this type of reflection is not immediately available, so the question remains: What method or procedure can make it available?

The obvious answer: Through the epoché. For as Husserl emphasizes again and again (with an obvious jab at introspectionism), unless the way has first been cleared by the epoché, we will be dealing with an objectified and mundanized experience regardless of how intensively or how carefully and attentively one reflects (Hua 8/79, 3/107). In contrast to the positive sciences, which can proceed directly to their different fields of research, the region that phenomenology is supposed to investigate is not immediately accessible. Prior to any concrete investigation it is necessary to employ a certain methodological reflection to escape the natural attitude. Only through a methodical suspension of all transcendent preconceptions, only through a radical turn toward that which in a strict sense is given from a first-person perspective, can transcendental analysis commence (Hua 3/136, 8/427).

One of the advantages of the Cartesian way to the reduction is its clarity. It is very easy to follow Husserl's description of the different modes of givenness. But this approach also confronts a number of problems, the chief being that it very easily gives rise to a serious misunderstanding of the proper aim and topic of phenomenology. By focusing on the immediate self-givenness of subjectivity and by stressing the difference between this givenness and the givenness of objects, one is easily led to the belief that the task of phenomenology is to investigate pure subjectivity in isolation and separation from both world and intersubjectivity.

In part, it is this distortion that Husserl seeks to address and overcome in his so-called *ontological way* to the reduction (Hua 6/158, 6/175). The ontological way does not take its point of departure in the immediate self-givenness of the subject, but starts with an analysis of the givenness of a specific ontological region (say, the region of ideal objects or of physical objects). This region is investigated qua appearing and the question concerning the condition of possibility for this appearance is then raised. The ontological description consequently serves as a guiding line for the subsequent transcendental analysis. If we restrict ourselves to that which shows itself (be it in a straightforward perception or in a scientific experiment), and if we focus more specifically on that which we tend to ignore in our daily life (because it is so familiar), namely the very appearance, we cannot avoid being led to subjectivity. Insofar as we are confronted with the appearance of an object, that is, with an object as presented, perceived, judged, or evaluated, we are led to the experiential structures and intentionality that these modes of appearance are correlated with. We are led to the acts of presentation, perception, judgment, and valuation, and thereby to the subject (or subjects) that the object as appearing must necessarily be understood in relation to. Through the phenomenological attitude we become aware of the givenness of the object. But we do not simply focus on the object exactly as it is given, we also focus on the subjective side of consciousness, thereby becoming aware of our subjective accomplishments and the intentionality that is at play in order for the object to appear as it does. When we investigate appearing objects, we also disclose ourselves as datives of manifestation, as those to whom objects appear. The epoché does not make us turn our attention away from the worldly objects, but permits us to examine them in a new light, namely in their appearance or manifestation for consciousness as constituted correlates.

First comes the straightforwardly given life-world, taken initially as it is given perceptually: as 'normal,' simply there, unbroken, existing in pure ontic certainty (undoubted). When the new direction of interest is established, and thus also in strict epoché, the life-world becomes a first intentional heading, an *index* or *guideline* for inquiring back into the multiplicities of manners of appearing and their intentional structures. A further shift of direction, at the second level of reflection, leads to the ego-pole and what is peculiar to its identity (Hua 6/175 [172, transl. modified]).

The attempt to reach a philosophical comprehension of the world leads, in other words, *indirectly* to a disclosure of subjectivity, since the phenomenological perspective on the world must necessarily be through the appearance of the world *for subjectivity*. However, the subjectivity we thereby encounter is no longer the empirical subject—the subject that is investigated by the positive sciences such as psychology, history, or neurophysiology. The empirical subject is an object in the world, and like all other appearing worldly objects it presupposes a subject to whom it appears. No, it is the transcendental subjectivity we are disclosing, the subjectivity that is the condition of possibility for appearance as such. This subjectivity remains hidden as long as we are absorbed in the prephilosophical natural attitude, where we live in self-oblivion among objects, but which the epoché and the reduction is capable of revealing.

Whereas Husserl's Cartesian way to the reduction seems to emphasize the subject's status as a separate and different region of being (as a thinking substance), thereby providing ammunition for the widespread misinterpretation that the task of phenomenology is to explore this autonomous, isolated, and worldless subject, his ontological way to the reduction makes it clear that the investigation of subjectivity is something that takes place in connection with and inseparable from a philosophical clarification of the world (Hua 4/107, 6/175).[7]

As it has occasionally been said, phenomenology is only interested in consciousness insofar as it is the field or dimension where the world appears.[8] It is worth emphasizing that on this account, although being no part of the world, transcendental subjectivity is not worldless. After all, as the subject of intentionality, it cannot be described without reference to the world; it is nothing in isolation from the world.

Through the epoché, which is neither less nor more than a focus on phenomena (appearing objects), we reach an understanding of the performance of subjectivity. The world is not something that simply exists. The world appears, and the structure of this appearance is conditioned and made possible by subjectivity. It is in this context that Husserl would say that it is absurd to speak of the existence of an absolutely mind-independent world, that is, of a world that exists apart from any possible experiential and conceptual perspective. For Husserl, this notion is simply contradictory. This might sound very idealistic (cf. p. 69 below), but this central thesis held by all phenomenologists, can also be formulated negatively. It is basically a rejection of a realistic and naturalistic objectivism that claims that the nature of meaning, truth, and reality can be understood without taking subjectivity into account.

Given what has been said so far, it is relatively easy to clarify Husserl's turn to transcendental philosophy. As I mentioned in Part 1, Husserl claims that we need to return to the things themselves, that is, to base our theories on that which shows itself and actually appears, rather than make do with empty and idle talk. But as we have also seen, a philosophical analysis of the object qua appearing must necessarily also take subjectivity into account. If we wish to truly understand what physical objects are, we will eventually have to turn to the subjectivity that experiences these objects, for it is only there that they show themselves as what they are. If we wish to understand reality, we ultimately have to return to the conscious acts in which it is given. In short, subjectivity is a condition of possibility for appearance or manifestation. Without subjectivity there can be no appearance. However, this dictum can be interpreted in two radically different ways. Either one claims that there is a fundamental gap between appearance and reality—that an object consequently is what it is quite regardless of how it appears, or whether it appears at all—or it is claimed that, although the distinction between appearance and reality can be maintained (after all, some appearances might be deceptive), this distinction is in reality a distinction internal to the phenomenal world, that is, to the world of appearances, and ultimately a distinction between how the objects might appear at a casual look and how they might appear in the best of circumstances, that is, in the light of a sophisticated scientific investigation. The reality of the object should not be sought behind its appearances, as if the latter were somehow hiding it; rather, it reveals itself in the optimal appearance. If the last interpretation is chosen we are faced with a transcendental philosophical position: Subjectivity (and as we will eventually see, intersubjectivity) is a condition of possibility for reality. Without subjectivity there can be no reality. The problem in *Logische Untersuchungen* is Husserl's failure to make a choice between these two interpretations. Later, however, he claims that only the latter interpretation is phenomenologically sound, whereas the first is bound up with an uncritical and naive distinction between reality and phenomenon.

Some Misunderstandings

As already indicated, Husserl's account of the epoché and the reduction is not always crystal clear. It is, therefore, not surprising that it has given rise to a number of misunderstandings concerning the precise aim and topic of phenomenology, misunderstandings that are still firmly rooted in the philosophical literature.

To take one example, Leslie Stevenson, in a popular introduction to different philosophical traditions, claims that phenomenology is an obscure philosophical method attempting to locate an unproblematic foundation by describing 'the phenomena' as they seem to be without making any presumptions about what they are in reality. Ultimately, he argues that Husserl ends up identifying philosophy with the study of human consciousness, thereby giving it a quasi-psychological twist.[9]

The key reason to mention Stevenson's bizarre reading is that he manages to reproduce a number of classical and widespread misunderstandings in a very few sentences:

I. In contrast to the objective or positive sciences, phenomenology is not particularly interested in the substantial nature of the objects, that is, in their weight, rarity, or chemical composition, but in the way in which they show themselves, that is, in their modes of givenness. And as we already saw in Part I, an important piece of Husserl's seminal work has been the mapping out of a whole variety of different types of phenomena. There are essential differences between the way in which a physical thing, a utensil, a work of art, a melody, a state of affairs, a number, an animal, a social relation, and so on, manifests itself. Moreover, it is also possible for one and the same object to appear in a variety of different ways: From this or that perspective, in strong or faint illumination, as perceived, imagined, wished for, feared, anticipated or recollected, demonstrated, described or communicated. Rather than disregarding the specific appearance of the object as something inessential and merely subjective, as something not worthy of closer inspection, Husserl has typically been interested in investigating objects exactly as they are given. However, the work of phenomenology does not stop here. The specific and unique *transcendental*-phenomenological question is: What are the conditions of possibility for appearance as such?

Insofar as phenomenology seeks to disclose the very conditions of possibility for appearance, it should be obvious that one cannot equate the phenomenological reflection with a psychological introspection, nor claim that phenomenology in toto can be threatened, replaced, or criticized by psychology. Why is the transcendental reflection not a form of introspection? Because introspection is ordinarily understood as a mental operation that enables us to report about our own current mental states. A claim like 'I am presently thinking about a red balloon' is normally taken to be based on introspection. But it is not at all claims of this type that phenomenology is concerned with, and more generally speaking, phenomenology is not at all interested in establishing what a given individual might currently be thinking about. The phenomenological field of research does not concern private thoughts, but intersubjectively accessible modes of appearance. This investigation, of course, also calls for an exploration of subjectivity, that is, of transcendental subjectivity in its constitutive correlation to the world, but in contrast to a private introspection, this exploration claims to be intersubjectively valid and therefore corrigible by any (phenomenologically tuned) subject.

In ordinary language one occasionally uses the terms *phenomenon* or *appearance* in the contrast phenomenon-essence or appearance-reality. The phenomenon is the immediate givenness of the object, it is how it *apparently* is. If one wishes to discover what the object is really like, however, one has to transcend the merely phenomenal. It is a version of this concept of phenomenon that one can find in large parts of the philosophical tradition. The phenomenon is how the object appears to us, seen with our eyes (and thought with our categories), but it is not the object as it is in itself. Had it been this concept of phenomenon that phenomenology were employing, it might have been nothing but a science of the merely subjective, apparent, or superficial. But obviously it is not. On the contrary, Husserl operates with a concept of phenomenon that can be traced back to Antiquity.[10] The phenomenon is understood as the manifestation of the thing itself, and phenomenology is therefore a philosophical reflection on the way in which objects show themselves—how objects appear or manifest themselves—and on the conditions of possibility for this appearance.

It could be claimed that Husserl is confusing a banality with a great philosophical discovery. When he claims that the world as we experience it—the world as we understand, describe, and conceptualize it—can only exist insofar as there are subjects, it could be replied that it is true that the world as it is conceived by us depends on us, but that this is quite uncontroversial. However, this reply overlooks Husserl's rebuttal of a two-world theory. According to him the world that appears to us, be it in perception, in daily concerns, or in scientific analysis, is the only real world. To claim that in addition, there exists a hidden world behind the phenomenal world, a hidden world that transcends every appearance and every experiential and conceptual evidence and that this world is the true reality, is, for Husserl, not only an empty speculative postulate that completely lacks phenomenological credibility. Ultimately, he even argues that such an argumentation is based on a category mistake.[11]

Phenomenology is not a theory about the *merely* appearing, or to put it differently, appearances are not *mere* appearances. For how things appear is an integral part of what they really are. If we wish to grasp the true nature of the object, we had better pay close attention to how it manifests and reveals itself, be it in sensuous perception or in scientific analyses. The reality of the object is not hidden behind the phenomenon, but unfolds itself in

the phenomenon. As Heidegger would say, it is phenomenologically absurd
to say of the phenomenon that it stands in the way of something more fundamental that it merely represents.[12] To repeat: Although the distinction
between appearance and reality can be maintained, according to Husserl it
is not a distinction between two separate realms, but a distinction internal
to the realm of appearances. It is a distinction between how the objects
might appear at a superficial glance, and how they might appear in the best
of circumstances.

In the light of these considerations, it seems rather problematic to
claim that Husserl was no longer interested in reality after the effectuation
of the epoché, but only concerned with an analysis of meaning and mental representations. Such a claim, however, is made by Dreyfus, who argues
that Husserl, in his search for an indubitable foundation, wished to investigate consciousness from a strictly internal perspective, and consequently
found it necessary to effectuate a procedure of purification which would re-
move all external or transcendent components from consciousness. Dreyfus,
consequently, interprets the reduction as a change of attitude that makes
us turn our attention away from the objects in the world, and away from
any psychological experiences of being directed at objects, in order to focus on the abstract mental representations which makes intentionality possible.[13] Dreyfus reads Husserl as a prototypical *internalist* who takes mental representations to have the function they have regardless of how the
world is, and as somebody who urges us to investigate mental content without any regard for whether that which we are intentionally directed at does
at all exist.[14] Since Dreyfus also takes Husserl to regard meaning as something purely mental and completely detached from the world, he claims
that Husserl is unable to account for how objects are given (*sic*), but only for
how they are intended,[15] ultimately defining Husserlian phenomenology as
an investigation that is exclusively interested in the mental representations
that remain in consciousness after the performance of the reduction has
bracketed the world.[16]

As should be clear from my own presentation, by no means am I in
agreement with Dreyfus. But Dreyfus is not alone in putting forth this interpretation. Some of his claims can also be found in the work of Smith
and McIntyre. According to their view, Husserl makes use of a special reflection in order to bracket all concern with the external world and focus on
the internal structures of experience.[17] Broadly defined, phenomenology

consequently becomes the study of the intrinsic features of consciousness or simply the study of human experience.[18] This definition easily leads to the conclusion that the phenomenological reduction is nothing but a sophisticated type of introspection, and phenomenology, in reality, a subdiscipline of psychology eventually to be defined—as Smith does—as an intentional psychology.[19] Both Smith and McIntyre do, however, acknowledge that Husserl operates with more than one reduction, and, according to them, the purpose of the *phenomenological-psychological* reduction is to focus our attention on consciousness and its experiences rather than on the various external objects with which it is typically occupied, whereas the purpose of the *transcendental* reduction is to eliminate from this study of consciousness all empirical or naturalistic considerations. Thus it becomes possible to speak more narrowly of a transcendental or pure phenomenology that is then defined as a study of the structures of consciousness purified from all empirical or naturalistic concerns.[20]

In Part 1, I presented some of the main features of Husserl's theory of intentionality. Obviously Husserl did not end his investigation of intentionality in *Logische Untersuchungen*. On the contrary, he continued to develop it, as instanced in parts of *Ideen 1* that are dedicated precisely to the elaboration of a far more complex theory. Giving a detailed account for this later theory would lead me too far afield, but since the interpretation of Husserl's phenomenology just outlined is often based on a certain interpretation of his theory of intentionality in *Ideen 1*, I will have to say a few words about it.

Already in *Logische Untersuchungen* it was clear that an analysis of intentionality would have to distinguish between the immanent (reell) content of the act and the transcendent correlate of the act. This immanent content was made up of two different components, the sensations and the concrete intentions qua psychical processes (cf. p. 25). In *Ideen 1*, Husserl continues to hold this position, but he now employes a new terminology. As he puts it: The stream of consciousness contains two different components: 1) A level of non-intentional sensuous content, be it visual or tactile sensations, sensations of pain, nausea, and so forth. Husserl speaks of sensuous matter (*hyle*) or simply of *hyletic* matter; 2) An intentional dimension of animating or meaning-giving components. Husserl speaks of intentional form (*morphe*), but also and more frequently of *noesis* or of the *noetic* component (Hua 3/192–196). Whereas both of these components are immanent to the act, the transcendent, constituted correlate is now called the *noema*. This noema is often identified with the object-as-it-is-intended. One of the crucial and much debated problems has been to specify the relation between the object-as-it-is-intended and the object-that-is-intended. Are we dealing with two quite different ontological entities, or rather with two different perspectives on one and the same?

This so-called noema-discussion began in earnest with Føllesdal's 1969 publication of 'Husserl's notion of noema.' Although this discussion has at times almost led a life of its own, generating countless articles, it cannot be ignored since it bears on a very important issue. The noema-interpretation one adheres to has ramifications for one's interpretation of Husserl's theory of intentionality, as well as for one's general understanding of his phenomenological project.[21] Let me give a very brief outline of the two most important interpretations.

It is widely acknowledged that the noema is something that is only discovered through the epoché and the reduction. It is only then that we thematize the intended qua intended, that is, the object exactly as it is meant and given (Hua 3/202–205). But does the epoché imply that we parenthesize the transcendent spatio-temporal world in order to account for internal mental representations, or does the epoché rather imply that we continue to explore and describe the transcendent spatio-temporal world, but now in a new and different manner? Is the noema, the object-as-it-is-intended, to be identified with an internal mental representation—with an abstract and ideal sense—or rather with the givenness of the intended object itself?

Føllesdal, Dreyfus, Miller, Smith and McIntyre (often known as the California school, or the West Coast interpretation) have defended a *Fregean* interpretation of Husserl's theory of intentionality. According to them, the noema must be sharply distinguished from both act and object. It is an ideal meaning or sense which mediates the intentional relation between act and object. Thus, and very importantly, the noema is not taken to be that toward which consciousness is directed, but that by means of which it is directed, and by virtue of which we achieve a reference to the external object. The decisive feature of the Fregean approach is, consequently, that the intentionality of consciousness is conceived in analogy with the reference of linguistic expressions. In both cases the reference is determined by the sense, that is, in both cases the reference is effectuated *via* the sense. In short, the noema is an intermediary ideal entity which is instrumental in our intending the objects themselves. As Smith and McIntyre write: 'Husserl's theory of intentionality is not an object-theory but a mediator-theory . . . : for Husserl, an act is directed toward an object *via* an intermediate "intentional" entity, the act's noema.'[22]

In contrast, Sokolowski, Drummond, Hart, and Cobb-Stevens (often known as the East Coast interpretation) argue that intentionality is a fundamental feature of conscious experience, and they therefore deny what seems to follow from the mediator theory favored by the West Coast interpretation, namely that the intentional directedness of the act is a function of the intensional nature of the meaning. In their view, the purpose of the epoché and reduction is not to replace the worldly objects with mental representations. After the reduction, we continue to be concerned with the worldly object, but we now no longer consider it naively, rather we focus on it precisely as it is intended and given, that is as a correlate of experience. But to examine the object-as-it-is-intended, that is, the object in its significance for us, is, as Sokolowski emphasizes, to examine the object itself, it is not to examine a structure of consciousness.[23] As a consequence, it is argued that the noema is neither to be understood as an ideal meaning, a concept, or a proposition, it is not an intermediary between subject and object, it is not something that bestows intentionality on consciousness (as if consciousness prior to the introduction of the noema would be like a closed container with no bearing on the world), rather it is the object itself considered in the phenomenological reflection (in contrast to a psychological or linguistic reflection). The noema is the perceived object as perceived, the recollected episode as recollected, the judged state of affairs as judged, and so on. The object-as-it-is-intended is the object-that-is-intended abstractly considered (namely in abstraction from the positing that characterizes our natural attitude), and thus something capable of being given only in a phenomenological or transcendental attitude.[24] Thus, the East Coast interpretation would criticize the West Coast interpretation for confusing what is an ordinary object considered abstractly in a non-ordinary (phenomenological) attitude with a non-ordinary abstract entity.[25] Insofar as an investigation of the noema is an investigation of any kind of object, aspect, dimension, or region, considered in its very manifestation, in its very significance for consciousness, the object and the noema turn out to be the same differently considered. This does not imply, however, that there is no distinction (within the reflective stance) between the object-as-it-is-intended and the object-that-is-intended, but this distinction is a structural difference within the noema, and not a distinction between two ontologically different entities.[26] The noema does not direct us toward an object that is ontologically distinct from the noema, rather the intended object is itself the most fundamental moment *in* the noema, is itself a noematic component. As Drummond puts it, we do intend the object through its sense, but not through it in the sense of going beyond it, but through it in the sense of penetrating it.[27]

Given the East Coast interpretation of Husserl's concept of noema, is Husserl still to be characterized as an internalist? He is certainly not one, if internalism is understood as a theory claiming that internal representations (existing in some wordless mental realm) are the necessary and sufficient condition for any kind of reference. In its resolute showdown with representationalism, the East Coast interpretation fully shares Dreyfus's rejection of the traditional view according to which our ability to relate to objects requires the existence of internal representations in the mind.[28] But at the same time it also strongly questions the claim that Husserl's theory of intentionality ignores our involvement with existing reality and that the noema has the function it has regardless of how the world is. After all, the noema is nothing but the worldly object-as-it-is-intended.

The discussion of the noema is a highly technical discussion, and it would lead us too far afield if I were to account in further detail for the arguments given by the different positions. I will not hide, however, that my own sympathy is with the East Coast interpretation. There are several reasons for this, one of them being that I believe the Fregean interpretation of the noema goes hand in hand with an interpretation of Husserl's phenomenology that I reject. In my view, it is not possible to discuss the noema in isolation. It must necessarily be integrated into a more general interpretation of Husserl's transcendental-philosophical theory of reduction and constitution. As Husserl himself points out in his introductory remarks to the discussion of the relation between noesis and noema in part three of *Ideen 1*, 'Without having seized upon the peculiar ownness of the transcendental attitude and having actually appropriated the pure phenomenological basis, one may of course use the word, phenomenology; but one does not have the matter itself' (Hua 3/200). However, if one accepts the interpretation of epoché and reduction that I have offered above, it is obvious that one must reject the claim that seems to follow from the Fregean interpretation, namely, that the proper field of phenomenology is the intrinsic features or structures of consciousness itself, and that the execution of the phenomenological epoché consequently demands abstention from ontological commitment and neutrality when it comes to all questions concerned with being or existence. Thus, it is problematic to claim that Husserl's phenomenology is only to be understood as a theory of meaning and not as an ontology.[29] This misunderstanding might be based on a failure to distinguish between Husserl's descriptive phenomenology and his transcendental phenomenology—in *Logische Untersuchungen*, Husserl himself actually claimed that the *existence* of the object was phenomenologically irrelevant (Hua 19/59, 358, 387, 672)—or it might have come about through overlooking that, although Husserl's epoché suspends unjustified metaphysical assumptions, his phenomenology does not lack metaphysical implications altogether. As Husserl points out already in *Ideen 1*, however, phenomenology eventually integrates and includes everything that it had at first parenthesized for methodological reasons (Hua 3/107, 3/159, 3/337). It is against this background that Husserl can eventually claim that a fully developed transcendental phenomenology is *eo ipso* the true and realized ontology (Hua 8/215), where all ontological concepts and categories are clarified in their correlation to constituting subjectivity,[30] just as he also rejects any antimetaphysical interpretation of phenomenology:

Finally, lest any misunderstanding arise, I would point out that, as already stated, phenomenology indeed *excludes every naïve metaphysics* that operates with absurd things in themselves, but *does not exclude metaphysics as such*. . . . The intrinsically first being, the being that precedes and bears every worldly Objectivity, is transcendental intersubjectivity: the universe of monads, which effects its communion in various forms (Hua 1/38–39).

Phenomenology is anti-metaphysical insofar as it rejects every metaphysics concerned with the construction of purely formal hypotheses. But like all genuine philosophical problems, all metaphysical problems return to a phenomenological base, where they find their genuine transcendental form and method, fashioned from intuition (Hua 9/253. Cf. 5/141.).

As Landgrebe writes, the transcendental reduction is Husserl's road to the core-problems of metaphysics.[31]

To avoid misunderstandings, let me emphasize that this attempt to argue for a metaphysical dimension to phenomenology should not be seen as an endorsement of every metaphysical endeavor. 'Metaphysics' is an unusually ambiguous term, which can be understood and defined in a variety of quite different ways, say as

- a speculatively constructed philosophical system dealing with the 'first principles'
- a science of supersensible or transphenomenal entities
- an objectivistic attempt to describe reality from a view from nowhere, that is, as an attempt to provide an absolute nonperspectival account of reality
- an answer to the old question of *why* there is something rather than nothing
- a mode of thinking founded on the 'logic' of binary oppositions
- an attempt to answer the perennial questions concerning the meaning of factual human life[32]
- or simply as a systematic reflection on the nature of existing reality

It is only if metaphysics is taken in the last 'minimal' sense, that I consider metaphysical neutrality as a questionable transcendental-phenomenological move, a move that threatens to reintroduce some kind of two-world theory—the world as it is for us, and the world as it is in itself.

It is true that transcendental phenomenology and metaphysics are two very different enterprises. Metaphysics remains to some extent precritical or naïve. In its attempt to map out the building stones of reality it never leaves the natural attitude. It doesn't partake in the reflective move that is the defining moment of transcendental thought. Whereas metaphysics has a straightforward object-oriented nature, transcendental phenomenology does have a distinctly reflective orientation. But it is one thing to make this point, and something different to claim that transcendental phenomenology has no metaphysical impact whatsoever, as if it is in principle compatible with a variety of different metaphysical views. To argue like this is to make transcendental phenomenology indistinguishable from something quite different, namely phenomenological psychology. Phenomenological psychology is a regional ontological enterprise, whose basic task is to investigate the a priori structures that any possible (intentional) subject must be in possession of. But this task, important as it might be, should not, as Husserl himself has persistently emphasized, be confused with the objective of transcendental phenomenology. Transcendental phenomenology is not merely a theory about the structure of subjectivity, nor is it merely a theory about how we understand and perceive the world. It is not even a theory about how the world appears to us, if, that is, such a theory is supposed to be complemented by a further investigation (left to metaphysics) of what the world itself is like. To construe Husserlian phenomenology in such a way would make it vulnerable to the objection that it engages in an unphenomenological abstraction. Something crucial would be missing from its repertoire, being and reality would be topics left for other disciplines. And as we have just seen, this interpretation does neither respect nor reflect Husserl's own assertions on the matter.

When Husserl speaks of the world's ontic meaning (*Seinssinn*) and gives a detailed description of its constitution, he is not engaged in a semantic investigation of a mere dimension of sense that is taken to be ontologically separate from the actually existing world, but, on the contrary, he is exploring the signification of the latter. Husserl is not preoccupied with meaning-theoretical reflections that lack metaphysical and ontological implications, so to describe Husserl's reflections in this way is not only to misunderstand the true nature of his theory of intentionality, but also to overlook the transcendental philosophical status of his thought. As Fink remarks in an article from 1939, only a complete misunderstanding of the aim of phenomenology leads to the mistaken but often repeated claim that Husserl's phenomenology is not interested in reality or the question of being, but only in subjective meaning-formations in intentional consciousness.[33] Consequently, any attempt to support this narrow meaning-theoretical, semantic interpretation by referring to the places where Husserl speaks explicitly about the constitution of *sense* is useless, since this maneuver overlooks that Husserl has transcended the objectivistic distinction between meaning and being through his effectuation of the transcendental reduction. This does not imply, of course, that every meaningful entity exists. When speaking of an existing object, we are talking about an object in a preeminent mode of givenness, an object that is or could be bodily present, that is, intuitively given *in propria persona*.

It is only within the limits of Husserl's pretranscendental phenomenology that the distinction between being and meaning can be maintained. As I mentioned at the end of Part 1, in *Logische Untersuchungen* Husserl still claimed that questions concerning the existence of a mind-independent world were metaphysical questions that did not belong to phenomenology (Hua 19/26). Similarly, he could argue that it was irrelevant to phenomenology whether a perception was true or deceptive (Hua 19/358) since the task of phenomenology was exclusively to describe the phenomena qua phenomena. As long as the question concerning the metaphysical status of the intentional object remained in suspension, however, Husserl's phenomenology remained characterized by some decisive shortcomings. But Husserl's understanding of the topic and extent of phenomenology changed the moment he took the step to a clear-cut transcendental phenomenology. In the last part of *Ideen 1*, which carries the title 'Reason and Actuality,' Husserl actually treats the questions concerning objective reality and its correlation to rational consciousness. It was this analysis that gradually led Husserl toward an understanding of transcendental *inter*subjectivity as the foundation of worldly objectivity and reality (cf. p. 115 below).

In *Ideen 1*, Husserl writes that the noematic correlate can be called a sense in a very extended use of that word (Hua 3/203). Obviously the question is, how extended? One answer is given by Fink in his article 'Die phänomenologische Philosophie Edmund Husserls in der gegenwärtigen Kritik' (from 1933)—an article that Husserl himself introduced with the words 'I explicitly recognize every single sentence in this article as expressing my own conviction and standpoint.' Fink writes:

> If the psychological noema is the *meaning* of an actual intentionality which is to be distinguished from the being itself to which it is related, then by contrast the transcendental noema is this being itself.[34]

Fink's point is that, whereas we might distinguish between the noema and the object itself as long as we remain within a psychological stance, such a distinction is no longer acceptable when we adopt a transcendental attitude. From this perspective, there is no longer any ontological distinction between the constituted validity and significance of an object and its reality and being. In the same article, Fink also argues that the attempt to define phenomenology as an intentional psychology merely reveals that one remains within the natural attitude. He claims that it is only possible to understand the transcendental, that is, truly phenomenological concept of the noema in the light of the phenomenological reduction, writing that the difference between noema and object is in reality a difference internal to the noema, since the object that is intended is nothing but a noematic identity.[35] As Husserl himself wrote in 1922:

> To claim that consciousness 'relates' itself to a transcendent object through its immanent noematic Sinn (i.e., the meaningpole X in its noematic determinations

and its positional mode as existing) is a problematic and, to be more precise, false way of speaking. I have never meant something like this. I would be surprised if this formulation could be found in 'Ideas', but in its proper context it would then surely not have this meaning (Ms. B III 12 IV, 82a).[36]

Despite these critical remarks, I am not claiming that the Fregean interpretation of Husserl is completely without merits, nor that it lacks every kind of textual evidence. In his article 'Husserls Begriff des Noema' Rudolf Bernet has argued that Husserl's early notion of the noema is highly ambigious, and that it is possible to distinguish no less than three different concepts of the noema in *Ideen I* alone: 1) the noema understood as the concrete appearance, 2) the noema understood as the ideal meaning, 3) the noema understood as the constituted object.[37] Thus, as an attempt at reconciliation, it might be claimed that Husserl's concept of the noema is so ambiguous that it offers itself to several different interpretations. To a certain extent, Fink's distinction between a psychological and a transcendental concept of the noema can serve as a similar argument. But, of course, the central question is then *which* concept of the noema represents Husserl's mature view. For Ströker, to mention one last view, Husserl's concepts of noesis and noema are transcendental-phenomenological concepts, and it is, properly speaking, meaningless to suppose that the intended object should lie beyond the noematic sphere since the claim of transcendental philosophy is exactly that there is no such beyond, but only a constituted transcendence. According to Ströker, however, the reason why it has nevertheless been possible to find support for the thesis that the noema is merely that by means of which we intend the transcendent object is exactly because Husserl's own presentation in *Ideen I* constantly slides between the natural and the (transcendental) phenomenological attitude.[38]

Let me just add that, apart from discussing the noema in the context of a Husserl interpretation, it is also possible and quite legitimate to discuss it in connection with a systematic attempt to develop the most plausible theory of intentionality. It should not come as a surprise, however, that both competing interpretations claim that their own favored account accomplishes both the most faithful Husserl interpretation as well as the most plausible theory of intentionality. As a consequence, each side would argue that their own interpretation is systematically superior to the other side. To give but one example, the Fregean interpretation will typically argue that the East Coast interpretation has a hard time accounting for cases of hallucination, whereas they themselves can easily do so. In contrast, the

East Coast interpretation will argue that by conceiving the intentional re-lation as involving some kind of mediation, the Fregean approach offers an account that is vulnerable to the standard problems facing classical men-talism and representationalism, whereas their own interpretation brings subjectivity and world much closer together, thereby making Husserl's the-ory more akin to the positions held by later phenomenologists.

To a certain extent it is undoubtedly this systematic angle on the noema that is the most interesting, but the scope of the present book does not allow me to pursue it any further.[39]

II. Husserl's Cartesian way to the reduction, which seeks to justify the difference between world and consciousness by appealing to the fact that consciousness is given with a different kind of evidence than worldly objects, has often led to the claim that Husserl advocates a kind of *foun-dationalism.*[40] More precisely, Husserl's phenomenology has been inter-preted as an attempt to disclose a number of certain and indubitable truths that could serve as the systematic foundation and point of departure for all other types of knowledge.

It is not only the title of one of Husserl's more popular writings, *Philosophie als strenge Wissenschaft*, that has given rise to this interpretation, but also and perhaps to an even greater extent, Husserl's continuous at-tempt to uncover deeper and deeper layers in the constitutive life. Particu-larly in some of the early writings (for instance in the Cartesian epistemo-logical–oriented lecture course *Die Idee der Phänomenologie*) this attempt is described in a way that could easily give rise to the impression that phe-nomenology should neutralize and suspend every transcendent intention and every positing of that which is given inadequately in order to focus ex-clusively on the adequately and apodictically given subjective immanence (Hua 2/44–45).

Needless to say, Husserl would claim that the phenomenological analysis of transcendental subjectivity has quite a different status than, say, an anthropological investigation of the sex role patterns among tribes in New Guinea. To the extent that he is a transcendental philosopher, Husserl does search for some kind of foundation. He would insist that a clarifica-tion of transcendental subjectivity is an investigation into the very frame-work that makes all other sciences comprehensible. Transcendental phe-nomenology investigates the condition of the possibility for experience, meaning, and manifestation, and thereby also the framework within which all other sciences take place.

Despite this, there is, however, something very misleading about calling Husserl a foundationalist, at least if the term is used in its traditional epistemological sense. As Husserl himself observes in *Formale und Transzendentale Logik*, the very attempt to establish a science which is based exclusively on absolutely certain truths is one that ultimately involves a misunderstanding of the very nature of science (Hua 17/169). As it was pointed out in Part 1, Husserl's own concept of evidence by no means excludes errors or subsequent corrections (cf. also p. 138).

Husserl's view also differs from traditional foundationalism in a number of other ways:

1. First of all, Husserl does not conceive of his own transcendental analysis as a conclusive, final analysis. It is an exploration of a field, which in an absolute sense, is unavoidable (*unhintergehbar*). But the analysis of this field can always be refined, deepened, and improved. According to Husserl, the full and conclusive truth about the transcendental dimension is a regulative ideal. Philosophy as a science based on ultimate justification is an idea which can only be realized in an infinite historical process (Hua 8/186, 6/439).

2. Secondly, Husserl explicitly distances himself from the axiomatic and deductive ideal of method that rationalistic foundationalism has normally been committed to (Hua 1/63) and consequently denies that the transcendental 'I' could ever serve as the starting point for a transcendental deduction (Hua 6/193). Phenomenology is not a *deductive* discipline, but a *descriptive* discipline, for which reason Husserl repeatedly emphasized that it belongs to a quite different type of science than mathematics (Hua 3/158). To put it differently, the truths that transcendental phenomenology might uncover does not make up a foundation that the contents of the positive sciences could be deduced from.

I have already mentioned that Husserl takes adequate and conclusive truth as a regulative ideal, that is, a goal attainable only in infinite endeavor. Nevertheless, it is correct that, to a far larger extent than the later phenomenologists, Husserl was concerned with questions concerning the condition of possibility for knowledge and objectivity. However, one should note Husserl's motive for doing philosophy. It is not primarily a theoretical motivation, but a practical, or more precisely an *ethical* one—the ethical striving for a life in absolute self-responsibility (Hua 8/197).

Consequently, it is important not to overlook the ethical dimension in Husserl's thinking. Husserl speaks of an evidence-based, self-responsible life that the phenomenological search for a transcendental foundation makes possible (Hua 8/167). To live in the phenomenological attitude is not a neutral impersonal occupation, but a praxis of decisive personal and existential significance (Hua 6/140). In other words, philosophy is closely linked to an ethical life. In *Erste Philosophie 1* Husserl explicitly refers to this Socratic-Platonic idea of philosophy:

Socrates' ethical reform of life is characterized by its interpreting the truly satisfying life as a life of pure reason. This means a life in which the human being exercises in unremitting self-reflection and radical accountability a critique—an ultimately evaluating critique—of his life-aims and then naturally, and mediated through them, his life-paths and his current means. Such accountability and critique is performed as a process of cognition, and indeed, according to Socrates, as a methodical return [*Rückgang*] to the original source of all legitimacy and its cognition—expressed in our terminology, by going back to complete clarity, 'insight,' 'evidence' (Hua 7/9).

This normative-ethical motivation is particularly important the moment we realize that the attempt to work out an adequate foundation is an infinite ideal. It is exactly the demand for absolute self-responsibility that can urge us onward in our search for absolute evidence (Hua 8/196, 244, 5/139, 1/53).

To put it differently, what is decisive for Husserl is not the *possession* of absolute truth, but the very *attempt* to live a life in absolute self-responsibility, that is, the very attempt to base one's thoughts and deeds on as much insight as possible. And, as Husserl states in one of his still unpublished manuscripts, the self-responsibility of the individual also entails a responsibility for the community. Self-responsibility is fully realizable only in relation to other subjects (Ms. E III 4 18a, E III 4 31a. Cf. Hua 8/197–98, 15/422.).

Husserl's Transcendental Idealism

According to Husserl, every object must necessarily be understood in its correlation to experiencing (constituting) subjectivity if dogmatic presuppositions are to be avoided. But if a decisive break with ontological dogmatism demands and implies a return to the field of givenness, any assertion concerning the existence of an absolutely mind-independent reality seems unacceptable. We are thus confronted with Husserl's *idealism*.

Already in *Logische Untersuchungen*, Husserl declared that only an idealistic epistemology was coherent (Hua 19/112). At that time, idealism meant merely a theory that defended the irreducibility of ideality, that is, a theory that claimed that ideality could not be reduced to psychical or physical entities or processes. In *Cartesianische Meditationen* one finds the same thesis (Hua 1/118), but now it should be taken in a far more radical sense. After Husserl's transcendental turn, idealism is understood as a position that defends the transcendental primacy of subjectivity (Hua 8/215), a primacy that Husserl considers to be so central to phenomenology that he even identifies phenomenology and transcendental idealism:

Only someone who misunderstands either the deepest sense of intentional method, or that of transcendental reduction, or perhaps both, can attempt to separate phenomenology from transcendental idealism (Hua 1/119. Cf. 8/181.).

However, Husserl also repeatedly emphasizes that his transcendental-phenomenological idealism is radically unlike any traditional idealism, which by its very opposition to realism simply manifests its confinement within the natural attitude (Hua 5/149–153, 17/178, 1/33–34, 118). And as we have already seen, Husserl also quite unequivocally condemns phenomenalism:

It is the fundamental defect of phenomenalistic theories that they draw no distinction between appearance (*Erscheinung*) as intentional experience, and the apparent object (the subject of the objective predicates), and therefore identify the experienced complex of sensations with the complex of objective features (Hua 19/371 [546]).

However we may decide the question of the existence or non-existence of phenomenal external things, we cannot doubt that the reality of each such perceived thing cannot be understood as the reality of a perceived complex of sensations in a perceiving consciousness (Hua 19/764–765 [862]).

Thus, Husserl vehemently criticizes the view that the intentional object can be reduced to a complex of sensations. His idealism certainly does not imply any dissolution of worldly reality into mental content (Hua 3/335). But how then should one understand it?

According to Husserl, reality is not simply a brute fact detached from every context of experience and from every conceptual framework, but is a system of validity and meaning that needs subjectivity, that is, experiential and conceptual perspectives if it is to manifest and articulate itself. It is in this sense that reality depends on subjectivity, which is why Husserl could claim that it is just as nonsensical to speak of an absolute mind-independent reality as it is to speak of a circular square (Hua 3/120). This is obviously not to deny or question the existence of the real world, but simply to reject an objectivistic interpretation of its ontological status.

What does it mean to be a transcendent object? For Husserl, this question can only be answered critically, that is, undogmatically, by turning to the phenomenologically given, namely to the objects qua appearing. To speak of transcendent objects is to speak of objects that are not part of my consciousness and that cannot be reduced to my experience of them. It is to speak of objects that might always surprise us, that is, objects *showing themselves* differently than we expected. However, it is not to speak of objects as independent of or inaccessible to my perspective in any absolute sense. On the contrary, Husserl believes that it only makes sense to speak of transcendent objects insofar as they are transcendent *for us*. The objects only have significance for us through our consciousness of them. To be real, to be an objectively existing object, is to have a specific regulated structure of appearance, it is to be given for a subject in a certain way, with a certain meaning and validity, not in the sense that the object can exist only when it actually appears, but in the sense that its existence is connected to the possibility of such an appearance. To claim that there are objects that are not actually experienced—stones on the backside of the moon, plants in the Amazon jungle, or colors in the ultraviolet spectrum, for instance—is to claim that the objects in question are embedded in a *horizon* of experience and could be given *in principle* (though there might be empirical or anthropocentric difficulties connected to this). It is precisely for this reason that every transcendent object is said to remain part of the phenomenological field of research.

Occasionally, Husserl describes his idealism as an attempt to comprehend and clarify the richness and transcendence of the world through a systematic analysis of constituting intentionality (Hua 1/34). In this sense, Husserl's transcendental idealism can be seen as an attempt to redeem rather than renounce the realism of the natural attitude. Or, to put it differently, Husserl would claim that the transcendental reduction enables us to understand and account for the realism that is intrinsic to the natural attitude. In fact, Husserl writes that his transcendental idealism contains natural realism within itself (Hua 9/254).[41]

[T]he transcendent world; human beings; their intercourse with one another, and with me, as human beings; their experiencing, thinking, doing, and making, with one another: these are not annulled by my phenomenological reflection, not devalued, not altered, but only understood (Hua 17/282 [275]).

That the world exists, that it is given as an existing universe in uninterrupted experience which is constantly fusing into universal concordance, is entirely beyond doubt. But it is quite another matter to understand this indubitability which sustains life and positive science and to clarify the ground of its legitimacy (Hua 5/152–153).

There can be no stronger realism than this, if by this word nothing more is meant than: 'I am certain of being a human being who lives in this world, etc., and I doubt it not in the least.' But the great problem is precisely to understand what is here so 'obvious' (Hua 6/190–191 [187]).

No ordinary 'realist' has ever been so realistic and so concrete as I, the phenomenological 'idealist' (a term that I by the way don't use anymore) (Husserliana Dokumente III/7, 16).

In making these claims, Husserl is not only approaching Kant's famous dictum about the compatibility of transcendental idealism and empirical realism,[42] he is also getting close to what has occasionally been called internal realism. To a certain extent, it might actually be said that Husserl's criticism of representationalism does support a kind of (direct) realism. We are 'zunächst und zumeist' directed at real existing objects, and this directedness is not mediated by any intramental objects. But if one wants to call this position realism, it has to be emphasized that it is a realism based on experience. It is an experiential realism or an internal realism not unlike the one espoused by Hilary Putnam,[43] having no affinities with a metaphysical realism.

In the same breath, and perhaps even more appropriately, one might say that Husserl's criticism of representationalism can be seen as a criticism of both realism and idealism. If one defines the opposition between realism and idealism with the use of the doublet internal representation/external reality, idealism claiming that the only entity existing is the intramental representation, while realism claims that the mental representation corresponds to an extramental and mind-independent object, it is obvious that Husserl must reject both. To put it differently, it is relatively easy to define realism and idealism in such a way that both of them are unsuitable when it comes to a characterization of Husserl's phenomenology. To provide another such definition: If one defines idealism as the position that claims that subjectivity can persist without the world, and realism as the position claiming that the world can persist without subjectivity, then it is obvious that a position (compare Husserl's ontological way to the reduction) that insists on a strict correlation between the two is beyond both realism and idealism. Indeed, given such a definition of realism, it is even possible to describe Husserl's position as a kind of idealism, or to be more exact, as a kind of *antirealism*, insofar as it is incompatible with the realism in question. The lesson to learn is undoubtedly that the very notions of realism and idealism are so elastic as to be nearly useless. It is no coincidence that both Hans-Georg Gadamer and Fink have praised Husserl for overcoming the old opposition between realism and idealism,[44] and it is certainly true that he was neither a subjective idealist nor a metaphysical realist.

The Concept of Constitution

One of the recurrent problems in Husserl research has been the question of how exactly to understand Husserl's notion of constitution, particularly in its implications for the discussion between realism and idealism. Many of Husserl's critics have claimed that constitution is a creative process, accusing Husserl of an untenable idealism. Philosophers who have been more favorably inclined toward Husserl have often tried to counter this criticism in one of two (or both) ways. Either it has been claimed that the process of constitution merely denotes the epistemic relation between the experiencing subject and the experienced object (for which reason it is fully compatible with a realism), or it has been claimed that the dimension that is constituted by the transcendental subject is a dimension of meaning and not of being.

All three interpretations are problematic however, ultimately leaving one to ask whether the standard criticism of Husserl—who himself never gave a clear-cut answer to the question of whether constitution is to be understood as a creation or a restoration of reality—is not presenting us with a false alternative.[45] To paraphrase a remark that Putnam once made: It is not that the mind makes up the world, but it doesn't just mirror it either.[46]

To claim that the subject is the condition of the possibility for objects is not to postulate a causal connection between the subject and objects. On the contrary, the conditioning in question is exactly of a noncausal kind. Constituting subjectivity should never be compared to a 'Big Bang'; it does not initiate a causal process that determines everything else. But then what exactly is *constitution*? To make a very concise suggestion: Constitution must be understood as a process that allows for manifestation and signification, that is, it must be understood as a process that permits that which is constituted to appear, unfold, articulate, and show itself as what it is (Hua 15/434, 14/47). As Heidegger was to observe: '"Constituting" does not mean producing in the sense of making and fabricating; it means *letting the entity be seen in its objectivity*.'[47] Contrary to another widespread misunderstanding, however, this process does not take place out of the blue, as if it were deliberately and impulsively initiated and controlled *ex nihilo* by the transcendental ego.[48] As Husserl points out in a manuscript from 1931, constitution has two primal sources, the primal ego and the primal non-ego. Both are inseparably one, and thus abstract if regarded on their own (Ms. C 10 15b). Both are irreducible structural moments in the process of constitution, the process of bringing to appearance. Thus, although Husserl insists that subjectivity is a condition of the possibility for manifestation, he apparently does not think that it is the only one. That is, although it might be a necessary condition, it is not a sufficient one. Since Husserl occasionally identifies the non-ego with the world (Hua 15/131, 287, Ms. C 2 3a)—thereby operating with a more fundamental notion of the world than the concept of an objective reality which he attempted to nihilate in § 49 of *Ideen I*—and since he even finds it necessary to speak of the world as a *transcendental non-ego* (Ms. C 7 6b), I think it justifiable to conclude that he conceives of constitution as a process involving several intertwined transcendental constituents, both subjectivity and world (and ultimately also intersubjectivity, cf. p. 115 below). What is particularly relevant in this context is that Husserl takes the process of constitution to presuppose an element of *facticity*, a passive pregivenness without any active participation or contribution by the ego (Hua 13/427, 11/386). Obviously, this should not be taken as a new form of dualism, on the contrary, the idea is exactly that subjectivity and world cannot be understood in separation from each other. Thus, Husserl's position seems very close to the one adopted by Merleau-Ponty in the following passage:

The world is inseparable from the subject, but from a subject which is nothing but a project of the world, and the subject is inseparable from the world, but from a world which the subject itself projects. The subject is a being-in-the-world and the world remains 'subjective' since its texture and articulations are traced out by the subject's movement of transcendence.[49]

Constitution is a process that unfolds itself in the structure subjectivity-world. For that reason constitution cannot be interpreted as a contingent animation of some meaningless sense data, nor as an attempt to deduce or reduce the world from or to a worldless subject.[50] To speak of transcendental subjectivity as the constituting and meaning-giving entity (Hua 8/457, 17/251, 15/366) and to speak of objects as being constituted by and dependent on subjectivity is formally to speak of the structure subjectivity-world as the transcendental framework within which objects can appear.

Against this background, it is once again possible to illustrate that Husserl's idealism differs from any traditional idealism. Although Husserl apparently claims that the world depends upon constituting subjectivity (Hua 3/104–106, 159, 5/153), one should pay attention to the transformation of the concepts 'subject' and 'world' that takes place through the transcendental reduction. As Husserl occasionally writes, being and consciousness are mutually interdependent and united in transcendental subjectivity (Hua 1/117). Similarly, Husserl's concept of the 'monad'—which is his term for the subject in its full concretion—encompasses not merely the intentional life, but also all the objects that are constituted through it (Hua 1/26, 102, 135, 14/46). Although Husserl does not always formulate himself in this manner, it cannot be doubted that his concept of subjectivity gradually expanded until it surpassed or even undermined the traditional opposition between subject and object (cf. Hua 6/265). To rephrase: Husserl operates with two different concepts of subjectivity, a narrow and abstract concept that resembles the one we normally use, and a broader and more concrete one that encompasses both consciousness and world. As Husserl writes (with a critical jab at his own presentation in *Ideen 1*), it is an abstraction to speak of a pure, worldless I-pole, for full subjectivity is a world-experiencing life (Hua 15/287). This is one of the reasons why Husserl eventually started using concepts like *lifeworld* and *life of world-consciousness* (*Weltbewußtseinsleben*) (Hua 29/192, 247).

Eventually, Husserl gave up the idea of a static correlation between the constituting and the constituted. As he points out in some of his later writings, the constitutive performance is characterized by a certain reciprocity insofar as the constituting subject is itself constituted in the very process of constitution. It is against this background that one should understand assertions from *Cartesianische Meditationen* to the effect that the constitution of the world implies a mundanization of the constituting subject (Hua 1/130), that is, that the subject's constitutive experience of the world goes hand in hand with the subject's constitutive experience of its own worldly being. This is why Husserl also speaks of the mutual interdependency between the constitution of space and spatial objects on the one side and the body's self-constitution on the other (Hua 5/128, 15/546). In short, it is a misunderstanding to claim that the transcendental subject remains unaffected by its own constitutive performance, just as it is a mistake to think that the subject could somehow abstain from constituting. The subject exists as constituting, and this constitution entails at the same time the self-constitution of the constituting subject:

The constituting consciousness constitutes itself, the objectivating consciousness objectivates itself—and indeed, in such a way that it brings about an objective nature with the form of spatiotemporality; within this nature, my own lived body; and, psychophysically one with the latter (and thereby localized in natural spatiotemporality according to place, temporal position, and duration), the entire constituting life, the entire *ego*, with its stream of consciousness, its ego-pole and habitualities (Hua 15/546).

Obviously these reflections question any thesis concerning the existence of a worldless transcendental subject.[51] They are reflections that one finds further developed by Husserl's assistant Eugen Fink, who writes that the true topic of phenomenology is neither the world nor a worldless subject, but the becoming of the world in the self-constitution of the transcendental subject.[52]

    One of the consequences of these reflections is that the empirical subject can no longer be regarded as a mere contingent appendix to the transcendental subject, and therefore no longer as something that transcendental phenomenology can allow itself to ignore. On the contrary, it is of decisive importance to understand why, as part of the constitutive process, the transcendental subject must *necessarily* conceive of itself as a worldly entity. As Husserl writes in the supplementary volume to *Krisis*, it is apodictically certain that the I must appear in the world as a human being (that is, as a mundane entity). The explanation offered by Husserl— and this is something I will pursue in Part 3—is that the transcendental subject can only constitute an objective world if it is *incarnated* and *socialized*, both of which entails a mundanization (Hua 29/160–165, 1/130, 5/128, 16/162).

To put it differently, in order to understand Husserl's final position it is (as already mentioned) not sufficient simply to operate with the subjectivity-world dyad. Intersubjectivity must also be taken into regard as the third indispensable element. As we have already seen, Husserl takes self- and world-constitution to go hand in hand, but he would also claim that the world- and self-constitution takes place intersubjectively (Hua 1/166). And when it comes to intersubjectivity, he explicitly states that it is unthinkable unless it is

explicitly or implicitly in communion. This involves being a plurality of monads that constitutes in itself an Objective world and that spatializes, temporalizes, realizes itself—psychophysically and, in particular, as human beings—within that world (Hua 1/166. Cf. 8/505–506.).

The constitution of the world, the unfolding of self, and the establishing of intersubjectivity are all parts in an interrelated and simultaneous process. As Husserl wrote in *Ideen 11*, I, we, and the world belong together (Hua 4/288). Ultimately, the constitutive process occurs in a threefold structure, *subjectivity-intersubjectivity-world*.

Husserl's formulations and terminology are not always crystal clear, but the main idea is relatively straightforward: Husserl consistently claims that reality can only appear thanks to subjectivity. But eventually he came to the realization that 1) the subject does not remain untouched by its constitutive performance, but is, on the contrary, drawn into it, just as 2) constitution is not simply a relation between a singular subject and the world, but an intersubjective process. The problem he then faced was to clarify the exact interrelation between subjectivity, world, and other. This is made most explicit in his last writings, where the three are increasingly intertwined. It does not matter which of the three one takes as a starting point, for one will still be inevitably led to the other two: Constituting subjectivity only gains its full relation to itself and to the world in relation to the other, that is, in intersubjectivity; intersubjectivity only exists and develops in the mutual interrelationship between subjects that are related to the world; and the world must be conceived as a common and public field of experience (cf. Hua 8/505, 15/373, 13/480, Ms. C 17 33a).

If Husserl's final position should remind some readers of elements in Hegel's thought, this is probably not without reason. However, as Fink has pointed out, Husserl's theory—no matter how speculative it might sound—

is no speculative construction, but a simple articulation of the fundamental insights of the phenomenological reduction.[53] It is certainly striking how many similarities there are between Husserl's account of the relation between self, world, and other, and the accounts to be found among the later phenomenologists (Heidegger, Sartre, and Merleau-Ponty). To conclude, let me illustrate this with a couple of passages in which Heidegger describes Dasein's being-in-the-world:

World exists—that is, it is—only if Dasein exists, only if there is Dasein. Only if world is there, if Dasein exists as being-in-the-world, is there understanding of being, and only if this understanding exists are intraworldly beings unveiled as extant and handy. World-understanding as Dasein-understanding is self-understanding. Self and world belong together in the single entity, the Dasein. Self and world are not two beings, like subject and object, or like I and thou, but self and world are the basic determination of the Dasein itself in the unity of the structure of being-in-the-world.[54]

Because being-in-the-world belongs to the basic constitution of the Dasein, the existent Dasein is essentially *being-with* others *as being-among* intraworldly beings. As being-in-the-world it is never first merely being among things extant within the world, then subsequently to uncover other human beings as also being among them. Instead, as being-in-the-world it is being with others, apart from whether and how others are factically there with it themselves. On the other hand, however, the Dasein is also not first merely being-with others, only then later to run up against intraworldly things in its being-with-others; instead, being-with-others means being-with other being-in-the-world—being-with-in-the-world. . . . Put otherwise, being-in-the-world is with equal originality both being-with and being-among.[55]

3

The Later Husserl: Time, Body, Intersubjectivity, and Lifeworld

In Parts 1 and 2, I first presented a number of central aspects of Husserl's theory of intentionality, and then went on to account for the more general character of his transcendental phenomenology. The underlying claim has been that it was Husserl's more and more radical analysis of intentionality that led him toward transcendental philosophy. To argue that subjectivity is not merely yet another entity in the world, but a condition of the possibility for appearance and meaning, and that it is the very dimension where reality can display and manifest itself in all its richness is, however, not the end but only the beginning of phenomenological work. As Husserl puts it, the nature of intentionality might seem obvious, particularly when defined as a consciousness *of* something. But this platitude merely conceals its enigmatic nature. In reality, 'intentionality' is the title of a problem, and not the answer to all the questions (Hua 3/200–201, 337). More thorough investigations are therefore called for.

This third part will be divided into four sections, each presenting different aspects of Husserl's continuing investigation of the constitutive process. Although all four topics can already be found in Husserl's early writings, nevertheless each increase in significance in the course of his writings. Each section, therefore, will also serve as a presentation of Husserl's later thinking.

A. Time

The analysis of time-consciousness is not simply one analysis among many. On the contrary, it concerns, in Husserl's own words, one of the most difficult and important areas in phenomenology (Hua 10/276, 334). It is not without reason, then, that Husserl begins his *Vorlesungen zur Phänomenologie des inneren Zeitbewußtseins* by quoting Augustine's famous words from *Confessions* book 11, chapter. 14: 'What then is time? If no one asks me, I know: if I wish to explain it to one that asketh, I know not.'

Why does Husserl ascribe such central importance to the investigation of temporality? First of all, Husserl's investigation of intentionality would remain incomplete as long as one ignored the temporal dimension of intentional acts and intentional objects. Without an investigation of time-consciousness it would not be possible to understand the crucial relation between perception and recollection, for instance, nor to understand the important *syntheses of identity*: If I move around an oak in order to obtain a more exhaustive presentation of it, then the different profiles of the oak do not present themselves as disjointed fragments, but are perceived as synthetically integrated moments. This process of synthesization is temporal in nature. Moreover, Husserl also claims that the intentional object is only constituted as an object—as act-transcendent—the moment we experience it as an identity in a manifold, that is, the moment we establish its identity across different acts and appearances. But this experience of the identity of the object across a change in acts (and appearances) is an experience that once again draws on the contribution of our time-consciousness (Hua 11/110–111, 10, 1/96, 155, 17/291). Ultimately, Husserl argues, temporality must be regarded as the formal condition of possibility for the constitution of any objects (Hua 11/125, 128).

Secondly, and even more importantly, Husserl's transcendental analyses cannot simply make do with a clarification of the constitution of objects. In *Ideen 1*, for instance, Husserl confined himself to an analysis of the relation between the constituted objects and the constituting consciousness. He accounted for the way in which the givenness of objects is conditioned by subjectivity, but apart from stressing that experiences are not given in the same (perspectival) manner as objects, he did not pursue the question concerning the givenness of subjectivity itself any further. However, such a silence is *phenomenologically* unacceptable. Any analysis of the conditioned appearance of objects necessarily lacks a foundation as long as the givenness of the subjective condition is left in the dark. Husserl was well aware of this, and in *Ideen I* he explicitly admits leaving out the most important problems, namely, those pertaining to inner time-consciousness. And as he adds, only an analysis of time-consciousness will disclose the truly absolute (Hua 3/182). Husserl speaks of a phenomenological absolute, and, more generally, of the analysis of temporality as constituting the bedrock of phenomenology exactly because it is not by any means to be taken as a mere investigation of the temporal givenness of objects. It is also an account of the temporal *self-givenness* of consciousness itself.

Primal Impression-Retention-Protention

What is time? In daily life time is spoken of in a variety of ways. The universe is said to have existed for many billions of years. In geology one can say that the Permian period, the most recent period of the Paleozoic period, lasted around 41 million years. One can also speak of the medieval age; one can refer to the German occupation of Denmark which began on April 9, 1940; and one can announce that the train will leave in twenty-two minutes. In other words, in daily life it is taken for granted that there is a datable, measurable, historical, and cosmic time. Husserl's analysis, however, is not primarily concerned with these forms of time, though by no means is he denying that one can speak of an objective time. Rather he claims that it is philosophically unacceptable simply to assume that time possesses such an objective status. The phenomenologically pertinent question is how time can appear with such a validity, that is, how it is constituted with such a validity: In order to begin this analysis, it is, however, necessary to perform an epoché. We will have to suspend our naive beliefs regarding the existence and nature of objective time, and, instead, take our point of departure in the type of time we are directly acquainted with. We have to turn to *experienced* or *lived time*.

In order to investigate the role and structure of time-consciousness, Husserl abandons his preferred examples of trees and tables in favor of what he calls temporal objects (*Zeitobjekte*), that is, objects that have a temporal extension and whose different aspects cannot exist simultaneously but only appear across time, for instance, melodies (Hua 10/23). The central question is: How can I experience such objects? Husserl's fundamental claim is that our experience of a temporal object (as well as our experience of change and succession) would be impossible if our consciousness were only conscious of that which is given in a punctual now, and if the stream of consciousness consequently consisted in a series of isolated now-points, like a line of pearls. If this were the case, were we only able to experience that which is given right now, we would, in fact, be unable to experience anything with a temporal extension, that is, anything that endured. This is obviously not the case, so consequently we are forced to acknowledge that our consciousness, one way or the other, can encompass more than that which is given right now. We can be co-conscious of that which has just been, and that which is just about to occur. However, the crucial question still remains, *how* can we be conscious of that which is no longer or not yet present to our consciousness?

According to Brentano, it is our *imagination* that enables us to transcend the punctual now. We perceive that which occurs right now, and imagine that which is no longer or which has not yet occurred. Husserl, however, rejects this proposal since he considers it to imply a counterintuitive claim: We cannot perceive objects with temporal extension, we can only imagine them. Thus, Brentano's theory seems unable to account for the fact that we are apparently able to hear, and not simply imagine, a piece of music or an entire conversation.

Husserl's own alternative is to insist on the *width of presence*. Let us imagine that we are hearing a triad consisting of the tones C, D, and E. If we focus on the last part of this perception, the one that occurs when the tone E sounds, we do not find a consciousness that is exclusively conscious of the tone E, but a consciousness that is still conscious of the two former notes D and C. And not only that, we find a consciousness that still *hears* the first two notes (it neither imagines nor remembers them). This does not mean that there is no difference between our consciousness of the present tone E and our consciousness of the tones D and C. D and C are not simultaneous with E, but, on the contrary, we are experiencing a temporal succession. D and C are tones that have been and are *perceived* as *past*, for which reason we can actually experience the triad in its temporal duration, rather than simply as isolated tones that replace each other abruptly.[1] We can perceive temporal objects because consciousness is not caught in the now. We do not merely perceive the now-phase of the triad, but also its past and future phases.

Let me introduce the technical terms used by Husserl to describe this case. Husserl operates, first of all, with a moment of the concrete act that is narrowly directed toward the now-phase of the object. He calls this moment the *primal impression*. On its own, this cannot provide us with a perception of a temporal object; it is, in fact, merely an abstract component of the act that never appears in isolation. The primal impression must be situated in a temporal horizon; and be accompanied by a *retention*, an intention that provides us with a consciousness of the phase of the object that has just been, and a *protention*, a more or less indefinite intention of the phase of the object about to occur (Hua 9/202, 33/46). Husserl, consequently, argues that in an implicit and unthematic manner we always anticipate that which is about to happen. That this anticipation is an actual part of our experience can be illustrated by the fact that we would be *surprised* if the wax figure suddenly moved or if the door we opened hid a stone wall. It only makes sense to speak of a surprise in the light of a certain anticipation, and since we can always be surprised, we always have a horizon of anticipation (Hua 11/7).

Both retention and protention have to be distinguished from proper (thematic) *recollection* and *expectation*. There is an obvious difference between retaining and protending the tones that have just sounded and are just about to sound, and remembering a past holiday or looking forward to the next vacation. Whereas the two latter intentions are independent intentional acts which presuppose the work of the retention and the protention, the protention and retention are dependent moments of an occurrent experience. They do not provide us with new intentional objects, but with a consciousness of the temporal horizon of the present object. If we compare the retention and the recollection, the first is an intuition, even if it is an intuition of something absent, something that has just existed (Hua 10/41, 118). The recollection, in contrast, is a re-presenting (*vergegenwärtigende*) intentional act directed toward a completed past occurrence (Hua 10/333).[2] Whereas the so-called retentional modification is a *passive* process which takes place without our active contribution, a recollection is an act which we can initiate ourselves.[3]

Since the presenting function of perception depends upon the contribution of the retention and its ability to retain that which has become absent, it would be wrong to identify the intuitively given with that which in a narrow sense is present, namely the punctual now-phase of the object.

It is, in part, for this reason that Husserl claims that the analysis of retention has led to a significant widening of the phenomenological field (Hua 11/324–325, 13/162). Whether Husserl's acknowledgment of the decisive contribution of retention does in fact commit him to a *metaphysics of presence* is something I will address later (cf. p. 93).

Let me emphasize that the primal impression (also known as the primal presentation) is Husserl's term for our *consciousness* of the now-phase of the object, not for this now-phase itself. It is, in fact, crucial to distinguish the different phases of the object from the following structure of consciousness: Primal impression-retention-protention (Hua 10/372, Ms. C 2 11a). The retention and the protention are not past or future in respect to the primal impression, but 'simultaneous' with it. Every actual phase of consciousness contains the structure primal impression (A), retention (B), and protention (C) (Ms. C 3 8a). The correlates of this triadic ecstatic-centered structure are the now phase (O2), the past phase (O1), and the future phase (O3) of the object (cf. Figure 1). The now-phase of the object has a horizon, but it is *not* made up of the retention and the protention, but of the past and future phases of the object.[4]

Let me return to the triad C, D, and E. When C is heard, it is intended by the primal impression. When it is succeeded by D, D is given in

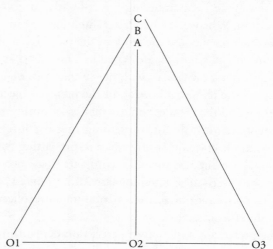

FIGURE 1. The relation between the primal
impression-retention-protention and the
different temporal phases of the object.

the primal impression, whereas C is now retained by the retention, and when E sounds, it replaces D in the primal impression, while D is now retained by the retention. The retention, however, is not simply a consciousness of the tone that has just been. When C is succeeded by D, then our impressional consciousness of D is accompanied by a retention of C (Dc). When D is replaced by E, then our impressional consciousness of E is accompanied by a retention of D (Ed), but also by a retention of the tone which was retained in D (Ec) (Hua 10/81, 100). This should be clear from Figure 2, where the horizontal line designates the series of tones (C, D, E, F); while the vertical line (say 'F, E, Ed, Ec) designates an actual phase of consciousness, consisting of protention, primal impression, and retentions; and where the diagonal line (say C, Dc, Ec, Fc) illustrates how a specific tone remains the same when it sinks into the past, though its mode of givenness is changing. The primal impression is 'simultaneous' with the whole series of retentions. But that which is given in the primal impression is not simultaneous with that which is conscious in the retention, and that which is retained by the first retention is not simultaneous with that which is retained in the retention of the retention. The order of the tones is preserved. They are not given simultaneously but in succession. A specific tone ceases to be present, and becomes past. But it keeps its position in the temporal order. One could say that the tone is always located at a certain point in time, but that the distance between this point and the actual now continues to increase (Hua 10/64). The fact that the tone is located in a temporal order with a certain unchangeable structure that can be recalled again and again and identified in recollection is, for Husserl, the first step toward the constitution of objective time, toward the constitution of the 'time of the clock.'

So far I have only described the constitution of temporal objects, but our very perception of these objects is, according to Husserl, also temporally constituted. Our acts and experiences are themselves temporal unities which arise, persist, and perish. They are also constituted in a network of primal impressional, retentional, and protentional intentions, and are only given, only self-aware within this framework (Hua 11/233, 293, 4/102, EU 205). Husserl, consequently, radicalizes his analysis of constitution. It is not only transcendent objects which are constituted. The subjective acts are also constituted and brought to appearance, and the difficult task is to disclose this last and absolute constitutive dimension. What is it that constitutes the intentional acts?

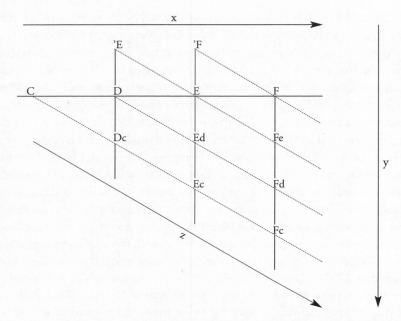

FIGURE 2. The structure of time-consciousness. This figure is a slightly simplified version of a diagram found in Hua 33/22.

Absolute Consciousness

The first and decisive point to make is that our consciousness of that which is given in constituted time (be it the constituted time of objects [objective time] or the constituted time of the experiences [subjective time]) is not itself given in the same kind of time, since this would lead to an infinite regress. If time-constituting consciousness were itself given in constituted time, it would be necessary to posit yet another higher-order time-constituting consciousness, and so forth. It is for this reason that Husserl denies that the time-constituting consciousness, the *absolute stream* as he also calls it, is *simultaneous* with that which is temporally constituted (Hua 10/96, 371). To speak of simultaneity is to posit a common temporal denominator, which is exactly what has to be avoided. The stream is not influenced by temporal change; it does not arise or perish in objective time, nor does it endure like a temporal object (Hua 10/113). Occasionally, Husserl will speak of the stream as if it were atemporal or supratemporal (Hua 10/112),[5] but this should not be misunderstood. The stream is atemporal in the sense of not being *in* time, but it is not atemporal in the sense of lacking any reference to time. On the contrary, the stream is always present, and this standing now (*nunc stans*) of the stream is itself a kind of temporality.[6] To put it differently, inner time-consciousness is not simply a consciousness *of* time, it is itself a temporal process of a very special nature.

Husserl consequently operates with three different types of temporality. The objective time of the appearing objects, the subjective or pre-empirical time of the acts and experiences, and, finally, the prephenomenal absolute streaming of inner time-consciousness (Hua 10/73, 76, 358).

The decisive difficulty that Husserl struggled with until the very end was to account for the relation between the subjective time and this absolute streaming. His reflections, which are primarily to be found in the so-called C and L manuscripts, are difficult and rather enigmatic. Therefore I must emphasize that the interpretation I am offering will be tentative.

As far as I can judge, it is only possible to understand Husserl's reflections on the relation between subjective time and the absolute streaming if they are connected to his analysis of the relation between *reflective* and *prereflective* self-awareness, that is, to the relation between the kind of self-awareness that comes about as a result of an explicit, thematic, objectifying reflection, and the kind of implicit self-awareness that characterizes all of our conscious acts and is a condition of the possibility for reflective self-awareness.[7] So, let me first say a few words about this distinction.

According to Husserl, to be a subject is to exist for-itself, that is, to be self-aware. Thus, rather than being something that only occurs during exceptional circumstances—that is, whenever we pay attention to our conscious life—self-awareness is a feature characterizing subjectivity as such, no matter which worldly entities it might otherwise be conscious of or occupied with.[8] In Husserl's words:

To be a subject is to be in the mode of being aware of oneself (Hua 14/151).

An absolute existent is existent in the form of an intentional life—which, no matter what else it may be intrinsically conscious of, is, at the same time, consciousness of itself. Precisely for that reason (as we can see when we consider more profoundly) it has at all times an essential ability to *reflect* on itself, on all its structures that stand out for it—an essential ability to make itself thematic and produce judgments, and evidences, relating to itself (Hua 17/279–280 [273, transl. modified]).

[E]very experience is 'consciousness,' and consciousness is consciousness *of*. . . . But every experience is *itself experienced* [*erlebt*], and *to that extent* also 'conscious' [*bewußt*] (Hua 10/291 [transl. modified]).

When Husserl claims that subjectivity is per se self-aware, he is not advocating a strong Cartesian thesis concerning total and infallible self-transparency, but simply calling attention to the intimate link between experiential phenomena and first-person givenness, in much the same way as Thomas Nagel and John Searle have later done. In his view, the subjective or first-person givenness of the experience is not simply a quality added to the experience, a mere varnish as it were. On the contrary, it constitutes the very mode of being of the experience. In contrast to physical objects that can exist regardless of whether or not they de facto appear for a subject, experiences are essentially characterized by their subjective givenness, by the fact that there is a subjective 'feel' to them. To undergo an experience necessarily means that there is something 'it is like' for the subject to have that experience.[9] But, insofar as there is something 'it is like' for the subject to have experiences, there must be some awareness of these experiences themselves. In short, there must be some minimal form of self-awareness. In fact, to be conscious rather than, say, in a coma, is exactly to be immediately and non-inferentially aware of one's occurrent experiences. To be acquainted with an experience in this first-personal mode of givenness is to be in possession of a primitive type of self-awareness, and, on this account, the only type of experience that would lack self-awareness would be an experience the subject was not conscious of, that is, an 'unconscious experience.'

If we now turn to the issue of reflection, Husserl considers the act of reflection—an explicit consciousness of an occurrent perception of a Swiss army knife, for instance—to be *founded* in a twofold sense. It does not present us with a self-enclosed subjectivity, but with a self-transcending subjectivity directed at an object, consequently presupposing the preceding act of object-intentionality (Hua 15/78, 8/157). Moreover, as an explicit self-awareness, it also relies on a prior, tacit self-awareness. To utilize a terminological distinction between perceiving (*Wahrnehmen*) and experiencing (*Erleben*) dating back to the *Logische Untersuchungen*: Prior to reflection one perceives the intentional object, but one experiences [*erlebt*] the intentional act. Although I am not intentionally directed at the act (this only happens in the subsequent reflection, where the act is thematized), it is not unconscious but conscious (Hua 3/162, 168, 251, 349, 9/29), that is, given in an implicit and prereflective manner (Hua 4/118).

According to Husserl, our acts are tacitly self-aware, but they are also accessible to reflection. They can be reflected on and thereby brought to our attention (Hua 4/248). An examination of the particular intentional structure of this process can substantiate this thesis concerning the founded status of reflection. Reflective self-awareness is often taken to be a thematic, articulated, and intensified self-awareness, normally initiated in order to bring the primary intentional act into focus. However, in order to explain the occurrence of reflection it is necessary that that which is to be disclosed and thematized is (unthematically) present, otherwise there would be nothing to motivate and call forth the act of reflection. As Husserl points out, it is in the nature of reflection to grasp something that was already given prior to the grasping. Reflection is characterized by disclosing, not by producing its theme:

When I say 'I,' I grasp myself in a simple reflection. But this self-experience [*Selbsterfahrung*] is like every experience [*Erfahrung*], and, in particular, every perception a mere directing myself towards something that was already there for me, that was already conscious, but not thematically experienced, nor noticed (Hua 15/492–493).

Whenever I reflect, I find myself 'in relation' to something as affected or active. That to which I am related is experientially conscious—it is already there for me as a 'lived-experience' in order for me to be able to relate myself to it (Ms. C 10 13a).[10]

In short, reflection is not an act sui generis, it does not appear out of nowhere, but presupposes, like all intentional activity, a *motivation*. According to Husserl, to be motivated is to be *affected* by something, and then to respond to it (Hua 4/217). I can thematize myself because I am already passively self-aware, I can grasp myself because I am already affected by myself (Hua 6/111, 15/78, 120).

When I start reflecting, that which motivates the reflection and which is then grasped has already been going on for a while. The reflected experience did not commence the moment I started paying attention to it, and it is not only given as still existing, but also and primarily as having already been. It is the *same* act that is now given reflectively, given to me as enduring in time—that is, as a temporal act (Hua 3/95, 162–164). When reflection sets in, it initially grasps something that has just elapsed, namely the motivating phase of the act reflected upon. The reason why this phase can still be thematized by the subsequent reflection is that it does not disappear, but is retained in the *retention*, for which reason Husserl can claim that retention is a condition of the possibility for reflection. It is, as he writes, because of the retention that consciousness can be made into an object (Hua 10/119). In other words, reflection can only take place if a *temporal horizon* has been established.

This brings us back to the issue of temporality and to the relation between the absolute streaming inner time-consciousness and the temporally constituted act. How should one conceive of this relation? One possibility is to conceive of it by analogy to the relation between the intentional act and the intentional object. Just as we have to distinguish between the constituted objects and the constituting acts that permit them to appear, we have to distinguish between the constituted acts and the deeper constituting time-consciousness that allows them to appear. Thus, it is the absolute streaming inner time-consciousness that makes us conscious of the acts qua temporal objects in subjective time. This has been the reigning interpretation for quite a while, but I find it problematic.[11]

One problem confronting Husserl's analysis was the threat of an infinite regress. When Husserl claims that the intentional act is constituted in inner time-consciousness, he does not mean that the act is brought to givenness by some other part of subjectivity. Inner time-consciousness is the prereflective self-awareness of the act, so to say that the act is constituted in inner time-consciousness simply means that it is brought to awareness thanks to itself. It is called *inner* time-consciousness because it belongs to the innermost structure of the act itself. To phrase it differently, Husserl's description of the structure of inner time-consciousness (primal impression-retention-protention) might be seen as an analysis of the structure of the prereflective self-manifestation of our acts and experiences. Thus, Husserl's position is relatively unequivocal: The intentional act is conscious of something different from itself, namely the intentional object, but the act also manifests itself. The object is given through the act, and if there were no awareness of the act, the object itself would not appear. Therefore, apart from being intentional, the act is also characterized by its 'internal consciousness,' '*Urbewußtsein*,' or 'impressional consciousness,' to mention three different terms for one and the same (Hua 4/118–119, 10/83, 89–90, 119, 126–127, 23/321).

Subjectivity is, as such, self-temporalizing, with intentional acts originally given as waves in this streaming experiencing, to use Husserl's own metaphor (Hua 10/75, Ms. C 17 63a). Originally, the intentional acts are moments of the self-temporalizing streaming and, therefore, *not* temporally constituted distinct and enduring *objects*. It is only the moment we start to thematize these acts, be it in a reflection or recollection, that they are constituted as objects in subjective, sequential time.[12] Prior to reflection, there is no awareness of internal objects, just as there is no distinction between the givenness of the act and the self-manifestation of the flow. As for the acts objectified by reflection, these cannot be separated from the flow either, since they are nothing but the flow's own *reflective* self-manifestation. That is, the absolute flow of experiencing and the constituted stream of reflectively thematized acts are not two separate flows, but simply two different manifestations of one and the same. Thus, Husserl can write:

> We say, I am who I am in my living. And this living is a lived-experiencing [*Erleben*], and its reflectively accentuated single moments can be called 'lived-experiences' [*Erlebnisse*], insofar as something or other is experienced in these moments (Ms. C 3 26a).[13]

Through inner time-consciousness one is aware not only of the stream of consciousness (prereflective self-awareness), but also of the acts as demarcated temporal objects in subjective time (reflective self-awareness) and of the transcendent objects in objective time (intentional consciousness). Inner time-consciousness is simply another name for the prereflective self-awareness of our experiences, a streaming self-awareness that is not itself an intentional act, a temporal unit, or an immanent object (Hua 10/127), but an intrinsic and irrelational feature of our consciousness. Therefore, no infinite regress is generated:

> The flow of the consciousness that constitutes immanent time not only *exists* but is so remarkably and yet intelligibly fashioned that a self-appearance of the flow necessarily exists in it, and therefore the flow itself must necessarily be apprehensible in the flowing. The self-appearance of the flow does not require a second flow; on the contrary, it constitutes itself as a phenomenon in itself (Hua 10/83).

In short, it is necessary to distinguish the prephenomenal being of the act, that is, its being prior to the reflective thematization, and its being as phenomenon (Hua 10/129). The prephenomenal being of the act, its original mode of prereflective self-manifestation, cannot be captured by a thinking that holds onto the distinction between subject and object, between act and object, between the experiencing and the experienced. In reaching these conclusions, Husserl is parting from a principle that has hitherto been fundamental—namely, the principle that the constituting and the constituted belong to two essentially different dimensions. The principles that hold true for the realm of object-intentionality fail when it comes to the self-manifestation of subjectivity.

As already mentioned, Husserl's investigation of time belongs among his most difficult but most fundamental analyses, and the topic has remained crucial to post-Husserlian phenomenology. Let me mention just one of the many problems that has subsequently been discussed. How is the absolute stream of time-consciousness ever to be made accessible for phenomenological description? Phenomenological description is based on reflection, but reflection is usually taken to be a *thematizing* and *objectifying* process. Reflection aims at capturing the prereflective functioning subjectivity, but doesn't it always arrive too late? Husserl, at least, frequently describes absolute constituting subjectivity as remaining *anonymous* (Hua 9/478, 14/29). And we are talking about an anonymity that can never be removed, neither through reflection nor through reduction.

This conclusion has repercussions for the very possibility of phenomenology. Concerning the investigation of the most fundamental constitutive dimension of subjectivity, the very source of the intentional life, it seems impossible to effectuate a faithful phenomenological description in accordance with Husserl's own methodological principles, particularly the so-called *principles of principles*, which states that our originary giving intuition should be the source of all knowledge (Hua 3/51). We cannot base all our considerations on that which is given intuitively in a phenomenological reflection since the reflection never manages to capture the functioning life, but is always too late. Either phenomenology has reached its limits, or the validity of the principles of principles must be reappraised.

What is certain is that a description of the absolute stream, which is so radically unlike any object, stretches language to its very limit.[14] This is repeatedly brought to the fore by Husserl, who continually stresses the fundamental shortcoming of the language at our disposal. We speak of absolute subjectivity in conformity with what is constituted (a strong affirmation of the thesis that it is impossible—and fundamentally misleading—to analyze absolute subjectivity in strict separation from that which it constitutes), and we describe it with predicates appropriate for temporal objects. For example, we call it streaming, standing, and present, although, properly speaking, it neither exists in the now nor as extended in time. But we simply lack more adequate words (Hua 10/75, Ms. C 3 4a, Ms. C 7 14a).[15] More generally, Husserl knew well that an investigation of lived subjectivity was beset with all kinds of difficulties. As he writes in a passage from the Bernau manuscripts:

In this sense it [i.e., the I] is not a 'being', but the antithesis to all that is, not an object (counter-stand) but the proto-stand (*Urstand*) for all objectivities. The I ought not to be called an I, it ought not to be called anything, since it would then

already have become an object; it is the ineffable nameless, not standing, not float-
ing, not existing above everything, but rather 'functioning' as apprehending, valu-
ing, etc. (Hua 33/277–278)

As already mentioned, we are here dealing with a problem that has occupied
phenomenologists ever since. To summarize one common insight: One cannot analyze and disclose the subjective dimension in the same way that one
investigates objects. Exactly for this reason, it is a mistake to think that phenomenology has failed because it parts from its usual principles the moment it has to account for absolute subjectivity. It must be realized that the
anonymity and elusiveness of functioning subjectivity does not reveal the
absurdity of the point of departure or the uselessness of the phenomenological method, but simply the nature of that which is investigated.[16]

Horizon and Presence

It will be natural to end the discussion of temporality with a look at
one of the most common charges made against Husserl, namely the charge
that he is an *intuitionist*. This criticism has been raised from both the
hermeneutical and the deconstructivistic holds, and the stumbling block
has often been Husserl's claim concerning the possibility of a presuppositionless philosophy.

More generally, Husserl's phenomenology has often been taken as a
classical example of what has been called a *metaphysics of presence*. That is,
it has been claimed that Husserl defines subjectivity as pure self-presence,
equating meaning, truth, and reality with that which can be given in intuitive immediacy for the subject.

The objections to this have been legion. Some have claimed that the
self-givenness of the subject is never immediate, but always mediated
through time, world, language, body, and intersubjectivity. Others have argued that one cannot account adequately for meaning, truth, and reality,
without taking language and tradition into account; we are situated within
a tradition that always transcends the individual. Finally, on a more fundamental level, it has also been claimed that the very notion of presence, far
from being simple and primary, presupposes a structural complexity. Ultimately, it is difference and absence that is constitutive of presence, and not
the other way around.

As for the first two objections, they will be answered indirectly by my
discussion of Husserl's analysis of the body, of intersubjectivity, and of the

lifeworld. As we will see, Husserl by no means succumbed to a naive adoration of presence. On the contrary, he was very well aware of the fact that even what appears as the most immediate experience might be permeated and influenced by earlier experiences as well as by acquired knowledge. In the years 1917–1921, Husserl began to distinguish between what he called a *static* and a *genetic* phenomenology. Static phenomenology is the type of phenomenology that we encounter in *Logische Untersuchungen* and *Ideen 1*, for instance. Its primary task is to account for the relation between the act and the object. It usually takes its point of departure from a certain region of objects (say, ideal objects or physical objects) and then investigates the intentional acts that these objects are correlated to and constituted by. This investigation must be characterized as static since both the types of objects and the intentional structures are taken to be readily available. But Husserl eventually came to realize that both of these types of objects as well as the intentional structures themselves had an origin and a history. Husserl speaks of a process of *sedimentation*, describing how patterns of understanding and expectations are gradually established and come to influence subsequent experiences. Certain types of experience (prelinguistic experiences, for example) condition later and more complex types of experience (scientific explorations, for instance), and the exact task of a genetic phenomenology is to explore the origin and formation of these different forms of intentionality (Hua 11/345). (It should be noted, though, that Husserl is concerned with the essential structures that such a formation is subordinated to. He is not interested in the investigation of any factual [onto- or phylogenetic] genesis.)

Moreover, both objections are partially misplaced. First of all, they confuse self-givenness in the formal sense of 'How can consciousness be aware of itself?' with self-knowledge in the substantial sense of 'Who am I?' Second, when Husserl speaks of a presuppositionless description of the phenomena, this should not be understood as a nonconceptual and atheoretical account, but simply as a description that is determined by the things themselves rather than by various extraneous concerns that might simply obscure and distort that which is to be analyzed. And, of course, the 'things' that concern Husserl are not concrete objects such as coins, anemones, television sets, or x-ray pictures, but regional-ontological and transcendental philosophical analyses of the fundamental structure of phenomena and of the conditions of the possibility for appearance. As we have already seen, this is by no means regarded by Husserl as an easy task. On the contrary, it calls for a number of methodological operations, a number of *reductions* or *destructions* (or to use another word from the phenomenological tradition, that one already encounters in Husserl a number of *deconstructions* [*Aufbau*]), since our understanding of what it actually means to be an object, a picture, a value, or something real or merely imagined is very often covered over and distorted by traditional prejudices.

Let me, instead, conclude this section with some comments about the last objection, which touches on the complexity of presence.

As already mentioned, it is true that Husserl does assign a privileged status to intuition. If we compare my perception of a flowering apple tree with my recollection or imagination of a flowering apple tree, it is correct that in all three cases we are directed toward a flowering apple tree (and not toward mental pictures or copies of an apple tree), but there are still crucial differences between the way in which the flowering apple tree appears in these three acts. There is a difference between the intention that intends the apple tree in an empty manner, and the intention that is fulfilled by the perceptually given apple tree. Husserl consequently claims that the flowering apple tree is given most *originarily* in the intuition, it is '*leibhaftig selbstgegeben*,' whereas in recollection or in imagination we lack that kind of presence. In the two latter acts, the givenness of the apple tree is *mediated*. This is clear, for instance, from the fact that the intentional structures of recollection and imagination refer to perception. A recollection, for instance, is for Husserl a consciousness of a prior perception and contains in that sense, qua derived mode of givenness, a reference to the original intuition.

All of this seems to support the thesis that Husserl ascribes to a metaphysics of presence. The more immediate the object shows itself for the subject, the more it *is* present. And the more present it is, the more real it is. This idea ultimately culminates in Husserl's persistent emphasis on the fact that the *existence* of the object (its being) is correlated to its intuitive givenness for a subject. That which distinguishes a fictive object from an existing object is exactly the fact that the latter can appear intuitively in *propria persona*.

But, and there is a but, as I have also already shown, Husserl always emphasizes the *transcendence* of the perceived object. That the object is not a part of my perceptual act is evident from the perspectival and horizonal givenness of the object. When I see an apple tree, it is necessary to distinguish that which appears and the appearance itself, since the apple tree is never given in its totality but always from a certain limited perspective. It is never the entire apple tree, including its front, backside, underside, and inside which is given intuitively, not even in the most perfect intuition, but only a single profile. Nevertheless, it is (normally) the appearing object and not the intuitively given profile that we intend and experience. The central question is: How is this possible?

According to Husserl, the reason why we perceive the apple tree itself although it is actually only a single profile that is intuitively present is because of the contribution of what he terms *horizonal intentionality*. Husserl claims that our intuitive consciousness of the present profile of the object is always accompanied by an intentional consciousness of the object's *horizon* of *absent* profiles (Hua 6/161). Were we only directed towards the intuitively given, no perceptual consciousness of the very object would be possible:

The improperly appearing objective determinations are co-apprehended, but they are not 'sensibilized,' not presented through what is sensible, i.e., through the material of sensation. It is evident that they are co-apprehended, for otherwise we would have no objects at all before our eyes, not even a side, since this can indeed be a side only through the object (Hua 16/55).

Every spatiotemporal perception (ordinarily termed 'external perception') can be deceptive, although it is a perception, that according to its own meaning, is a direct apprehension of the thing itself. According to its own meaning it is anticipatory—the anticipation [*Vorgriff*] concerns something cointended—and, in such a radical fashion, that even in the content of that which is perceptually given as itself, there is, on closer inspection, an element of anticipation. In fact, nothing in perception is purely and adequately perceived (Hua 8/45. Cf. 9/486.).

It is crucial not to underestimate Husserl's argument. He is not merely arguing that every perception of an object must necessarily include more than that which is intuitively present; in order to see something *as* a tree, we will have to transcend the profile that is intuitively given and unthematically co-intend the absent profiles of the tree (for which reason every perception, in Husserl's words, entails a '*Hinausdeutung*' [Hua 11/19]). The apple tree, in other words, can only appear as an intuitively given transcendent object in this play between presence (the intuitively given profile) and absence (the manifold of profiles that are not given intuitively).[17] Ultimately, Husserl is also claiming that the intuitively given profile is only presenting the object because of its horizonal reference to the absent profiles of the object, it is only because of its embeddedness in a horizon (of absence) that the present profile is constituted as a present profile. Husserl would never, however, go so far as to assign primacy to absence. The very claim that there is an absence that is not an absence for somebody and in relation to something present can hardly be defended phenomenologically.

It is important to emphasize the central role played by this concept of horizon in Husserl's theory of intentionality. It is not merely aspects of our thematically experienced object that are horizonally co-given. The very object is situated in a far more extensive horizon. A lemon that I am occupied with is lying on a kitchen table surrounded by different utensils. In the background the tap is dripping, and through the kitchen window I hear the cries of playing children. When I am concerned with the lemon I am also more or less co-conscious of its surroundings, and both the actually perceived and its co-conscious surroundings are penetrated by references to a vague and indeterminate horizon (Hua 3/57). We are here facing the inexhaustible and never fully thematizable *world-horizon*.

If we turn toward the self-givenness of the subject, we re-encounter the claim concerning the impossibility of a pure presence. As I have already mentioned, the primal impression is always situated in a temporal horizon. The living now has a triadic structure—primal impression-retention-protention—which is why Husserl writes that every consciousness has retentional and protentional horizons (Hua 11/337). For the very same reason, there is no isolated primal impression, there is no pure self-presence.

By now the claim that Husserl is the philosopher of presence par excellence should strike one as more and more unwarranted. Let me conclude this digression with a single additional remark.

One of Husserl's important discoveries is that the retention does not merely retain the tone, but also the primal impression. If $P(t)$ is the designation for the primal impression of a tone, then $P(t)$ is retained in the retention $Rp(t)$ when a new primal impression occurs. As this notation makes clear, it is not only the tone that is retained, but also our consciousness of the tone. In other words, the actual phase of the flow is not only retaining the tone that has just been, but also the elapsing phase of the flow.[18] The enduring object and the streaming consciousness are, consequently, given together, and can only appear in this interdependent fashion. I can only be prereflectively aware of my stream of consciousness when I am conscious of the duration of my object, and vice versa (Hua 10/83). To put it differently, consciousness can only be temporally self-given when it relates to something foreign (Hua 14/14, 379). But, of course, that point was already made in Husserl's theory of intentionality:

> The I is not thinkable without a non-I that it is intentionally related to (Hua 14/245. Cf. 13/170, 14/51, 13/92.).

If, however, the self-givenness of the subject goes hand in hand with an encounter with alterity, subjectivity cannot be defined as pure self-presence. Once again, the claim that Husserl should advocate a naive philosophy of presence has consequently been proven wrong.[19]

B. The Body

As I have mentioned several times, a pervasive feature of Husserl's analysis of perception is his reflection on the perspectival givenness of the perceptual (spatio-temporal) object. The object is never given in its totality, but always in a particular profile. A careful consideration of this apparently banal fact reveals several implications that are of direct relevance for an understanding of the importance attributed to the body by Husserl. These reflections can be traced all the way back to the lecture course *Ding und Raum* from 1907.

The Body and Perspectivity

Every perspectival appearance not only implies something that appears, it also implies someone that it appears for. In other words, an appearance is always an appearance of something for someone. Every perspectival appearance always has its *genitive* and *dative*.[20] When we realize that what appears spatially always appears at a certain distance and from a certain angle, the point should be obvious: There is no pure point of view and there is no view from nowhere, there is only an embodied point of view. Every perspectival appearance presupposes that the experiencing subject is itself given in space. Since the subject possesses a spatial location only because of its embodiment (Hua 3/116, 4/33, 13/239), Husserl can claim that spatial objects can only appear for and be constituted by *embodied subjects*.[21] The body is characterized as being present in any perceptual experience as the zero point, as the indexical 'here' in relation to which the object is oriented. It is the center around which and in relation to which (egocentric) space unfolds itself (Hua 11/298, 4/159, 9/392). Husserl consequently argues that the body is a condition of the possibility for the perception of and interaction with spatial objects (Hua 14/540), and that every worldly experience is mediated by and made possible by our embodiment (Hua 6/220, 4/56, 5/124).

These reflections concerning the body's function as a condition of the possibility for perceptual intentionality are radicalized the moment Husserl no longer analyzes the body simply in its function as a center of orientation, but also starts to examine bodily *mobility* and its contributions to the constitution of perceptual reality. As James Gibson points out, we see with 'mobile' eyes set in a head that can turn and is attached to a body that can move from place to place; a stationary point of view is only the limiting case of a mobile point of view.[22] In a similar manner, Husserl calls attention to the role played by movement (the movements of the eye, the touch of the hand, the step of the body, and so on) for our experience of space and spatial objects (Hua 11/299), and, ultimately, he argues that perception presupposes a particular type of bodily self-sensitivity. Our experience of perceptual objects are accompanied by a co-functioning but unthematic experience of the position and movement of the body, termed *kinaesthetic experience*.[23] When I play the piano, the keys are given in conjunction with a sensation of finger-movement. When I watch a horse race, the running horse is given in conjunction with the sensation of eye movement. This kinaesthetic experience amounts to a form of bodily self-awareness and, according to Husserl, it should not be considered as a mere accompanying phenomena. On the contrary, it is absolutely indispensable when it comes to the constitution of perceptual objects (Hua 16/189, 11/14–15, 4/66, 16/159, 6/109).

Husserl's reflections on these issues were originally motivated by the following question: What is it that enables us to take several different appearances to be appearances of one and the same object? What is it that enables us to perceive one and the same object in a series of changing appearances? Needless to say, these appearances must have certain qualities in common. The appearance of the underside of a dining table and the appearance of the front of a haystack are too diverse to be taken as appearances of one and the same object. But even a qualitative matching is merely a necessary and not a sufficient condition. After all, the front of one piece of paper and the back of another match excellently, but we nevertheless conceive of them as being appearances of two similar but different objects (Hua 16/155). A further necessary condition is that these appearances are experienced as belonging to the same continuum. Different appearances are only taken to present us with one and the same object if the appearances can be given in a continuous synthesis, that is, if there exists a sliding transition between them. According to Husserl, our awareness of such a continuity presupposes the contribution of kinaestheses.

Let me illustrate Husserl's line of thought with a concrete example. Whereas the actually given front of the wardrobe is correlated with a particular bodily position, the horizon of the cointended but momentarily absent profiles of the wardrobe (its backside, bottom, and so on) is correlated with my kinaesthetic horizon, that is, with my capacity for possible movement (Hua 11/15). The absent profiles are linked to an intentional if-then connection. If I move in this way, then this profile will become visually or tactually accessible (Hua 6/164). The absent backside of the wardrobe is only the backside of the same wardrobe I am currently perceiving because it can become present through a specific bodily movement.

All possible profiles of an object, as a spatial object, form a system that is coordinated to one kinaesthetic system, and to this kinaesthetic system as a whole, in such a way that 'if' some kinaesthesis or other runs its course, certain profiles corresponding to it must 'necessarily' also run their course (Hua 9/390).

It is against this background that Husserl can claim that every perception contains a double performance. On the one side, we have a series of kinaesthetic experiences and, on the other side, a motivated series of perceptual appearances that are functionally correlated to these experiences. Although the kinaesthetic experiences are not interpreted as belonging to the perceived object, and although they do not themselves constitute objects, they manifest bodily self-givenness and, thereby, a unity and framework that the perceptual appearances are correlated with (Hua 11/14), and which furnish them with a coherence allowing them to gain object-reference and become appearances *of* something (Hua 4/66, 16/159, 6/109). One might, consequently, say that perceptual intentionality presupposes a moving and therefore incarnated subject (Hua 16/176).[24] In short, the crucial point made by Husserl is not that we can perceive movement, but that our very perception presupposes movement.

The Body as Subject and the Body as Object

Once we realize that the body, qua subjective 'organ of experience,' plays a constitutive role in every type of perception (Hua 4/144, 11/13), one still needs to clarify the relation between subjectivity and embodiment, just as the relation between the functioning, subjective body (*Leib*), and the experienced, objective body (*Leibkörper*) needs to be analyzed. We immediately encounter the problem, however, that Husserl's entire argumentation seems to be threatened by a vicious circularity. How can one claim that the body is a constitutive condition of the possibility for spatial objects when the body is itself a spatial object? Husserl repeatedly emphasizes, however, the importance of distinguishing between 1) the unthematic prereflective lived body-awareness that accompanies and conditions every spatial experience, and 2) the subsequent thematic experience *of* the body as an object. One needs to distinguish between the *functioning* body and the *thematized* body and clarify their relation of foundation. My original body awareness is not an experience of the body as a spatial object (Hua 13/240). On the contrary, we are here dealing with a self-objectivation—which just like any other perceptual experience—is dependent on and conditioned by an unthematic co-functioning body awareness:

> Here it must also be noted that in all experience of things, the lived body is co-experienced as a functioning lived body (thus not as a mere thing), and that when it itself is experienced as a thing, it is experienced in a double way—i.e., precisely as an experienced thing and as a functioning lived body together in one (Hua 14/57. Cf. 15/326, 9/392.).

Husserl, consequently, argues that I originally do not experience my body as an object in objective space. The body is not given perspectivally, and I am not given for myself as belonging in a spatial object. Originally I do not have any consciousness *of* my body as an object. I am not perceiving it, I am it. Originally my body is experienced as a unified field of activity and affectivity, as a volitional structure, a potentiality of mobility, an 'I do' and 'I can' (Hua 11/14, 1/128, 14/540, 9/391). When the body moves and acts, *I* am moving and acting (Hua 14/540). To put it differently, the constitution of the body as an object is not performed by a disincarnated subject. On the contrary, we are dealing with a self-objectivation of the functioning body. It is performed by a subject that already exists bodily.

How does this constitution of the body as a spatial object take place? According to Husserl, there is an intimate connection between the constitution of an objective, that is, intersubjective communal space, and the self-objectivation of the lived body. Objective space is exactly a space that is *constituted* as transcending egocentric space. Its coordinates are no longer taken to depend upon my indexical 'here,' but are independent of my orientation and movement. But it is exactly by objectifying the body, by viewing it as a mere object among objects, that its indexicality is surmounted or suspended, something that has already happened when we have an experience of walking *through* space. The constitution of objective space as a homogeneous system of coordinates consequently presupposes an objectivation of the functioning body, where the indexical reference to my absolute here is suspended. But once again, how does this objectivation take place?

As already mentioned, Husserl claims that the body is originally given as a unified volitional structure, as a potential of movement—as an 'I can' and 'I do.' Subsequently this system is split up and apprehended as belonging to different bodily parts, it is only subsequently that the sensing is *localized* and that we are confronted with the experiencing subsystems of the fingers, eyes, legs, and so forth (Hua 4/56, 155, 5/118).

If I touch a table, I am confronted with a series of appearances that are apprehended as belonging to the table. When my hand slides over the table, I perceive the hardness, smoothness, and extension of the table. It is also possible, however, to undertake a change of attention (a kind of reflection) so that, instead of being preoccupied with the properties of the table, I thematize the touching hand and am then aware of feelings of pressure and movement that are not apprehended as objective properties of the hand, but that are, nevertheless, localized in the hand and that manifest its function as an experienc*ing* organ (Hua 4/146). One and the same sensation can, consequently, be interpreted in two radically different ways, that is both as an appearance of the experienced object and as a localized sensing in the correlated experiencing bodily part (to denote this duality Husserl makes use of the terms *Empfindung* and *Empfindnis*) (Hua 15/302, 13/273, 5/118–119). However, as Husserl is well aware, the touched object and the touching hand do not at all appear in the same manner. Whereas the properties of a material object are constituted adumbrationally, this is not the case for the localized sensations (Hua 4/149–150). As Husserl quite aptly remarks, 'Sensations of touch are not in the skin as if they were parts of its organic tissue' (Hua 13/115). In fact, the *Empfindnis* is not at all a material property of the hand, but the very embodied subjectivity itself. Thus, rather than to say that one and the same sensation can be interpreted in two different ways, it might be better to say that the sensation contains two radically different dimensions to it, namely, a distinction between the *sensing* and the *sensed*, and that we can focus upon either.

In the course of the localization, that is, the interpretation of the sensations as belonging to specific bodily parts, the kinaesthetic sensations become associated with the visually perceived movement of the body, a movement that can be interpreted both as the expression of a willed intention and as simple movement in space (Hua 15/268, 13/283). As a tentative illustration of the difference between these two apprehensions of one and the same movement, one can compare the experience of a gesture as seen and as felt. While the visual experience in its objectivation of the hand presents space as something existing independently of the gesture—as something that the hand moves through—the kinaesthesis does not furnish us with an experience of space independent of the experience of the gesture. Space is experienced precisely as the hand's field of mobility.

When I realize that my hand feels something or moves itself, that my ankle is throbbing or that my back hurts, I am localizing the sensing in different parts of the body. In itself this process of localization does not yet confront us with the body as an object. When my hand touches the table and when I pay attention to the very touching, I am, after all, conscious of an *experiencing* organ and not of an *experienced* organ. However, this changes the moment the body objectifies itself, as will happen if I gaze at my foot or if one hand touches another.

Thus, Husserl is anxious to emphasize the peculiar two-sidedness of the body (Hua 9/197, 14/414, 462, 4/145). My body is given as an *interiority*, that is, as a volitional structure and a dimension of sensing (Hua 14/540, 9/391), as well as a visually and tactually appearing *exteriority*. But what is the relation between that which Husserl calls the '*Innen-*' and the '*Aussenleiblichkeit*' (Hua 14/337)? In both cases I am confronted with my own body. But why is the visually and tactually appearing body at all experienced as the exteriority of *my* body? If we examine the case of the right hand touching the left hand, the touching hand feels the surface of the touched hand. But when the left hand is touched, it is not simply given as a mere object, since it feels the touch itself (Hua 4/145). (Had the touched hand lacked this experience, it would have lacked bodily self-givenness and would no longer have been felt as *my* hand. Anybody who has tried to fall asleep with his arm as a pillow will know how strange it is to wake up with an insensible arm. When it is touched, it doesn't respond and could just as well be the arm of an Other.) The decisive difference between touching one's own body and everything else, be it inanimate objects or the body of Others, is, consequently, that it implies a *double-sensation*. Husserl also speaks of a *bodily reflection* taking place between the different parts of the body (Hua 1/128. Cf. 15/302.). What is crucial, however, is that the relation between the touching and the touched is reversible, since the touching is touched, and the touched is touching. It is this reversibility that demonstrates that the interiority and the exteriority are different manifestations of the same (Hua 14/75, 13/263, Ms. D 12 III 14). The phenomenon of double sensation consequently presents us with an ambiguous setting in which the hand alternates between two roles, that of touching and that of being touched. That is, the phenomenon of double sensation provides us with an experience of the dual nature of the body. It is the very same hand that can appear in two different fashions, as alternately touched and touching. Thus, in contrast to the self-manifestation of, say, an act of judging, my bodily self-givenness permits me to confront my own exteriority. For Husserl this experience is decisive for empathy (Hua 15/652), serving as the springboard for diverse alienating forms of self-apprehension. Thus, it is exactly the unique subject-object status of the body, the remarkable interplay between *ipseity* and *alterity* characterizing double-sensation, which permits me to recognize and experience other embodied subjects (Hua 8/62, 15/300, 14/457, 462, 9/197, 13/263). When my left hand touches my right, I am experiencing myself in a manner that anticipates both the way in which an Other would experience me and the way in which I would experience an Other. This might be what Husserl is referring to when he writes that the possibility of sociality presupposes a certain intersubjectivity of the body (Hua 4/297).

Although the body as touched or seen has a number of properties in common with objects in the world, such as extension, mass, softness, smoothness, and so on, it is still important to emphasize that, qua field of localization for kinaesthetic and tactile sensations, it is radically different from ordinary objects (Hua 4/151–152, 16/162). Although our exploration of the body entails an objectivation of it, it does not imply a complete suspension of its subjectivity, exactly because the touched hand feels the touch. This does not imply that it is impossible to view one's own body as a mere object, but, according to Husserl, this self-understanding is not immediately accessible: It is only via another subject's perception of my body (which, in certain respects, is superior to my own [Hua 5/112], for instance when it comes to a visual presentation of my neck and eyes), and through an appropriation of this perspective that I can adopt a reifying and abstractive view on my own body (Hua 14/62–63), regarding it as an object among other objects, situated in and determined by a causal network.

Husserl occasionally speaks of the reciprocal co-dependency existing between the constitution of spatial objects, on the one hand, and the constitution of the body, on the other. The very exploration and constitution of objects implies a simultaneous self-exploration and self-constitution. This is not to say that the way we live our body is a form of object-intentionality, but merely that it is an embodied subjectivity characterized by intentionality that is self-given. The body is not first given for us and subsequently used to investigate the world. On the contrary, the world is given to us as bodily investigated, and the body is revealed to us in this exploration of the world (Hua 5/128, 15/287). To phrase it differently, we are aware of perceptual objects by being aware of our own body and how these two interact. That is, we cannot perceive physical objects without having an accompanying bodily self-awareness, be it thematic or unthematic (Hua 4/147). But the reverse ultimately holds true as well: The body only appears to itself when it relates to something else—or to itself as Other (Hua 13/386, 16/178, 15/300). As Husserl writes, 'We perceive the lived body but along with it also the things that are perceived "by means of" it' (Hua 5/10 [transl. modified]). This reciprocity between self-affection and hetero-affection is probably nowhere as obvious as in the tactual sphere—the hand cannot touch without being touched and brought to givenness itself. In other words, the touching and the touched are constituted in the same process (Hua 14/75, 15/297, 15/301), and, according to Husserl, this holds true for our sensibility in general.[25]

If, however, the self-givenness of the touch is inseparable from the manifestation of the touched, if, more generally, self-affection is always penetrated by the affection of the world (Hua 10/100), it seems untenable to introduce a founding-founded relation between subjectivity and world, since they are inseparable and interdependent. As Husserl himself says, every experience possesses both an egoic and a nonegoic dimension (Ms. C 10 2b). These two sides can be distinguished, but not separated:

The ego is not something for itself and that which is foreign to the ego, something severed from it, so that there is no room for the one to turn toward the other; rather, the ego is inseparable from what is foreign to it . . . (Ms. C 16 68a. Cf. Ms. C 10 2b.).[26]

As Merleau-Ponty would put it (with Husserl's approval, I believe), subjectivity is essentially oriented and open toward that which it is not, be it worldly entities or the Other, and it is exactly in this openness that it reveals itself to itself. What is disclosed by the cogito is, consequently, not an enclosed immanence or a pure interior self-presence, but an openness toward alterity, a movement of exteriorization and perpetual self-transcendence. It is by being present to the world that we are present to ourselves, and it is by being given to ourselves that we can be conscious of the world.[27]

So far I have only described the constellation subjectivity, body, world. Husserl, however, also claims that our body plays a crucial role when it comes to an understanding of intersubjectivity, just as intersubjectivity can have a significant impact on the constitutive function exerted by the body. I will, however, postpone this aspect until the next section.

Husserl argues that the constitution of an egocentric space presupposes a functioning body, and that the constitution of objective space presupposes a bodily self-objectivation (Hua 16/162). In short, the constituting subject is embodied, and since this bodily subject is always already interpreting itself as belonging to the world, it must once again be concluded that the thesis concerning a worldless subject is highly problematic. To put it differently, in his analysis of the body Husserl himself is providing arguments against his Cartesian position in *Ideen I*.

To forestall misunderstandings, let me just add that I am not arguing that Husserl would claim that every type of experience is a bodily experience. I am only claiming that he takes the lived body to be indispensable for sense experience and, therefore, of crucial (founding) significance for other types of experience. As Husserl writes in *Ideen II* and *III*:

Hence in this way *a human being's total consciousness is in a certain sense, by means of its hyletic substrate, bound to the lived body*, though, to be sure, the intentional lived experiences themselves are *no longer* directly and properly *localized*; they no longer form a stratum on the lived body. (Hua 4/153 [transl. modified]).

Of course, from the standpoint of pure consciousness sensations are the indispensable material foundation for all basic sorts of noeses . . . (Hua 5/11).

By now it should be clear that Husserl's analysis of the body is more than a mere regional-ontological investigation. On the contrary, we are faced with a transcendental philosophical investigation with extensive implications for the more fundamental understanding of the relation between subjectivity and world. Let me conclude my treatment of Husserl's phenomenology of the body by mentioning two further arguments in support of this interpretation.

1. In Part 1, I mentioned the role played by the sensations in Husserl's theory of intentionality. According to Husserl, the sensations were nonintentional, that is, they lacked reference to objects and only acquired this the moment they were subjected to an objectifying interpretation. This theory has often been criticized by later phenomenologists, who claimed that formless and meaningless sensations, far from being the result of a proper phenomenological analysis, merely reflect a theoretical prejudice that Husserl inherited from British empiricism.[28] Not only does it seem very difficult to locate these (supposedly) meaningless sensations in ordinary life, in which we are always already faced with meaningful experiences: that which we perceive is always already interpreted *as* something. Additionally, the attempt to interpret our sensation as a per se meaningless affection also makes it incomprehensible how the sensed could ever guide and limit our interpretation. If the sensations are taken to be meaningless, the mediation between sensuous experience and conceptual thinking becomes arbitrary.

To a certain extent this criticism is justified, but it does not tell the whole story. Husserl's concept of sensation is notoriously ambiguous, and it changed during the course of his philosophical development. When speaking of a sensation, one can refer to the very process of sensing, but also to that which is sensed. And, needless to say, it makes a difference whether one is speaking about an impressional episode in one's own sensibility or about the sensible presence of something transcendent.[29] To put it differently, Husserl's investigation of the body makes it clear that one should distinguish between two very different types of sensations. On the one hand, we have the kinaestheses that should be interpreted noetically. These constitute bodily self-awareness and do not intend objects. On the other hand, we have hyletic sensations, which Husserl occasionally describes as *Mermalsempfindungen* or *Aspektdaten*. These sensations are neither formless nor senseless, but are always imbued with meaning and configured in correlation to the kinaesthetic field.[30] As sensed, the hyletic datum is not an immanent or worldless content or quality, nor is it a medium between subjectivity and world. Rather, our sensing is already an openness toward the world, even if it is not yet a world of objects, and the hyletic datum is the primordial manifestation of this worldly being. Nevertheless, the differentiation between hyletic sensations and objects remain. It remains possible to distinguish between hearing an increasing loudness and hearing an approaching car, feeling a local pain and feeling the prick of the needle. The sensation itself is underdetermined, for it is only by apprehending and interpreting it as something that a full-fledged object is constituted.

2. When Husserl writes that the transcendental subject is embodied, it should be clear that we are dealing with a significant departure from the concept of transcendental subjectivity that Kant originally introduced. According to Kant, transcendental subjectivity is a transpersonal abstractly deduced principle of justification, whereas for Husserl it is a concrete and finite subject. Against this background it is quite understandable that Husserl's analysis of the body eventually led him to the problems concerning the *birth* and *death* of transcendental subjectivity.

Initially, Husserl considered it to be something of a category mistake to discuss the birth and death of the transcendental subject. Qua constitutive principle, qua being the source of temporality and the condition for every kind of presence and absence, transcendental subjectivity was simply not the kind of 'thing' that could arise and perish. Since the body does die, however, Husserl was forced to say that transcendental subjectivity can persist disembodied and that 'death' should therefore be regarded as a separation from the world, something analogous to a dreamless sleep (Hua 11/379–381, 13/399). It should be clear, however, that in this case we are talking about an impoverished subject (Hua 13/464–465), or, to be more exact, the notion of subjectivity that we thereby approach is an absolute limit-concept.[31]

In the beginning of the 1930s, Husserl seems gradually to have changed his mind, however, no longer regarding birth and death as something that pertains only to the empirical subject, for, as he writes, birth and death, as well as generativity (the change of generations), are all conditions of the possibility for the constitution of an objective and historical world (Hua 15/171–172). In my analysis of Husserl's notion of lifeworld, I will attempt to interpret this surprising claim, but already now it can be mentioned that Husserl conceived of our situatedness in a living *tradition* as having constitutive implications.

It would be an exaggeration to claim that Husserl managed to solve the very perplexing problem about the birth and death of subjectivity, but his sporadic reflections on these issues can nevertheless serve as an illustration of the constant development of his thinking. Ultimately, it must remain an open question whether we are dealing with an issue that can be treated by phenomenology at all, or whether, rather, we are faced with something that can only be addressed by speculative metaphysics.[32]

C. Intersubjectivity

Husserl considered intersubjectivity to be a topic of immense importance, and, from a purely quantitative point of view, he devoted more pages to this issue than any of the later phenomenologists.[33] For a number of reasons, Husserl's analysis of intersubjectivity deserves a detailed treatment, not the least because it constitutes an important corrective to his 'system.' To be more precise: Only a consideration of his analysis of intersubjectivity permits a correct understanding of Husserl's transcendental-idealistic position. Although Husserl has often been regarded as a *methodological solipsist*,[34] he in fact undertook what Karl-Otto Apel and Jürgen Habermas have later become known for: *An intersubjective transformation of transcendental philosophy*.

Solipsism

Husserl's phenomenology has very frequently been accused of being solipsistic in nature. By solipsism one normally understands a position that either claims that there only exists one single consciousness, namely one's own, or that argues that it is impossible to know whether there are in fact any other subjects besides oneself. But why this criticism? Because the very effectuation of the epoché and the transcendental reduction seem to restrict the field of research of phenomenology in advance to the phenomenologizing individual's own consciousness and phenomena. If the purpose of the intentional-constitutive analysis is to investigate the world's givenness for me, how should it then ever be capable of disclosing the world's givenness for another subject, not to speak of the self-givenness of this foreign subject? If one is meaningfully to speak of a foreign subject, of an Other, it is evident that we are dealing with something that cannot be reduced to its mere givenness for me. But if phenomenology calls for a return to that which is evidentially given to me, there appears to be a problem.

To be more precise, Husserl's phenomenology of intersubjectivity seems to be confronted with two interrelated difficulties: 1) How should I ever be able to constitute the Other, since the Other qua Other must be more than a mere product of constitution? 2) How should it phenomenologically be possible to describe the givenness of the Other, since the Other qua foreign subjectivity is characterized by its inaccessibility, by always transcending its givenness *for me*?

These problems are increased the moment Husserl begins arguing that the phenomenologist must start as a solipsist (Hua 8/176, 17/276) and necessarily, at least initially, effectuate a so-called *primordial* reduction, that is, a reduction that has the aim of isolating the *sphere of ownness*—the totality of all that which can be constituted by an isolated ego without the contribution of any other subjects (Hua 1/124, 17/248). For, as he writes, only thereby will it be possible to comprehend the *constituted* ontological validity of the Other (Hua 15/270–271).

All in all, these considerations seem to unequivocally support the standard criticism: Husserl remained caught in a solipsistic paradigm, and, in contrast to later phenomenologists, failed to appreciate the importance of intersubjectivity.

However, the actual situation is considerably more complex. Let me show why.

Transcendental Intersubjectivity

The easiest way to introduce Husserl's analysis of intersubjectivity is in connection with his theory of intentionality. According to Husserl, my perceptions present me with intersubjectively accessible being, that is, being that does not exist for me alone, but for everybody (Hua 9/431, 14/289, 390, 17/243, 6/469). I *experience* objects, events, and actions as public, not as private (Hua 1/123, 15/5). Husserl consequently claims that an ontological analysis, insofar as it unveils the being-sense (*Seinssinn*) of the world as intersubjectively valid, leads to a disclosure of the transcendental relevance of foreign subjectivity and thus to an examination of *transcendental intersubjectivity* (Hua 15/110). As he ultimately formulates it:

Concrete, full transcendental subjectivity is the totality of an open community of I's—a totality that comes from within, that is unified purely transcendentally, and that is concrete only in this way. Transcendental intersubjectivity is the absolute and only self-sufficient ontological foundation [*Seinsboden*], out of which everything objective (the totality of objectively real entities, but also every objective ideal world) draws its sense and its validity (Hua 9/344, transl. modified).

It is in the light of such considerations that Husserl can characterize the intersubjective-transcendental sociality as the source of all real truth and being (Hua 1/35, 182, 8/449, 9/295, 474), and occasionally even describes his own project as a *sociological* transcendental philosophy (Hua 9/539), writing that the development of phenomenology necessarily implies the step from an egological to a *transcendental-sociological* phenomenology.[35] Transcendental phenomenology is only *apparently* solipsistic, and the reason for introducing the primordial reduction is methodological in nature. It is only possible to realize the full extent of the significance of intersubjectivity when we realize how *little* the single subject can manage on its own. In other words, a radical implementation of the transcendental reduction will eventually lead to a disclosure of transcendental intersubjectivity (Hua 1/69, 9/245–246, 8/129).

Given this background, it is fairly easy to show why Husserl occupied himself so intensively with the issue of intersubjectivity. He was convinced that it contained the key to a comprehension of the *constitution* of objective reality and transcendence, and since Husserl regarded that as one of the most important tasks of transcendental phenomenology (Hua 8/465), it should be obvious what kind of systematic importance his analyses of intersubjectivity possess and how much is actually at stake. If transcendental phenomenology for some reason were prevented in principle from accounting for intersubjectivity (eventually because of its alleged methodological solipsism or subjective idealism), the consequence would not merely be its inability to carry out an investigation of a specific and clearly demarcated problem, but its failure as a fundamental philosophical project.

Husserl's phenomenological investigation of intersubjectivity is an analysis of the *transcendental* or constitutive function of intersubjectivity, and the aim of his reflections is precisely to formulate a theory of transcendental intersubjectivity and *not* to give a detailed examination of the concrete sociality or the specific I-Thou relation. The reason why this must be emphasized is that the major part of the critical assessment of Husserl's phenomenology of intersubjectivity (which has often restricted itself to an analysis of his account in the Fifth *Cartesian Meditation*) has focused on exactly these aspects. Thus, it has been customary to discuss, on the one hand, whether Husserl's concept of empathy (*Einfühlung*) implies a direct

or an indirect experience of the Other, and whether this account is phenomenologically sound; or, on the other, whether Husserl's (idealistic)
model of constitution could at all establish a symmetrical relation between
the I and the Other, a discussion that was often quite inadequate, since one
did not at the same time analyze the actual meaning of constitution, but
simply presupposed a (flawed) interpretation of it.[36]

It would be wrong to claim that these problems are completely irrelevant, especially since Husserl's concept of intersubjectivity is in fact a concept of *inter*-subjectivity, that is, the relation between subjects. Consequently,
it implies an examination of empathy—how can I experience another subject? According to the phenomenological approach, intersubjectivity cannot
be examined adequately from a third-person perspective, but must be analyzed in its experiential manifestation from a first-person perspective. As
Husserl writes in *Krisis*, intersubjectivity can only be treated as a transcendental problem through a radical 'mich-selbst-befragen' (Hua 6/206); only
my experience of and relation to another subject, as well as those of my experiences that presuppose the Other, really merit the name 'intersubjective.'

The reason why it is still problematic to proceed in the customary
manner is that one confuses the way to and the aim of Husserl's analysis of
transcendental intersubjectivity. One overlooks that the latter, to some extent, is independent of his analysis of the actual process and constitutive
structure of empathy. Even if his account of empathy were to fail, it would
not have meant the wreck of the rest of his investigation. Furthermore, as
will be shown in a moment, Husserl's theory of intersubjectivity is more
complex than normally assumed. He operates with several *kinds* of intersubjectivity and is, for that reason, able to guard against the type of critique
which, by questioning his account of the bodily-mediated intersubjectivity, assumed that the entire foundation of his analysis would break down.[37]

Let me say a few words about Husserl's description of the concrete
experience of the Other before I turn to what I believe is the really essential part of his analysis of intersubjectivity—his account of constitut*ing*
intersubjectivity.

The Experience of the Other

The concrete experience of the Other is, for Husserl, always an experience of the Other in its bodily appearance, for which reason concrete intersubjectivity must be understood as a relation between incarnated sub-

jects. I will not account in detail for Husserl's precise analysis of the complex structure of empathy (which would imply an extended discussion of such notions as appresentation [*Appräsentation*] and pairing [*Parrung*]),[38] but let me merely mention that Husserl takes empathy to presuppose a certain similarity between the foreign embodied subject I encounter and myself. Were I not myself a bodily subject, I would never be able to recognize other embodied subjects. This does not imply, however, that my experience of the Other is, in reality, a case of an analogical inference (Hua 1/141, 13/338–339). We are not dealing with any kind of inference, but with an actual *experience*, the structure of which Husserl attempts to uncover. He therefore refuses to take the experience of the Other as a basic, unanalyzable fact (something he accuses Max Scheler of doing [Hua 14/335]). On the contrary, its genesis and specific presuppositions have to be clarified. We need to uncover the conditions of possibility for empathy, particularly those that concern the nature of the experiencing subject. Thus, as Husserl for example points out, it is exactly the unique subject-object status of my body that permits me to recognize another body as a foreign embodied subjectivity (Hua 8/62). As I already mentioned in my presentation of Husserl's phenomenology of the body, when my left hand touches my right hand, I experience myself in a way that anticipates the way in which I would experience an Other and an Other would experience me.

This focus on the importance of the body also comes to the fore when Husserl writes that the experience of the body (one's own as well as the body of the Other) constitutes the foundation and norm for all other experiences (Hua 14/126). Thus, Husserl occasionally speaks of the mother-child relation as the most original of all relations (Hua 15/511, 15/582, 15/604–605), claiming that it precedes the experience of physical objects. In other words, the central question is not how I can get from the experience of a physical object to the experience of a foreign subject, but how my experience of incarnated subjectivity (my own as well as foreign) conditions the experience of mere objects (Hua 15/637).

That I have an actual experience of the Other, and do not have to do with a mere inference, does not mean that I can experience the Other in the same way as the Other experiences himself or herself, nor that the consciousness of the Other is accessible to me in the same way as my own is. But this is not a problem. On the contrary, it is only because the foreign subject eludes my direct experience in this way that he or she is experienced as an Other at all. As Husserl writes, had I the same access to the consciousness of the Other as I have to my own, the Other would have ceased being an Other and instead have become a part of myself (Hua 1/139). The self-givenness of the Other is inaccessible and transcendent to me, but it is exactly this limit that I can experience (Hua 1/144, 15/631). When I have an *authentic* experience of another subject, I am exactly experiencing that the Other—in contrast to objects—eludes me. To demand more, to claim that I only experience an Other the moment I can gain access to the first-personal givenness of the Other's experiences is a fundamental misunderstanding that far from respecting the *transcendence* of the Other as Husserl is constantly doing, seeks to abolish it.[39]

Thus, although Husserl would argue that we do experience the Other, this does not imply that the Other is reduced to a mere intentional object. On the contrary, we are dealing with a subject-subject relation insofar as the Other is exactly experienced in its subjective inaccessibility. It is essential to the phenomenological description of the subject-subject relation that it involves an *asymmetry*. There is a difference between the experiencing subject and the experienced subject. But this asymmetry is a part of any correct description of intersubjectivity. Without asymmetry there would be no intersubjectivity, but merely an undifferentiated collectivity.

This clarification makes it possible to understand what Husserl actually meant when he said that the ego constitutes the Other. It is impossible to meet the Other and to respect the irreducible alterity of the Other unless the Other appears. One cannot speak meaningfully of the absolutely foreign unless this alterity appears as a phenomenon one way or another.[40] To speak of an Other or of something foreign is to use concepts of relation whose meaning presupposes the ego as contrast. The foreign is exactly foreign for me, the Other is exactly an Other in relation to me—and not in relation to itself. When Husserl speaks of the constitution of the Other, he is referring precisely to this fact. But Husserl would never claim that the ego constitutes the *self-givenness* of the Other, a self-givenness that is characterized by the same kind of immediacy and certainty as my own self-givenness (Hua 15/43). As Husserl repeatedly emphasizes, I do not create, invent, or produce the Other when I constitute him (Hua 1/168, 17/244, 258, 15/13). If this were not the case, it would have implied a denial of foreign subjectivity and Husserl would not have been able to escape solipsism.

These considerations will have to be corrected on one single point. To a certain extent, the self-being of the Other does, in fact, depend upon me, namely, to the extent that the self-being of each and every subject depends upon its relation to other subjects. As will become clear in the following, Husserl attributes a decisive importance to intersubjectivity when it comes to the self-constitution of the transcendental ego. This holds true for all egos, not only for my own. In its full concretion no subject (not even the Other) can exist independently of Others. In this regard, Husserl advocates a strong symmetrical relation between the ego and the Other.

The Constituting Intersubjectivity

Let me now turn toward the central issue. As already mentioned, Husserl claims that the objectivity and transcendence of the world is constituted intersubjectively and that a clarification of this constitution consequently demands an analysis of transcendental intersubjectivity, and more concretely an examination of my experience of another subject. Why is it, however, that a subject can only constitute objectivity after having experienced an Other? Why is the Other a necessary condition of possibility for my experience of an objective world? Why is my experience of objects changed radically the moment I experience foreign subjectivity? Basically, Husserl's thesis is that my experience of objective validity is made possible by my experience of the transcendence (and inaccessibility) of foreign subjectivity, and that this transcendence, which Husserl designates as the first real alterity and as the source of all kinds of real transcendence, endows the world with objective validity (Hua 14/277, 15/560, 1/173).

Here we have the only transcendence that is genuinely worthy of its name, and everything else that is also called transcendent, such as the objective world, rests upon the transcendence of foreign subjectivity (Hua 8/495).

All Objectivity, in this sense, is related back constitutionally to what does not belong to the Ego proper, to the other-than-my-Ego's-own in the form, 'someone else'—that is to say: the non-Ego in the form, 'another Ego' (Hua 17/248 [241, transl. modified]).

Why is foreign subjectivity such a fundamental condition of the possibility for the constitution of transcendent objects? Why are objects only able to *appear* as transcendent through the Other? The explanation offered by Husserl is that the objects cannot be reduced to being merely my intentional correlates if they can be experienced by Others as well. The intersubjective experienceability of the object guarantees its real transcendence, so my experience (constitution) of transcendent objects is necessarily mediated by my experience of its givenness for another transcendent subject, that is, by my experience of a foreign world-directed subject. (It is exactly for this reason that the Other's *transcendence* is so vital. If the Other were only an intentional modification or an eidetic variation of myself, the fact that he experienced the same as I would be just as conclusive—to use a Wittgensteinian example—as if one found the same report in several copies of the same newspaper.) Only insofar as I experience that Others experience the same objects as myself do I really experience these objects as objective and real. Only then do the objects appear with a validity that makes them into more than mere intentional objects. Now they are given as real (objective, that is, intersubjectively valid) intentional objects. Whereas every concrete encounter with an Other is fallible—what I took to be a valid experience of an Other could turn out to be a mere hallucination— the very constitutive relation between intersubjectivity and objectivity is a priori in nature.

That which in principle is incapable of being experienced by Others cannot be ascribed transcendence and objectivity. But even if one is willing to concede that there is a connection between intersubjectivity and reality there is, however, an unsolved problem. Under normal circumstances, I still experience that which I accidentally experience alone (for instance this computer that I am writing on now) as transcendent, objective, and real, although I am not simultaneously experiencing this object as being experienced by Others. And this is even implicitly admitted by Husserl, who writes that, even if I knew with absolute certainty that a universal plague had destroyed all life but my own, my worldly experience would still be dependent upon co-functioning transcendental intersubjectivity (Hua 1/125, 15/6, 6/81). The problem can be solved, however, if one differentiates between our first primal experience of Others—which once and for all makes the constitution of objectivity, reality, and transcendence possible, thus *permanently* transforming our categories of experience—and all subsequent experiences of Others. This does not mean that all these subsequent experiences are insignificant, but their contribution is of a different nature. They no longer make the constitution of the categories of objectivity and transcendence possible, but rather, *fulfill* them. To phrase it differently: Although my solitary experience of the computer is an experience of it as real and objective, these components of validity are at first only given *signitively*. Only the moment I experience that Others are, in fact, also experiencing it is the validity-claim of my experience fulfilled intuitively, that is, in evidence.

As I have indicated, it is important that my experience of another subject be an experience of another *experiencing* subject. Indeed, Husserl even claims that the validity of the other subject's experience is accepted along with my experience of that subject (Hua 14/388).[41] This can be illustrated by reference to Husserl's analysis of the body, where Husserl claims that the experience of another as incarnated subject is the first step toward the constitution of an objective (intersubjectively valid) shared world (Hua 14/110, 15/18, 15/572). The reason for this is that my experience of something as the body of another must be accompanied by another's experience of the *same* as her own body (Hua 13/252, 14/485). In the experience of the body of another, one is confronted with a congruity between one's own experience and the Other's experience—a congruity which, according to Husserl, is the foundation of every subsequent experience of intersubjective objects, that is, objects that are also experienced (experienceable) by Others.

Husserl continues his analysis by describing a special kind of experience of the Other, namely, those situations where I experience the Other as experiencing myself. This kind of 'original reciprocal co-existence'—which Michael Theunissen has named '*Veranderung*'[42]—in which I take over the Other's objectifying apprehension of myself, in which my self-apprehension is mediated by the Other, and in which I experience myself as alien, is of decisive importance for the constitution of an objective world. When I realize that I can be an *alter ego* for the Other just as he can be it for me, a marked change in my own constitutive significance takes place:

The difference between oneself and the foreign I vanishes; the other apprehends me as foreign, just as I grasp him as foreign for me, and he himself is a 'self,' etc. Parity thus ensues: a multiplicity of feeling, willing I's that are alike in kind and each independent in the same sense (Hua 13/243–244; cf. 15/635).

In my encounter with an Other I come to realize that my perspective on the world is only one among many, but in coming to this realization, I can no longer uphold my privileged status in relation to the objects of experience. Whether I or an Other is the subject of the experience makes no difference in principle for the validity of that experience (Hua 17/245, 15/645, 1/157).

Husserl consequently claims that my experiences are changed when I experience that Others experience the same as I, and when I experience that I myself am experienced by Others. From then on, my object of experience cannot any longer be reduced to its mere being-for-me. Through the Other, it has been constituted with a subject-transcendent validity. No longer do I experience it as being dependent on me and my factual existence. On the contrary, as an intersubjective object, it is endowed with an autonomy of being that transcends my own finite existence (cf. Hua 15/218, 8/495, 13/242).[43]

To summarize: Husserl claims that the sense and the categories of *transcendence, objectivity,* and *reality* are constituted intersubjectively. These categories of validity can only be constituted by a subject that has experienced other subjects. Husserl also stresses, however, that the same is the case for the categories of *immanence, subjectivity,* and *appearance*. His line of thought is the following: When I realize that my object of experience can also be experienced by Others, I also realize that there is a difference between the thing in itself and its appearance for me (Hua 6/167, 4/82). Thus, it only makes sense to speak and designate something as a mere appearance, as merely subjective, when I have experienced other subjects and thus acquired the concept of intersubjective validity (Hua 9/453, 13/382, 388–389, 420–421).

The structures that have been emphasized so far (my experience of the world-directed transcendent foreign subject, and my experience of the Other's experience of myself) take up a decisive place in Husserl's account of the transcendental-constitutive function of intersubjectivity. It would be a mistake, however, to assume that Husserl understands intersubjectivity as something that is exclusively attached to concrete bodily mediated interaction. If this had been the case, one might criticize him by pointing to the fact that exactly this kind of experience seems to be both contingent and fallible—which Husserl himself admits (Hua 14/474–475)—and exactly for that reason, not the most convincing foundation for a transcendental philosophy.[44] Husserl, however, does not operate with only one kind of transcendental intersubjectivity—a common assumption—but with several different kinds. Apart from the kind that has already been described, Husserl also argues for a place for intersubjectivity in the very intentional relation to the world, that is, he occasionally argues that my intentionality already implies a reference to other subjects prior to any concrete experience of them, that is, *a priori*. Finally, Husserl also claims that one should ascribe a constitutive function to the anonymous community, which manifests itself in our inherited linguistic normality (in our tradition).

To account in detail for these last two kinds of intersubjectivity would exceed the limits of this section. Let me, however, briefly outline Husserl's ideas.[45] Concerning the first and most fundamental kind of intersubjectivity, Husserl writes that the analysis of the transcendental ego ultimately leads to a disclosure of its *apodictic* intersubjective structure (Hua 15/192).[46] Why is that? Because, as Husserl claims, each and every one of my perceptual objects not only implies a reference to myself as experiencing subject, but also to the Others as co-subjects (Hua 6/468). As he puts it in the manuscript C 17:

> My experience as mundane experience (that is, already each of my perceptions) does not only entail Others as mundane objects, but also and constantly in existential co-validity as co-subjects, as co-constituting, and both are inseparably intertwined (Ms. C 17 36a).[47]

Husserl's reasoning seems partly to be based on an investigation of horizonal intentionality. My perceptual objects are characterized by their horizonal givenness. They are not exhausted in their appearance for me; rather, each object always possesses a horizon of co-existing profiles which, although being momentarily inaccessible to me—I cannot see the front and the back of a chair simultaneously, for instance—could very well be perceived by other subjects. Since the perceptual object is always there for others, too, whether or not such other subjects do in fact appear on the scene, the object refers to those other subjects, and is, for that very reason, intrinsically intersubjective. It does not merely exist for me, but refers to a plurality of possible subjects, as does my intentionality whenever I am directed at these intersubjectively accessible objects. That is, my perceptual intentionality contains a reference to Others, regardless of whether or not I experience these Others, and, indeed, regardless of whether they actually exist or not. Thus my perceptual intentionality can be said to contain an *a priori* reference to something that Husserl occasionally calls 'open intersubjectivity.' As he writes in *Zur Phänomenologie der Intersubjektivität II*:

> Thus everything objective that stands before me in experience—and primarily in perception—has an apperceptive horizon of possible experience, my own and foreign. Ontologically speaking, every appearance that I have is from the very beginning a

part of an open, endless, but not explicitly realized, totality of possible appearances of the same, and the subjectivity belonging to this appearance is open intersubjectivity (Hua 14/289. Cf. 9/394 and 15/497.).

If these considerations are combined with Husserl's account of the actual, *horizonal* experience of another bodily subject, it is obvious that the a priori reference to the open intersubjectivity is already presupposed. Prior to my concrete encounter with the Other, intersubjectivity is already present as co-subjectivity, for which reason Husserl's analysis of perceptual intentionality can be said to demonstrate the untenability of a solipsistic position. Perhaps Husserl was referring to this when in the manuscript C 17 he wrote: 'When empathy occurs, is the community, the intersubjectivity there already in advance, and is empathy merely a disclosing performance?' (Ms. C 17 84b).[48] A question Husserl then goes on to answer in the affirmative.

So far we have been dealing with two types of intersubjectivity, and it is important to emphasize that the concrete experience of the Other, although it presupposes the intersubjectivity at work in horizonal intentionality, is still transcendental, that is, constitutive. Thus, the concrete experience of the bodily Other is not a mere intramundane episode, since it is only here that I can experience the true alterity and transcendence of the Other and take over his objectifying apprehension of myself. According to Husserl, it is precisely these experiences that are conditions of the possibility for the constitution of true objectivity.

Husserl, however, also operates with a third type of transcendental intersubjectivity different in kind from the previous two, although it presupposes both.[49] Thus, as I will show in more detail in the next section dealing with Husserl's concept of the *lifeworld*, Husserl also claims that certain types of self-and world-apprehension are only made possible by a linguistically sedimented and traditionally handed-down *normality*. Thus, normality qua anonymous community also possesses constitutive implications.

Subjectivity—Inter/subjectivity

So far it has been amply demonstrated that Husserl took intersubjectivity very seriously. Thus, when he claims that the subject can only be world-experiencing insofar as it is a member of a community (Hua 1/166), that the ego is only what it is as a *socius*, that is, as a member of a sociality

(Hua 15/193) and that a radical *self*-reflection necessarily leads to the discovery of absolute intersubjectivity (Hua 6/275, 472), the general line of thought is indicated. Husserl takes transcendental subjectivity to be (at least in part) dependent on transcendental intersubjectivity. This interpretation can be substantiated by numerous passages in Husserl's work. In *Erste Philosophie II*, for instance, he writes that transcendental subjectivity in its full universality is exactly *inter*-subjectivity (Hua 8/480). In a research manuscript from 1927 (published in *Zur Phänomenologie der Intersubjektivität I*) Husserl writes that the absolute reveals itself as the intersubjective relation between subjects (Hua 13/480). Thus, Husserl's recurrent point is that a sufficiently radical carrying out of the transcendental reduction leads not only to subjectivity, but also to intersubjectivity (Hua 9/344), and it is no coincidence, that at certain points, with reference to Leibniz, he called his own theory a *transcendental monadology* (Hua 8/190), thereby stressing the *plurality* of constitutive centers.[50]

As already mentioned, Husserl's view on the transcendental ego differs from Kant's. Husserl not only advocates the heretical standpoint that it is possible, that is, *coherent*, to talk about a plurality of transcendental egos, ultimately he even strengthens this assertion, claiming that it is *necessary*, insofar as 'subjectivity is what it is—an ego functioning constitutively—only within intersubjectivity' (Hua 6/175 [172]). The claim that subjectivity only becomes fully constitutive, that is, fully transcendental through its relation with Others is in striking contrast with any traditional Kantian understanding of transcendental subjectivity. Curiously enough, it is exactly this traditional understanding which A. Schütz tacitly accepts in his well-known criticism of Husserl's theory of intersubjectivity. Thus Schütz writes:

It must be earnestly asked whether the transcendental Ego in Husserl's concept is not essentially what Latin grammarians call a 'singulare tantum,' that is, a term incapable of being put into the plural. Even more, it is in no way established whether the existence of Others is a problem of the transcendental sphere at all, i.e., whether the problem of intersubjectivity does exist between transcendental egos . . . ; or whether intersubjectivity and therefore sociality does not rather belong exclusively to the mundane sphere of our life-world.[51]

Husserl, however, takes issue with this position in a manuscript now published in the supplementary volume to *Krisis*, where he explicitly states that the possibility of a transcendental elucidation of subjectivity and world is

lost if one follows the Kantian tradition in interpreting transcendental subjectivity as an isolated ego, thereby ignoring the problem of transcendental
intersubjectivity (Hua 29/120). This remark could easily have been ascribed to Apel. It is of utmost importance to notice, however, that Husserl,
in contrast to the philosophers of language, does not conceive of his own
phenomenology of intersubjectivity as a break with (a correctly understood) philosophy of subjectivity. Moreover, it is possible to find reflections
concerning the fundamental significance of intersubjectivity in his manuscripts side by side with remarks concerning the importance of the transcendental ego, and even statements saying that the transcendental primal
ego (*Ur-Ich*) cannot be pluralized (Hua 6/188).

To say the very least, this seems to imply an inconsistency at the very
core of Husserl's reflections. Two popular 'solutions' have consisted in claiming either that Husserl changed his mind within a few years, alternately at-
tributing priority to the ego (in *Cartesianische Meditationen*) and to intersubjectivity (in *Krisis*); or, alternatively, that Husserl never abandoned his
egological point of departure, for which reason his treatment of intersubjectivity remained superficial and without any real radicality. Both of these
interpretations are, however, encumbered with some obvious problems. The
first is problematic because it is possible to find the alleged alternatives
within both *Cartesianische Meditationen* and *Krisis*. In both works Husserl
speaks about the fundamental importance of both ego and intersubjectivity. The second is also problematic since it is confronted with a large number of passages (some already quoted) where Husserl seems quite unam-
biguously to ascribe a fundamental and decisive role to intersubjectivity.

A closer reading reveals that the ascribed inconsistency is only apparent. It disappears the moment we realize that Husserl's emphasis on the
uniqueness of the primal ego does not clash in any way with his intersubjective transformation of the transcendental philosophical project. Quite
the contrary. Once more the character of Husserl's phenomenology of intersubjectivity has to be stressed. Transcendental intersubjectivity is not an
objectively existing structure in the world that can be described and analyzed from a third-person perspective, but a relation between subjects in
which the ego itself participates. To phrase it differently: Transcendental
intersubjectivity can only be disclosed through a radical explication of the
ego's structures of experience. This indicates not only an intersubjective
structure to the ego, but also the egological rootedness of intersubjectiv-

ity.[52] Husserl's accentuation of the fundamental importance of the ego must, in other words, be seen as an accentuation of the fact that intersubjectivity, my relation to the Other, presupposes my own subjectivity as one of the relata. Only from this point of view is intersubjectivity and the plurality of constitutive centers phenomenologically accessible.

The remaining problem is to explain how Husserl can persist in designating the transcendental primal ego as unique. An examination of the manuscript B I 14, however, can solve this problem. Husserl writes that the 'I' does not admit of any plural as long as the word is used in its original sense. Others can experience themselves as I, but only I can experience myself as I. Besides myself there is no other I about which I can say 'this is me.' Precisely for that reason, it is impossible to speak about *an* I as long as 'I' really means I. I is absolutely unique and individual (Ms. B I 14 138a). When Husserl mentions the absolute uniqueness of the ego and denies that it can be put into plural, he is obviously referring to the unique egocentric givenness of my own consciousness. I am only self-aware of myself and can never ever be self-aware of anybody else. This uniqueness, however, is of a kind that admits of Others: 'The unique I—the transcendental. In its uniqueness it posits 'other' unique transcendental I's—as 'others', who themselves posit others in uniqueness once again' (Ms. B I 14 138b.[53] Cf. Hua 14/212.). Of course, Husserl would deny that this first-personal uniqueness is merely a contingent linguistic fact. On the contrary, we are dealing with a transcendental necessity ultimately connected to the crucial issue of self-givenness and inner time-consciousness. 'I am' is the intentional ground for the ego that thinks it. It is, as Husserl says, the primal fact that, as a philosopher, I must never overlook (Hua 17/243–244, 14/307, 29/165).

This is offered merely as a demonstration of the consistency of Husserl's position. When he speaks about the absolute priority of the ego, this does not contradict his reflections concerning transcendental intersubjectivity as the absolute field of being. Transcendental intersubjectivity is a transcendental foundation, but, as Husserl says, it possesses a necessary I-centering (Hua 15/426). Intersubjectivity can unfold itself only in the relation between unique subjects, and it is for this reason that Husserl writes that the disclosure of transcendental subjectivity effectuated by the reduction is ambiguous, since it leads to subjectivity as well as to intersubjectivity (Hua 15/73–75). Far from being competing alternatives, subjectivity and intersubjectivity are in fact complementary and mutually interdependent notions.

At this point, it would have been appropriate to provide a more detailed investigation of the role played by intersubjectivity on the most fundamental level, namely, when it concerns the self-temporalization of the subject. On the one hand, it is important to emphasize the significance of intersubjectivity when it comes to the self-constitution of the subject. On the other hand, it is also important to insist on the fact that each single subject must possess a certain amount of ontological autonomy—since a complete elimination of this would make the very concept of intersubjectivity impossible. If the difference between the subjects were negated, there would not be any plurality and consequently no inter-subjectivity (Hua 15/335, 339). Thus, if one wants to preserve intersubjectivity and keep the plurality of individual and transcendent subjects, it is necessary to reject the proposal that they have their ground of being in a prior unity.[54] However, a detailed analysis of Husserl's complex account of the ego's many structural moments (including a differentiation between those that are intersubjectively constituted and those that must be presupposed sui generis in order for the notion of intersubjectivity to be at all coherent) would be beyond the scope of this book. Let me only mention that Husserl's position apparently is that the very temporal flow of consciousness, which constitutes the most basic level of subjectivity, is a process that does not depend on the relation to the Other (Hua 14/170–175). At the same time, however, he occasionally seeks to found the very openness toward Others in the very structure of temporality. As he points out, there is a structural similarity between empathy and recollection (cf. Hua 1/144, 3/325, 8/175, 6/189, 13/188, 15/447, 15/641, 15/416). Recollection entails a self-displacement or self-distanciation, qualities that are needed if I am to be capable of empathy, that is, if I am to meet the Other as a self. This line of thought is continued when Husserl speaks of the affinity between the de-presentation effectuated by original temporalization and the self-alienation taking place in empathy:

Self-temporalization through de-presentation [*Ent-Gegenwärtigung*], so to speak (through recollection), has its analogue in my self-alienation [*Ent-Fremdung*] (empathy as a de-presentation of a higher level—de-presentation of my primal presence [*Urpräsenz*] into a merely presentified [*vergegenwärtigte*] primal presence) [transl. modified] (Hua 6/189 [185]. Cf. Hua 15/642, 634).

Thus, Husserl appears to regard the step from de-presentation to self-alienation as an intensification of alterity, and, more generally, he seems to consider the ecstatic-centered self-differentiation brought about by the process of temporalization to be a condition of the possibility for empathy, for an openness toward the Other.[55]

D. The Lifeworld

Husserl's analysis of the lifeworld (the prescientific world of experience) constitutes one of his best-known investigations and is among those that have found widest acceptance outside of phenomenology—for instance, in parts of sociology.[56] In attempting a brief summary of the main ideas to be found in these extensive analyses, it is natural to emphasize three lines of thoughts: 1) First of all, Husserl's analysis of the lifeworld is a clarification of the relation between scientific theory and the prescientific practically oriented experience. This clarification questions the rampant *objectivism* and *scientism* that is so widespread today. 2) Second, Husserl's analysis of the lifeworld can be regarded as a new introduction to or way toward the transcendental-phenomenological reduction, a way that radically questions a number of Cartesian motives in Husserl's thinking and that understands the relation between subjectivity and world in a very different manner than *Ideen 1*. 3) Finally, Husserl's analysis of the lifeworld can be seen as a radicalization of his analysis of intersubjectivity, insofar as concepts like *historicity*, *generativity*, *tradition*, and *normality* are given a central transcendental-philosophical significance.

The Lifeworld and the Crisis of Science

Although Husserl's concept of the lifeworld and its accompanying topics can already be found early on in his writings,[57] its most systematic treatment is to be found in his last work, *Die Krisis der europäischen Wissenschaften und die transzendentale Phänomenologie*. What 'crisis' is Husserl referring to? To put it slightly paradoxically, one could say that the positive sciences, and, more specifically, the objectivistic paradigm of science, have been too successful. A crisis not only reveals itself in dramatic breakdowns, but also in a smoothly functioning mindlessness. According to Husserl, the positive sciences have had such immense success that they are no longer reflecting on their own foundations and eventual limitations, but merely concerned with advanced technical issues. The fundamental problems pertaining to the very (metaphysical) framework within which these sciences operate have been lost from sight, as have questions like 'What is truth?,' 'What is knowledge?,' 'What is reality?,' 'What is a good and meaningful life?,' and the like. To put it differently, not only are the positive sciences in need of an ontological and epistemological clarification, they have also lost their existential relevance. This is why Husserl accuses the sciences of having gone bankrupt ethically as well as philosophically.

According to Husserl's diagnosis, this crisis is a direct consequence of the objectivism that has dominated since the Scientific Revolution in the Renaissance, a revolution characterized by its quantitative ideal of method, its sharp distinction between facts and values, and its insistence that science and science only can describe reality as it is in itself. To quote Galileo, who, according to Husserl, personifies this entire enterprise:

Philosophy is written in this grand book, the universe, which stands continually open to our gaze. But the book cannot be understood unless one first learns to comprehend the language and read the letters in which it is composed. It is written in the language of mathematics, and its characters are triangles, circles, and other geometric figures without which it is humanly impossible to understand a single word of it; without these, one wanders about in a dark labyrinth.[58]

According to Husserl, the only way to overcome the present scientific crisis and to heal the disastrous rupture between the world of science and the world of everyday life is by criticizing this reigning objectivism. This is why Husserl commences his analysis of the lifeworld, a lifeworld which, although it constitutes the historical and systematical foundation of science, has been forgotten and repressed by it.

*

In our prescientific experience, the world is given concretely, sensuously, and intuitively. In contrast, the scientific world is a system of idealities that in principle transcends sensuous experience. Whereas the lifeworld is a world of situated, relative truths, science seeks to realize an idea about strict and objective knowledge that is freed from every relation to the subjective first-person perspective. Whereas the objects in the lifeworld are characterized by their relative, approximate, and perspectival givenness—when I experience the water as cold, my friend might experience it as warm; my perspective on the table is not completely identical with my neighbor's—the objects of science are characterized as irrelative, nonperspectival, univocal, and exact (Hua 6/309). Science—and we are primarily talking about natural science—is, consequently, characterized by its attempt to transcend the vagueness and relativity that characterizes our bodily and practical interaction with and experience of the world. It seeks to acquire knowledge not of how the world is for us, but of how it is mind-independently, that is, 'in itself' (Hua 13/381, 4/207).

It is considerations like these that are behind the classical distinction between *primary* and *secondary* sensory qualities. Thus, it has traditionally been taken for granted that the form, size, and weight of the object, that is, all of those properties that can be described quantitatively and with mathematical precision, are objective properties, whereas the color, taste, smell, and so on, of the object are mere subjective epiphenomena lacking any objective, that is, mind-independent reality.[59] But, as Husserl points out, this classical distinction has been radicalized in the course of time. It is not merely specific qualities of the appearing object that are now taken to be subjective, but everything that appears. It is the very appearance that is taken to be subjective, and it is this appearance, this phenomenal dimension, that science seeks to transcend in its attempt to grasp the true nature of the object. If we wish to analyze water, the fact that we drink it and swim in it is considered irrelevant, just as its color, taste, and smell are quite inessential. But, more generally, this is also the case for the entirety of sensuous appearance, since this is taken to be nothing but a subjective distortion of the underlying true reality. Ultimately our goal must be to disclose the physical structure of the object: Water = H_2O. True reality— that which really exists objectively and mind-independently—is, consequently, claimed to be completely different from that which we encounter in our prescientific experience. Although science initially set out to rescue the world from the onslaught of skepticism, it apparently did so by returning us a world we barely recognize.

It should not come as a surprise that Husserl disagrees with this account, and, already in *Ideen 1* (§§ 40 and 52), he calls attention to a number of category mistakes that it involves. As the analysis of intentionality has shown, it is simply wrong to claim that the appearing object, i.e., our intentional object, is subjective in the sense of being *intramental.* This even holds true for something as patently unreal as a hallucinated pink moose, and even more so for the green grass or the tasty, sweetly fragrant peaches.

The claim that the appearing, intuitively given object is a mere representation of the real physical object must also be questioned. Husserl's criticism of the representative theory of perception, which was presented in Part 1, is still valid. To be a representation of something is not a natural property of an object. On the contrary, the object is only endowed with its representative function through an intentional interpretation (cf. p. 18). More generally, Husserl would claim that any justified theoretical claim should be supported directly or indirectly by experience. This is no less true for arithmetics than for astrophysics or botany. Thus, one should not overlook the very broad concept of experience used by Husserl (cf. p. 37). Ideal objects can also appear intuitively, though not in a sensuous manner, but rather in a categorial fashion.

Let me emphasize that Husserl is by no means suggesting that the scientific exploration of reality is false, invalid, or superfluous. On the contrary, all he wishes to criticize is certain elements in the inflated self-understanding of science. On the one hand, he wishes to challenge the scientistic assumption that reality is defined by science, that is, that reality is identical with that which can be grasped and described by physics, and that our commonsense belief in the existence of such everyday objects as tables and chairs, books, and nations, is consequently nothing but a grand illusion. On the other hand, he wishes to question its bland objectivism—its attempt to define reality in terms of that which is absolutely independent of subjectivity, interpretation, and historical community.

Husserl does acknowledge the validity of scientific theories and descriptions, and would even concede that they attain a higher degree of objectivity than our daily observations. But, as he repeatedly points out, we are faced with a faulty inference if against that background, we conclude that 1) only scientific accounts can capture true reality, or that 2) these accounts manage to grasp something which, in a very radical sense, is independent of our experiential and conceptual perspective. To think that science can give an *absolute* description of reality, that is, a description from a view from nowhere, is simply a misunderstanding. We must reject the assumption that physics is the sole arbiter of what there is, and that all notions to be taken seriously should be reducible to the vocabulary and the conceptual apparatus of the exact sciences.

As Husserl points out, natural science by itself undermines the categorical distinction between the sensuously given and the physically described. After all, it does insist that it investigates the water I am drinking, or the diamond I am admiring, rather than a completely different object. It maintains that it is the true nature of the *experienced* object that it seeks to capture.

> The physical thing which he [the physicist] observes, with which he experiments, which he continually sees, takes in his hand, puts on the scale or in the melting furnace: that physical thing, and no other, becomes the subject of the predicates ascribed in physics, such as weight, temperature, electrical resistance, and so forth (Hua 3/113).

According to Husserl, physics does not present us with an entirely new physical object, but rather with a different, higher, and more exact objective determination of the very same object that we encounter in our daily life (Ms. A III 9 8b). In contrast to my own estimation of whether the water is warm or hot or whether it tastes strange, a definition of water as H_2O is not only valid for me personally, but for all subjects. Even the most exact and abstract scientific results, however, are rooted in the intuitively given subject-relative evidence of the lifeworld—a form of evidence that does not merely function as an unavoidable, but otherwise irrelevant, way point toward scientific knowledge, but as a permanent and quite indispensable source of meaning and justification (Hua 6/142).

In its urge toward idealization, in its search for exact and objective knowledge, science has made a virtue out of its decisive showdown with subject-relative evidence, but it has thereby overlooked that its own more refined measurements inevitably continue to draw on the contribution of intuition, as when one sets up the experiment, reads the measuring instruments, or interprets, compares, and discusses the results with other scientists. We should not forget that empirical theories are based on experimental and experiential evidence (Hua 6/128). Although scientific theory in its idealization transcends the concrete, intuitively given lifeworld, the latter remains as a reference point and meaning-foundation (Hua 6/129).

But then what exactly is the lifeworld? Unfortunately, it is impossible to give a simple answer. Husserl's concept is equivocal, and the precise meaning of the term depends on the context. Quite generally, one should distinguish between an *ontological* and a *transcendental* concept of the lifeworld. When it comes to the ontological concept, it can be subdivided in the following manner: 1) At times, the concept simply refers to the prescientifically given world of experience, the world which we take for granted in daily life, with which we are familiar, and which we do not question. 2) Occasionally, however, Husserl modifies this description, writing that the lifeworld gradually absorbs scientific theories (Hua 6/132). Science is founded on the lifeworld, and will eventually sink down into the ground it is standing on. As time goes by, theoretical assumptions are assimilated into daily praxis, becoming part of the lifeworld: We all assume that the Earth is round, for example, although few of us have seen it; we frequently employ aids whose use is scientifically motivated, say vitamins or sun oil. One of the characteristic features of this modified concept of the lifeworld is that it is not static. The concrete lifeworld has a *genesis* and is under permanent transformation.

To a certain extent the distinction between these two concepts can be related to a development internal to Husserl's thinking. Whereas Husserl already thematized the connection and relation of foundation between the ideal scientific theories and the prelinguistic world of experience in *Ideen 1*, it was only later, particularly in *Krisis*, that he became concerned with the actual historicity of scientific theories.

These issues are further complicated by the fact that Husserl does not believe it sufficient to undertake a merely empirical investigation of the lifeworld. The philosophical task must be to disclose the a priori of the lifeworld, that is, its ontological essence. Given the concrete and relative nature of the lifeworld, it could be asked whether this task is not doomed to failure from the very start. Is the lifeworld not exactly something that evades theoretical fixation? However, although the lifeworld is characterized by its perspectival and relative nature, Husserl still takes it to be in possession of a basic invariant *morphological* structure.

Here, Husserl employs a distinction between *morphological* and *ideal* essences. If we take our point of departure in the perceptual world, and if we investigate the objects we are normally surrounded by, be it utensils such as knives, pens, or glasses, or natural objects such as birds, trees, or stones, they are all characterized by an essential vagueness, and our classification of these objects are, by nature, approximative. If we seek to impose on the phenomena of the lifeworld the exactness and precision that we find in, say, geometry, we violate them.

The geometer is not interested in *de facto* sensuously intuitable shapes, as the descriptive natural scientist is. He does not, like the latter, fashion *morphological con-*

cepts of vague configurational types which are directly seized upon on the basis of sensuous intuition and which, in their vagueness, become conceptually and terminologically fixed. The *vagueness* of such concepts, the circumstances that their spheres of application are fluid, does not make them defective; for in the spheres of knowledge where they are used they are absolutely indispensable, or in those spheres they are the only legitimate concepts. If the aim is to give appropriate conceptual expression to the intuitionally given essential characteristics of intuitionally given physical things, that means precisely that the latter must be taken as they are given. And they are given precisely as fluid; and typical essences can become seized upon as exemplified in them only in immediately analytic eidetic intuition. The most perfect geometry and the most perfect practical mastery of it cannot enable the descriptive natural scientist to express (in exact geometrical concepts) what he expresses in such a simple, understandable, and completely appropriate manner by the words 'notched,' 'scalloped,' 'lens-shaped,' 'umbelliform,' and the like—all to them concepts which are *essentially, rather than accidentally, inexact* and *consequently* also non-mathematical (Hua 3/155).

Whereas our vague and inexact descriptions of the phenomena in the lifeworld have an ontological correlate in the morphological structure of the phenomena, the exact sciences seek to overcome this vagueness, thereby making use of something Husserl calls *idealization*. It is not possible to draw a perfectly straight line, since a sufficiently detailed measurement will always reveal small aberrations. It is, however, possible to transcend these imperfections in thought. We can construe an idea about an absolutely straight line and take it as an ideal that can be approximated. In contrast to a morphological concept like the concept 'dog,' which refers to something we can actually see a concrete instantiation of, the concept of a perfectly straight line is an exact (and abstract) concept. It does not describe anything that actually exists in nature, but is an ideal construction.

As we have seen, Husserl takes the lifeworld to be characterized by its morphological typicity. In his view, this not only makes possible a theoretical exploration of the lifeworld itself, it also makes possible every other science. Had the lifeworld been completely chaotic, systematic theories would have had nothing to build upon and would have had no foundation (Hua 6/142–145). Thus, Husserl actually argues that there is a universal and essential structure to every possible lifeworld, regardless of how different it might otherwise be, geographically, historically, or culturally. And—to deliver Husserl's contribution to the discussion of relativism—it is exactly this universality which, although not actually guaranteeing transhistorical and intercultural understanding, does at least make it possible.

What exactly does this essential structure consists of? Again, Husserl's answer is equivocal. He often emphasizes a number of rather formal features such as a common spatiotemporal worldform (Hua 1/161–162, 4/83), and speaks of nature as that which is unconditionally universal and identical (Ms. C 17 45a). But at some places he chooses a rather different and far more concrete approach. Thus, Husserl calls attention to the fact that every lifeworld is correlated to a *functioning body*. He then goes on to claim that it is this corporeality with all that belongs to it (such as sexual drives, nutritional needs, birth and death, community and tradition) that makes up the universal framework that any conceivable lifeworld is structured in accordance with (Hua 15/433).

I earlier mentioned the distinction between an ontological and a transcendental concept of the lifeworld. It is exactly this distinction that now needs to be addressed. Although there is a difference between an ontological analysis of the lifeworld and an ontological analysis of different scientific regions (the region of chemistry, biology, physics, and so on), there is also a common denominator. In both cases, we are dealing with ontological analyses which belong within the natural attitude and which, consequently, don't presuppose the effectuation of the transcendental reduction. In itself this is a clear indication that we are not yet at the end of the investigation. And, in fact, Husserl's enterprise in *Krisis* is exactly the same as in a number of his earlier works, namely, to provide us with an introduction into transcendental phenomenology. More precisely, the characteristic feature of *Krisis* is that the way toward transcendental phenomenology proceeds via a criticism of objectivism. By first showing that scientific theories are rooted in the lifeworld, and then by taking the ontology of the lifeworld as a guiding line for a constitutive analysis (cf. p. 50), Husserl seeks to demonstrate that both lifeworld and science are constituted by transcendental (inter)subjectivity, for which reason both objectivism and scientism must be rejected. Any claim to the effect that Husserl's analysis of the lifeworld constitutes a break with his transcendental project is, consequently, mistaken. The lifeworld is constituted by subjective perspectives and correlated to transcendental (inter)subjectivity, or, to use a term from Husserl's last years, to the intersubjective life of world-consciousness (*Weltbewußtseinsleben*) (Hua 15/539).

Husserl's central argument against scientific objectivism is, consequently, transcendental in nature. It is not only perceptually given objects that are intentional correlates, this is also true for theoretical idealities. The latter are also constituted intentional objects that only acquire full intelligibility when they are investigated in correlation to transcendental (inter) subjectivity.

Normality and Tradition

If one accepts Husserl's conviction that reality is intersubjectively constituted, one is bound to take not only the consensus but also the *dissent* of the world-experiencing subjects seriously. Husserl's extended analyses of this problem, which can be seen as an elaboration of his theory of intersubjectivity, eventually made him enter fields that have traditionally been reserved for psychopathology, sociology, anthropology, and ethnology. Whereas a strict Kantian transcendental philosophy would have considered such empirical and mundane domains to be without any transcendental relevance, because of his interest in transcendental intersubjectivity, Husserl was forced to consider these from a transcendental point of view (Hua 15/391). Thus, I believe that Husserl's late thinking is characterized by a decisive reexamination of the relation between the transcendental and the empirical that ultimately led to an expansion of the transcendental sphere, a reexamination that was, in part, brought about by his interest in intersubjectivity, and that forced him to consider the transcendental significance of *generativity, tradition, historicity,* and *normality.*[60]

Let me focus on the problem of *normality*, which Husserl took up in a number of different contexts and which he considered to be a constitutional core concept. Basically, Husserl claims that our experiences are guided by anticipations of normality. Our apprehension, experience, and constitution are shaped by those normal and typical structures, models, and patterns which have been established by earlier experiences (Hua 11/186). If that which we experience happens to clash with our earlier experiences—if it is different—we have an experience of *anormality*, which may subsequently lead to a modification of our anticipations (Ms. D 13 234b, 15/438).

To start with, Husserl examines this influence of normality in connection with his analysis of the *passive synthesis* that occurs in the life of a single solitary subject. But as Husserl eventually realized, intersubjectivity has a crucial role to play. I have been among people as long as I remember, and my anticipations are structured in accordance with the intersubjectively handed-down forms of apperception (cf. 14/117, 125, 15/136). Normality is also *conventionality*, which, in its being, transcends the individual (Hua 15/611).[61] Thus, already in *Ideen II* Husserl pointed to the fact that, next to the tendencies originating from other persons, there also exist indeterminate general demands made by custom and tradition: 'One' judges thus, 'one' holds the fork in such and such a way, and so forth (Hua 4/269). I learn what is normal from Others (and, first and foremost, from my closest relatives, that is, from the people who raised and educated me [Hua 15/428–429, 569, 602–604]), and, thereby, I am involved in a common tradition which stretches back through a chain of generations into a dim past.

As I have just mentioned, one consequence of Husserl's treatment of intersubjectivity is that he also has to take the *disagreement* between world-experiencing subjects seriously. If my constitution of objectivity is dependent on my assurance that Others experience or can experience the same as I, it is a problem if they claim to be experiencing something different—although the fact that we can agree on there being a disagreement already indicates a kind of common ground (Hua 15/47). It is in this context, however, that Husserl emphasizes that only the (dis)agreement between the *normal* members of the community are of relevance. When it is said that real being has to be experienceable by everybody, we are, as he says, dealing with a certain averageness and idealization (Hua 15/141, 231, 629). 'Everybody' is the person who belongs to a normality of subjects and who is exactly normal in and through the community (Hua 15/142). Only with him do we fight over the truth and falsity, being and nonbeing of our common lifeworld. Only the normal is apprehended as being co-constitutive (Hua 15/162, 166, 9/497), whereas my disagreement with an anormal is (at first) considered inconsequential.[62]

Let me give a concrete and quite simple illustration. Let us imagine that I am standing on a bridge admiring an old sailing ship. I then turn to one of my friends and ask 'Don't you think it is beautiful?' If he agrees, an implicit confirmation of the validity of my experience has taken place. I do perceive a really existing sailing ship. If he looks bewildered and asks 'what sailing ship?,' the validity of my own experience will undergo certain modifications. I cannot maintain my belief that I am experiencing a real sailing ship (in contrast to simply hallucinating one) if the object in question is not accessible to Others. But the Others in question are normal Others. If, after his question, my friend asks whether I have forgotten that he is blind, our disagreement would no longer be relevant (cf. Hua 1/154, 15/48).

It quickly proves necessary to differentiate between at least two fundamental types of normality. First, we speak of normality when we are dealing with a mature, healthy, and rational person. Here the anormal will be the infant, the blind, or the schizophrenic. Secondly, we speak of normality when it concerns our own *homeworld*, whereas anormality is attributed to the foreigner, who can, however, provided certain conditions are fulfilled, be apprehended as a member of a *foreign normality*.[63]

It is precisely in this context that disagreement gains a vital constitutive significance. According to Husserl, the experience of discrepancy between normal subjects (including the experience of the existence of a plurality of normalities, each of which has its own notion of what counts as true) does not merely lead to a more comprehensive understanding of the world, insofar as we are able to incorporate these different perspectives. The disagreement can also *motivate* the constitution of *scientific* objectivity, insofar as we aim toward reaching a truth that will be valid for us all. As already mentioned, the task of science is to determine the nature of reality, such as it is, with unconditional validity for all (rational) subjects (Hua 6/324). But a decisive motivation for this enterprise is exactly those situations where we realize that we don't experience the world in the same way. Without such an experience there would be no incentive to start the scientific search for irrelative knowledge.

Husserl also claims that it is possible to distinguish several different levels of objectivity. When a community of color-blind subjects jointly examines a painting, they are dealing with an intersubjectively constituted object. When people with normal vision examine the 'same' painting, they are also dealing with an intersubjectively constituted object. The apprehension of both groups can, however, be mediated by a geometrical description which, due to its more formal (and empty) validity, possesses a higher degree of objectivity.

Thus, eventually it becomes necessary to differentiate between 1) the kind of objectivity that suffices in daily life and that might simply be correlated to a certain limited intersubjectivity, and 2) 'rigorous' or scientific objectivity, which is unconditionally valid for all subjects (Hua 14/111). It should be emphasized, however, that this ideal of irrelative truth is in fact irrelevant to most daily concerns. In daily life we do not interact with ideal theoretical objects, but with tools and values, with pictures, statues, books, tables, houses, friends, and family (Hua 4/27), and our interest is guided by practical concerns. That which is sufficient in praxis counts as the thing in itself (Hua 11/23).

In connection with the last and highest level of constitution—the constitution of theoretical scientific objectivity—Husserl touches on the significance of *writing*. It is not merely the case that meaning only acquires full objectivity the moment it is written down and detached from its in-dexical connection to person, time, and place. As written down, meaning can be handed down to later generations and incorporated into the body of knowledge, which generations of scientists draw on and add to. As Husserl observes in the famous appendix *Ursprung der Geometrie*, compre-hensive and complex theories are developed through centuries and would not have been possible were it not for the documenting, preserving func-tion of writing (Hua 6/369–374, 17/38, 349).

By serving as a kind of collective memory and reservoir of knowl-edge, writing has a major constitutive impact (Hua 15/224), but it is also, in Husserl's opinion, connected with two dangers. First of all, Husserl calls attention to the *seductive* powers of language (Hua 6/372). Instead of liv-ing and acting responsible on the basis of proper evidence, we are easily se-duced by the handed-down assumptions, structures of understanding, and forms of interpretation that are rooted in language (cf. Hua 4/269).[64] Sec-ond, one needs to be attentive to a threatening objectivism. The moment idealities are detached from their subject-relative origin, it is easy to forget about constituting subjectivity altogether. In the end, Husserl takes both of these dangers to be responsible for the modern crisis of science.

According to Husserl, scientific theories gradually arise out of practi-cal life. Historically speaking, a number of horizon-expanding 'primal in-stitutions' (*Urstiftungen*) have taken place, that is, a series of episodes have occurred where new types of objects, geometrical idealities, for instance, were constituted for the first time. Gradually, these new types of under-standing have become more and more widely employed; they have been handed down from generation to generation and have ultimately become so familiar and obvious, that they are simply taken for granted, for which reason their historical and subjective origin has been forgotten. Galileo and his contemporary mathematicians already had a highly developed mathematics at hand. It was taken for granted and even regarded as representing true reality. However, this view cannot be maintained when one realizes the transcendental-historical function of the lifeworld. The objectivistic ideal of science and the theoretical, idealizing attitude that we find in mathematics are not natural in any sense, but rather products of a historically developed method, a fact that has subsequently been forgotten.

It is important to understand that Husserl's accentuation of the historical origin of science does not entail any attempt at reducing scientific idealities to empirical and factual realities. Nor is he trying to ground the validities of these idealities in factual circumstances. Husserl's so-called '*Rückfrage*' (which can be translated as 'a backward directed investigation' or a 'return inquiry') is not an attempt to identify the actual discoverer of geometry, nor is it an attempt to reconstruct the factual development of the theory—Husserl has not suddenly become friendly toward historicism, psychologism's cousin. On the contrary, Husserl is striving to answer the following question: What implications does it have for our appraisal of science that it, by necessity, arose at a certain point in history, and that it has been developed and handed down over generations? Husserl's conclusion, which can be seen as a criticism of the static nature of Kantian transcendental philosophy—for Kant the transcendental categories are given once and for all—is that the constitutive performance made possible by scientific rationality has a *genesis* and has developed over time. In its present form science is a tradition, a cultural formation that has been constituted by a historical community of transcendental subjects.[65]

Husserl's criticism of objectivism can also be seen as an attempt to delimit the validity of the scientific notion of truth, allowing us to acknowledge the existence of several different and equally valid types of description. With an argumentation resembling that of the later Wittgenstein,[66] Husserl writes:

What if the relativity of truth and of evidence of truth, on the one hand, and, on the other hand, the infinitely distant, ideal, absolute, truth beyond all relativity— what if each of these has its legitimacy and each demands the other? The trader in the market has his market-truth. In the relationship in which it stands, is his truth not a good one, and the best that a trader can use? Is it a pseudo-truth, merely because the scientist, involved in a different relativity and judging with other aims and ideas, looks for other truths—with which a great many more things can be done, but not the one thing that has to be done in a market? It is high time that people got over being dazzled, particularly in philosophy and logic, by the ideal and regulative ideas and methods of the 'exact' sciences—as though the In-itself of such sciences were actually an absolute norm for objective being and for truth (Hua 17/284 [278]).

Husserl, consequently, argues that there exists a correlation between different levels of normality and objectivity (Hua 15/155). Even absolute, objective being and truth are correlated with a subject-relative normality, namely, the normality of rational subjects (Hua 15/35–36).

Husserl's treatment of normality as a transcendental philosophical category can also serve to throw light on some of the more far-reaching consequences of his phenomenology of intersubjectivity. The dimension of historicity in Husserl's thinking, for instance, becomes visible. My own home-worldly normality is instituted through tradition and generativity, and is therefore historical. Normality is a tradition-bound set of norms. Thus, Husserl even designates the normal life as generative and claims that any normal person is historical as a member of a historical community (Hua 15/138–139, 431).

What I generate from out of myself (primally instituting) is mine. But I am a 'child of the times'; I am a member of a we-community in the broadest sense—a community that has its tradition and that, for its part, is connected in a novel manner with the generative subjects, the closest and the most distant ancestors. And these have 'influenced' me: I am what I am as an heir (Hua 14/223).

Moreover, the very constitution of objectivity and of a common objective world is seen as a historical process (Hua 15/421). Far from being already constituted (Hua 15/220), the meaning-formations 'objectivity' and 'reality' have the status of intersubjective presumptions, which can only be realized in an infinite process of socialization and horizon-fusion. To phrase it differently—and here Husserl is speaking, neither Apel nor Habermas—absolute truth (real being) designates an idealization; we are dealing with a regulative ideal with a correlate to the ideal consensus of an open intersubjective community that can be approximated in a process of permanent correction, although it can never be reached, since every factually realized consensus is in principle open for further corrections (Hua 8/52, 3/331, 6/282, 1/138, 15/33).[67] Consequently, Husserl can write that there is no stagnant world, since it is only given for us in its relativity of normality and anormality (Hua 15/212, 381, 6/270. Ms. C 17 31a). The being of the world is only apparently stable, while, in reality, it is a *construction of normality*, which in principle can collapse (Hua 15/214).

That Husserl tried to add a historical dimension to transcendental philosophy can also be illustrated in a different way. At one place Husserl writes that the transcendence of the world is constituted through Others and through the generatively constituted co-subjectivity (Ms. C 17 32a). It is exactly this concept of *generative intersubjectivity* (Hua 15/199) that indicates that Husserl no longer regarded the birth and death of the subject as mere contingent facts, but as transcendental conditions of the possibility for the constitution of the world (Hua 15/171). As he says in *Krisis*, the incorporation into a historical generative context belongs just as inseparably to the ego, as its very temporal structure (Hua 6/256). In other words, Husserl considered the subject's embeddedness in a living tradition to have constitutive implications, and, as I mentioned earlier (cf. p. 120), it is consequently possible to speak of an *anonymous normality* as a *third kind* of transcendental intersubjectivity. It is not merely the case that I live in a world, which, as a correlate of normality, is permeated by references to Others and which Others have already furnished with meaning, or that I understand the world (and myself) through a traditional, handed-down, linguistic conventionality. The very category 'historical reality' implies a type of transcendence that can only be constituted insofar as I take over traditional meaning, which has its origin outside of me in a historical past.

Is it on this background possible to conclude that Husserl, in the last phase of his thinking, substituted the transcendental ego as the phenomenological point of departure for the historical community of the lifeworld? No, of course not. Although he does take transcendental intersubjectivity as the transcendental foundation, it is crucial not to forget Husserl's phenomenological approach. There is no community without I-centering, and consequently no generative intersubjectivity without a transcendental primal ego in which intersubjectivity can unfold itself (Hua 15/426). As Husserl has emphasized several times, the 'we' stretches *from me onward* to the simultaneous, past, and future Others (Hua 15/61, 139, 142, 499); the historically primary is our present (Hua 6/382). In other words, the transcendental analysis of the historical past, of previous generations, and more generally any analysis of meaning that transcends the finiteness of the subject, must always take its point of departure in the first-person perspective.

There is probably no one who would claim that Husserl managed to integrate historicity and transcendentality in a definite and conclusive manner. This is, nevertheless, what he attempted to do in the last phase of his thinking, which must be appreciated when it comes to an evaluation of the scope and comprehensiveness of his philosophy. Whether it is a fruitful approach that can be developed further, or a final aporetical draft, can be discussed. That Husserl did not advocate a classical Cartesian-Kantian subject-philosophy, and that he was not a solipsist, but, on the contrary, treated intersubjectivity as a transcendental philosophical notion of utmost importance should, however, have been demonstrated.[68]

Conclusion

That Edmund Husserl is a central figure in twentieth-century philosophy is undisputed. It is well known that he was the founder of phenomenology, that he developed a theory of intentionality and a concept of the lifeworld, and, last but not least, that he was the teacher of Heidegger. For a long period it has also been common knowledge, however, that despite his best intentions, he was unable to free himself from the framework of a classical metaphysics of presence. Husserl never abandoned the conviction that reality and the Other were constituted by a pure (disincarnated and worldless) transcendental subject, and his thinking, consequently, remained foundationalistic, idealistic, and solipsistic. Thus, although Husserl must still be respected as an initiator, his position was irrevocably surpassed by Heidegger, and later phenomenologists, hermeneuticists, deconstructivists, and philosophers of language have distanced themselves from him, with good reason.

As should have become clear from my presentation, this widespread Husserl interpretation must now be regarded as outdated. One of the reasons why it survived for such a long time has to do with events in recent German history. Because of Husserl's Jewish origin, his philosophy was not taught during the Nazi era (1933–1945). This meant that an entire generation of German philosophers was trained in Heideggerian phenomenology instead. And although there had been an initial interest in Husserl in France in the 1930s, after the war even the French read Husserl through the eyes of Heidegger. With very few exceptions, it was only from the 1960s onward, when a number of young philosophers (including Held and Claesges) did their doctoral dissertations on themes in Husserl's research manuscripts, that Husserl scholarship took a decisive step forward.

The continuing publication of Husserliana has made—and continues to make—an increasing number of Husserl's research manuscripts available, and a study of these has made it necessary to revise and modify a number of widespread and dominant interpretations. This is a result not only of the fact that the publication of Husserl's research manuscripts has made a complementary understanding of Husserl's phenomenological core concepts possible, but also because these manuscripts have disclosed aspects of his thinking that it would have been difficult, if not impossible, to anticipate through a mere study of the works originally published by Husserl himself.

A few examples can serve as an illustration. As early as 1966, when *Analysen zur passiven Synthesis* was published, it became obvious that Husserl was not at all preoccupied with the analysis of a purely active and spontaneous subjectivity. On the contrary, the clarification of the depth-dimension of passive genesis was given an absolutely central importance. Seven years later, when Kern published *Zur Phänomenologie der Intersubjektivität I–III*, a wealth of material was released, which not only made those prior discussions of Husserl's analysis of intersubjectivity—which had been restricted to the account given in *Ideen II* and, above all, in *Cartesianische Meditationen*—obsolete, but ultimately, to quote Strasser, made all current views about the content of Husserl's philosophy inadequate.[1] The volume *Vorlesungen über Ethik und Wertlehre 1908–1914*, published in 1988 by, Ullrich Melle made a number of texts available that revealed Husserl's interest in ethics and value theory. It disclosed the practical field of Husserl's research, thus modifying the standard interpretation, which took him to be exclusively concerned with pure *theoria*.

It has been customary to divide Husserl's thinking in different phases: The decisive breaks were supposed to have happened in the period between *Philosophie der Arithmetik* (1891) and *Logische Untersuchungen* (1900–1901) insofar as Husserl started criticizing his own initial psychologism; in the period between *Logische Untersuchungen* and *Ideen zu einer reinen Phänomenologie und phänomenologischen Philosophie I* (1913), to be precise around 1905–1908, when Husserl abandoned a purely descriptive phenomenology in favor of a transcendental phenomenology; in the years 1917–1921 where the so-called *static* phenomenology was complemented with a *genetic* phenomenology; and, finally, in the period between *Cartesianische Meditationen* (1929) and *Die Krisis der europäischen Wissenschaften und die transzendentale Phänomenologie* (1936), where Husserl supposedly abandoned his subject-centered transcendental philosophy in favor of a phenomenology based on the lifeworld.

This traditional account is misleading. Although all of the remarks contain a greater or, in some cases, smaller core of truth, the idea that Husserl's work is characterized by a series of decisive ruptures is a relic from a time where one had access only to his published works. When one reads his lectures and research manuscripts, the continuity in Husserl's thinking becomes evident. That there is a development and a decisive difference between his early and later works is, of course, undisputable. But, first of all, the changes that occur later are often anticipated in the earlier works and, second, the changes are never so radical that one can speak of a veritable rupture.

In contrast to earlier times when the core texts were made up of the obligatory classical volumes such as *Logische Untersuchungen*, *Ideen I*, *Cartesianische Meditationen*, and *Krisis*, this is no longer the case. The focus and scope have expanded to include all of the volumes of Husserliana currently available, and, apart from volumes already mentioned, *Erste Philosophie II*, *Phänomenologische Psychologie*, and *Ergänzungsband zur Krisis* have proven especially decisive lectures. This change of focus has brought about a new type of interpretation, which is not only characterized by an emphasis on the dimensions of facticity, passivity, alterity, and ethics in Husserl's thinking; it has also enabled reinterpretations of the classical volumes, thus revealing a unity and consistency in the development of his thinking that would otherwise have remained concealed.[2]

*

My presentation has focused on a few central topics in Husserl's thinking. That I have spent time refuting a number of widespread misunderstandings is not the result of an attempt to immunize Husserl against criticism. On the contrary, I have tried to clear away a number of distracting misinterpretations that for a long time have cast a shadow over the truly central topics in his thinking. I have done this in the hope of thereby making room for a novel and more constructive criticism that can carry the discussion forward.

Among the many aspects that I have not had time to treat, one can mention a few, namely Husserl's far more complex investigation of intentionality; his discussion of the structure of the ego and the personality; his analysis of the relation between linguistic and prelinguistic meaning; his investigation of the role of passivity, including his analysis of the instincts and the unconscious; his analyses of the foundation of logic and mathematics, not to speak of his reflections on politics, ethics, aesthetics, and religion.

Nevertheless, I hope this book has been able to demonstrate the scope, fertility, and contemporary relevance of Husserl's thinking. I hope my presentation can stimulate the reader to turn to Husserl's own writings, not only because a study of these writings remains an indispensable presupposition for a correct understanding of phenomenology, but also because of their intrinsic philosophical value.

It is not without reason that philosophers like Scheler, Heidegger, Sartre, Merleau-Ponty, Levinas, Schütz, Ricoeur, Henry, and Derrida (to mention but a few) owe a lot to Husserl. Although there has been a tendency among his philosophical successors to criticize him in order to emphasize their own merits, these days one can perceive an increased appreciation of the uniqueness of Husserl's phenomenology. He is no longer regarded as a mere precursor to Heidegger, Merleau-Ponty, or Levinas; he is no longer simply regarded as a surpassed chapter in the history of phenomenology.

REFERENCE MATTER

Notes

1. This is Levinas, Peiffer, and Koyré's French translation of *Cartesianische Meditationen*. The work was written in 1929, but was only published in German in 1950.

2. Husserl has often been characterized as a very monological and monolithic thinker. There is probably a certain truth in this characterization, but there are also indications that point in a different direction. First of all, there can be no doubt that Husserl's discussions with his last two assistants, Ludwig Landgrebe and Eugen Fink, were of decisive importance for the development of the final phase of his philosophy (cf. Fink 1933, Cairns 1976, Bruzina 1989, Zahavi 1994c). Second, the publication of Husserl's extensive correspondence (in ten volumes) demonstrates that throughout his life Husserl kept in touch with a large number of leading intellectuals. Among the published correspondence one finds letters to Bergson, Binswanger, Bühler, Cantor, Cassirer, Dilthey, Frege, Gurwitsch, Hartshorne, Hilbert, Hofmannsthal, Horkheimer, Jaspers, Koyré, Lask, Lévy-Bruhl, Lipps, Löwith, Mach, Marcuse, Masaryk, Natorp, Otto, Patočka, Russell, Schestow, Schütz, Sigwart, Simmel, Stumpf, Twardowski, and Wertheimer.

3. Cf. Van Breda's preface to Husserliana I, and Van Breda 1959.

4. Cf. Ricoeur 1985, 44.

5. References to the Husserliana edition are cited by volume number, with the page number(s) following a slash. Where an English translation exists, several different conventions are used. In cases where the translation includes the Husserliana page numbers in the margin, only the German page numbers are provided. But where the marginal page numbers in the English translation refer to a different edition or no marginal page numbers are provided, the corresponding English page number is added in square brackets immediately following the Husserliana citation—for example, 18/87 [109–110], 6/154–5 [152]. (The same principle has also been applied in those cases where I am quoting from authors other than Husserl, that is, Heidegger, Fink, Merleau-Ponty, and so on.) For the most part, I have used the standard English translations of Husserl's works. Where no English

translation was available, I have provided one myself (with the help of numerous colleagues), and in all cases where Husserl's unpublished manuscripts are quoted, the original German text can be found in the notes. When referring to these latter manuscripts the last number always refers to the original shorthanded page.

PART I

1. It can be added that Husserl's criticism of psychologism was also directed against his own earlier position in *Philosophie der Arithmetik* (1891). It has occasionally been claimed that it was Frege's severe review of this work that made Husserl change his mind. But this interpretation is probably anachronistic, and more recent research points at Husserl's studies of Lotze and Bolzano as being the decisive factor. Cf. for instance Mohanty 1977; Bernet, Kern, and Marbach 1989, 20.

2. After the publication of the *Prolegomena*, Husserl was accused of being a platonist. But this is only a partial truth. As Husserl himself points out, he was engaged in a defense of the validity of ideality and was not trying to argue for the existence of ideal objects in a separate supernatural realm. In short, he was advocating a *logical* and not an *ontological* platonism (Hua 22/156).

3. Cf. Cobb-Stevens 1990.

4. It was Brentano, in his *Psychologie vom empirischen Standpunkt* (1871), who initially argued the need for a purely descriptive analysis of consciousness.

5. In a passage from *Ideen II* Husserl makes this point in a relatively clear manner: When the subject is directed toward an object and experiences this object, we are not dealing with a *real* relation, but with an *intentional* relation to something real. Under certain circumstances the object in question might also be affecting me in a real manner (causally). If the object in question does not exist, the real relation will not exist either, whereas the intentional relation will remain. That the intentional relation might be complemented by a real relation if the object exists, that is, that the object in certain circumstances might affect my sensory organs is, however, a mere psychophysical fact, and has no influence on the structure of the intentional relation (Hua 4/215–216).

6. Cf. Sokolowski 1992, 5.

7. The representative theory of perception is also strained by a number of additional difficulties. Let me just mention one: If one makes a distinction between the extramental object and the intramental representation of the object it is difficult to avoid the following question: How do we know that the representation that is in consciousness actually corresponds to something outside of consciousness? Not only do we not have any access to a neutral position where we can compare the two, but there is much reason to believe that they cannot at all be alike, as a number of epistemologists at the turn of the century concluded. As Brentano writes, the physical phenomena brought forth when our sensory apparatus is causally influenced are *signs* of something real, namely the molecular os-

cillations (Brentano 1924–1925, 13–14, 28, 66–67). Since the phenomena obviously have nothing in common with these oscillations, Brentano concludes that the physical phenomena do not at all represent their causes in a veridical manner, for which reason sensory experience must be condemned as being misleading. We do not, in other words, experience reality as it is in itself (Brentano 1924–1925, 14, 86–87, 128).

8. In *L'être et le néant*, Sartre claims that the subject is directed at something that is different from the subject, therefore maintaining that the theory of intentionality contains an ontological proof of the existence of a mind-independent reality (1943, 28–29). To be different from and independent of is not the same, however, rendering Sartre's 'proof' of questionable validity.

9. This passage has often been taken as evidence for Husserl's metaphysical realism in *Logische Untersuchungen*. I will return to this misinterpretation later (cf. p. 40).

10. It is in this context that Husserl introduces a distinction between objectifying and nonobjectifying acts. The first types of act are those that contain a reference to an object in themselves. Examples of such acts might be perceptions or judgments. There are, however, also intentional acts such as aesthetic evaluations and feelings of love or hatred which, although they refer to an object ('that vase is beautiful,' 'I love Paris'), do so only in a founded manner. They are supported by an underlying objectifying act: 'The joy is not a concrete act in its own right, and the judgment an act set up beside it: the judgment rather underlies the joy, fixes its content, realizes its abstract possibility for, without some such foundation, there could be no joy at all' (Hua 19/418 [581]). Every intentional experience is, in other words, either an objectifying act or it has such an act as its foundation (Hua 19/514). In addition to speaking of objectifying and nonobjectifying acts, Husserl also speaks of primary and secondary intentions.

11. In *Logische Untersuchungen*, Husserl did not yet distinguish between meaning (*Bedeutung*) and sense (*Sinn*), but later on he understood *Bedeutung* narrowly as linguistic meaning, and *Sinn* as a more comprehensive concept that also included prepredicative and perceptual meaning (Hua 3/285).

12. A related point had been made earlier by Twardowski and Frege.

13. For an interesting elaboration of this point, cf. Smith 1981, 1982a, 1982b, 1984.

14. A concise analysis of the reasons why Husserl abandoned this conception around 1908 replacing it with a theory that understood meaning as the *correlate* of the act, can be found in Bernet 1979.

15. Although pictorial consciousness (imagination) and fantasy both imply a consciousness of something absent, there remains an obvious difference between the two. In pictorial consciousness I intend something via something else. This *representative* function is not a part of fantasy. If I think about a dancing faun, this faun is not taken to be a representation of a real faun. On the contrary, we are

dealing with an intentional object that is not taken to be real, but that merely appears 'as if' it were real (Hua 8/112–113).

16. Husserl's concept of founding has certain similarities with the contemporary notion of supervenience.

17. One can encounter the claim that, in his thesis about prelinguistic experience, Husserl sought to uncover an immediate level of experience which was prior to every interpretation, and that Husserl therefore overlooked the fact that *all* experience involves interpretation. This hermeneutical criticism itself, however, makes the mistake of thinking that all interpretation is linguistic. But as both Husserl and Heidegger have shown, there are also types of prelinguistic interpretation (cf. Heidegger 1976, 144–145).

18. This position can easily lead to relativism: What is real is completely determined by our current language game.

19. Cf. Stern 1985.

20. A more detailed analysis of Husserl's view on language can be found in Mohanty 1964; Sokolowski 1974; Derrida 1989; Cobb-Stevens 1990; Klausen 1994.

21. Rang 1973, 23. Cf. Hua 19/56–57.

22. For this happy phrase, cf. Sokolowski 2000, 158.

23. Cf. Rosen 1977, § 19.

24. For a more extensive argumentation, cf. Zahavi 2002b.

25. Husserl's account of the phenomenological project in the first edition of *Logische Untersuchungen* was also marred by some unfortunate ambiguities. Husserl appears to identify phenomenology with the analysis of the immanent (reell) content of mental acts, and asserts that one has to turn the theoretical interest away from the objects and toward the acts (Hua 19/14, 28). This methodological restriction is frequently repeated later in the work. In the Third and Fifth Investigations, for instance, where Husserl distinguishes between the immanent and phenomenological content on the one hand and the intentional content on the other (Hua 19/237, 411), thereby stressing the importance of discounting the intentional object in a description of the act because of its act-transcendence (Hua 19/16, 427). This account, however, is incompatible with Husserl's actual analysis of intentionality, in which the intentional act is characterized by its directedness toward something different from itself. It is therefore even according to the account in *Logische Untersuchungen* impossible to investigate the act properly without taking its intentional object into consideration. By the second edition of *Logische Untersuchungen*, Husserl had realized these problems and rectified the errors (cf. Hua 18/13–14). As Heidegger was later to remark: '[W]hen he wrote the introduction to these investigations, Husserl was not in a position to survey properly what he had actually presented in this volume' (Heidegger 1979, 31 [25]). This mismatch between the actual content of Husserl's analyses and his own self-interpretation is a recurrent problem not only in *Logische Untersuchungen*, but also in his later works.

26. Husserl 1939, 110, 117.

27. This turn was already initiated in *Logische Untersuchungen* (cf. Hua 24/425, 2/90–91, and Zahavi 1992a).

28. Sokolowski 1970, 159.

29. For more extensive analyses of *Logische Untersuchungen*, see Sokolowski 1967–1968, 1970, 1971; De Boer 1978; Zahavi 1992a; Benoist 1997; Zahavi and Stjernfelt 2002c. For a more detailed investigation of Husserl's concept of truth, see Tugendhat 1970; Rosen 1977. For a more elaborate discussion of Husserl's theory of meaning, see Mohanty 1964, 1977; Bernet 1979; Cobb-Stevens 1990. For more details on Husserl's theory of intentionality, see Mohanty 1972; Sokolowski 1974; Smith and McIntyre 1982; Drummond 1990.

PART 2

1. The first time Husserl mentions the reduction is in manuscripts from the summer of 1905 (the so-called *Seefelder Blättern*). Cf. Hua 10/253.

2. Husserl does recognize, however, that these deficiencies are part of what enables science to progress as fast as it does, and his criticism is not primarily meant as an attempt to revise science itself, but rather as an argument to the effect that philosophy has a task of its own. For some similar considerations, see Heidegger 1989, § 9.

3. Husserl renders this in a form that remains of contemporary relevance: When natural science speaks we are willing to learn. But natural science does not always speak when the natural scientists speak, and in particular not when they talk of a 'philosophy of nature' or of a 'naturalized epistemology' (Hua 3/45).

4. Cf. Kern 1962.

5. It is important to emphasize that Husserl does not thereby deny the intentionality of consciousness. It is one thing to imagine a worldless subject, and something else to imagine a subject without any intentional experiences. We cannot imagine the latter without changing the overall concept of subjectivity radically, but Husserl would claim that it is possible to imagine an intentional subject that merely has incoherent experiences, and that therefore lacks an *objective* world (cf. Tugendhat 1970, 263).

6. For a recent discussion of this issue, cf. Carr 1999.

7. Cf. Kern 1962 and Drummond 1975.

8. The attentive reader might have noticed that there is an interesting similarity between Husserl's ontological way to the reduction and the way in which phenomenology was introduced in *Logische Untersuchungen*. Although there has been a tendency to regard the Cartesian way as Husserl's early approach and the ontological way as his later, this is a simplification. Ultimately we are dealing with two different approaches that crisscross each other in a number of Husserl's writings.

9. Stevenson 1974, 79.

10. For a concise discussion of the phenomenological concept of phenomenon see § 7 in Heidegger's *Sein und Zeit*.

11. Cf. my account of Husserl's concept of the lifeworld in Part 3.

12. Heidegger 1979, 118.

13. Dreyfus 1982, 2, 6.

14. Dreyfus 1982, 14.

15. Dreyfus 1982, 108; Dreyfus 1988, 95.

16. Dreyfus 1991, 50.

17. Smith and McIntyre 1982, xiv, 87–88.

18. Smith and McIntyre 1982, 93; Smith 1989, 14.

19. Smith 1989, 14.

20. Smith and McIntyre 1982, 93–95.

21. This claim can easily be exemplified. Dreyfus, for instance, who basically accepts Føllesdal's noema-interpretation, argues that it was Føllesdal who first realized what Husserl's was actually up to. It was Føllesdal who pointed out that Husserl's noema is an abstract structure by virtue of which the mind is directed toward objects, and as Dreyfus puts it, it is thanks to Føllesdal's work that Husserl is now finally seen as the first to have developed a general theory of mental representation (Dreyfus 1982, 1–2).

22. Smith and McIntyre 1982, 87.

23. Sokolowski 1987, 525.

24. Sokolowski 1987, 526–527.

25. Drummond 1992, 89.

26. Drummond 1990, 108–109, 113.

27. Drummond 1990, 136.

28. Dreyfus 1988, 95; 1991, 51.

29. This is assumed, for instance, by Hutcheson 1980 and Hall 1982.

30. It is occasionally claimed that Husserl—in contrast to later phenomenologists, such as Heidegger—did not deal with ontological questions. At first this claim seems absurd, but it cannot simply be refuted by appeal to the quotations already given, since a comparison of Husserl and Heidegger will show that they do not understand the same when speaking of ontology. When Husserl speaks of ontology he is normally referring to either formal or material ontology, that is, to theories concerned with the properties of objects, whereas Heidegger typically understands the true *fundamental-ontological* question as a question pertaining to the Being of beings: What is it that conditions that something *is*, what is the condition of possibility of beings? Since Heidegger himself emphasizes that ontology is only possible as phenomenology (Heidegger 1986, 35), it seems permissible, however, to reformulate his central question into the following: What is the condition of possibility for appearance and manifestation? If the question is reformulated in this way, it is clear that Heidegger's fundamental-ontological question and Husserl's

transcendental-phenomenological question are not that far apart (this is even clearer if one takes Husserl's analysis of temporality into consideration). But of course, this does not imply that their answers to the question are identical.

31. Landgrebe 1963, 26.

32. In some of his later works, Husserl does in fact use the term 'metaphysics' in this slightly idiosyncratic manner, defining it as the philosophical treatment of the ultimate questions concerning the meaning of factual human life, that is, as reflections on such issues as facticity, birth, death, fate, history, and so forth (Hua 1/182). Ultimately, it is this line of thought that leads to Husserl's philosophical theology (cf. Hart 1986). However, this is not an aspect of Husserl's thinking that I intend to consider in any further detail, and none of my references to 'metaphysics' should be taken as referring to this particular enterprise.

33. Fink 1939, 257.

34. Fink 1933, 364 [2000, 117].

35. Fink 1933, 363–364.

36. "Zu sagen, daß das Bewußtsein sich durch seinen immanenten noematischen Sinn (bzw. den Sinnespol X in seinen noematischen Bestimmungen und seinem Setzungsmodus als seiend) auf einen transzendenten Gegenstand 'beziehe,' ist eine bedenkliche und, genau genommen, falsche Rede. Ist so verstanden nie meine Meinung gewesen. Ich würde mich wundern, wenn diese Wendung sich in den 'Ideen' fände, die im Zusammenhang dann sicher nicht diesen eigentlichen Sinn hätte." (Ms. B III 12 IV, 82a). I owe this reference to Rabanaque 1993.

37. Bernet 1990, 71.

38. Ströker 1987, 194–200.

39. Among the contributions to the noema-discussion one should mention Gurwitsch 1966; Føllesdal 1969; Smith and McIntyre 1975 and 1982; Sokolowski 1984 and 1987; Drummond 1990; Bernet 1990; Fisette 1994.

40. Cf. Habermas 1985, 129; Rorty 1980, 4, 166–168.

41. Fink writes that the truths in the mundane sphere do not clash with the truths in the transcendental sphere, since we are dealing with truths on two different levels. Thus, the transcendental understanding of the world does not deny the truths which are obtained in the natural attitude, but on the contrary makes them radically, i.e., constitutively, comprehensible (Fink 1988a, 129).

42. Kant 1956, A 370.

43. Cf. Putnam 1988.

44. Gadamer 1972, 178; Fink 1988a, 179. Although many interpreters would agree with this claim there are, as always, different ways to interpret it. 1) One interpretation argues that transcendental idealism is beyond both realism and idealism in the sense that it, strictly speaking, is concerned with quite different matters altogether, that is, transcendental idealism simply lacks metaphysical impact. 2) Another possibility is to argue that transcendental idealism is beyond the traditional

alternative between realism and idealism insofar as it actually seeks to combine elements from both positions. 3) Finally, it might also be argued that Husserl's transcendental idealism transcends the alternative insofar as it makes us realize that both metaphysical realism and subjective idealism (together with a lot of traditional metaphysical heritage) are, strictly speaking, absurd.

45. It is slightly surprising that the advocates of a creationistic interpretation of Husserl's concept of constitution have often referred to Fink's famous article 'Die phänomenologische Philosophie Edmund Husserls in der gegenwärtigen Kritik.' It is true that in this article Fink refers to the productive character of transcendental intentionality, writing that the essence of constitution must be defined as a productive creation. But immediately following this claim, Fink also adds that this definition is important only in order to pass beyond a merely receptive (epistemological) interpretation of the concept of constitution. And, as he then concludes, constitution is therefore neither a receptive nor a productive process, but something that cannot be captured with the use of these ontic concepts (Fink 1933, 373).

46. Putnam 1978, 1.

47. Heidegger 1979, 97.

48. It is important to notice the differences between the diverse types of constitution, be it the constitution of physical, ideal, or cultural objects. The latter implies a higher amount of creativity.

49. Merleau-Ponty 1945, 491–492 [1962, 430].

50. Cf., for instance, Tugendhat 1970, 177, 212, 217, and Sokolowski 1970, 138, 159, 197–198, 217.

51. Cf., for instance, Brand 1955, 47; Claesges 1964, 100, 143; Landgrebe 1982, 81.

52. Fink 1933, 370; Fink 1988a, 49. Cf. 15/403.

53. Fink 1933, 378.

54. Heidegger 1989, 422.

55. Heidegger 1989, 394; cf. 1989, 421. For further discussions of these similarities, cf. Zahavi 1996/2001 and Zahavi 1999b. For further analyses of Husserl's concept of reduction and epoché, see Kern 1962; Landgrebe 1963; Drummond 1975; Lenkowski 1978. For a more detailed presentation of Husserl's transcendental philosophy, see Fink 1933; Seebohm 1962; Sokolowski 1970; Aguirre 1970; Ströker 1987.

PART 3

1. The precise span of perception depends on our interest. If we are listening to a (short) melody we can claim to perceive the entire melody in its temporal extension, but if we are paying attention to the individual notes, one tone will cease being perceived the moment it is replaced by a new one (Hua 10/38).

2. Duval has argued that retention on its own cannot lead to a perception of the past, but only to a consciousness of duration. Past proper is constituted in the dialectic between forgetfulness and recollection (Duval 1990, 62, 67).

3. But, as Proust has illustrated with his famous example with the madeleine in *Remembrance of Things Past*, there are also recollections that arise quite unbidden.

4. Brough 1972, 302, 314–315.

5. Cf. Held 1966, 116–117.

6. Cf. Kern 1975, 40–41.

7. For an extensive discussion of these different types of self-awareness, cf. Zahavi 1999b.

8. One can find numerous statements to this effect. See for instance, Hua 1/81, 4/318, 8/189, 412, 450, 13/252, 462, 14/151, 292, 353, 380, and Ms. C 16 81b.

9. Cf. Searle 1992, 131–132, 172; Nagel 1974, 436; Nagel 1986, 15–16.

10. 'Wenn immer ich reflektiere, finde ich mich "in bezug auf" ein Etwas, als affiziertes bzw. aktives. Das, worauf ich bezogen bin, ist erlebnismäßig bewußt— es ist für mich etwas schon als "Erlebnis," damit ich mich darauf beziehen kann.' (Ms. C 10 13a).

11. This interpretation has been advocated by Brough and Sokolowski. For an extensive discussion and criticism, cf. Zahavi 1998d and 1999b.

12. For passages that might corroborate this interpretation, see Hua 4/104, 10/36, 51, 112, 33/166, 176, Ms. A V 5 4b–5a, Ms. C 10 17a, Ms. C 16 59a, Ms. C 12 3b.

13. 'Wir sagen, ich bin, der ich bin in meinem Leben. Und dieses Leben ist Erleben, seine reflektiv als einzelne abzuhebenden Bestandstücke heißen rechtmäßig "Erlebnisse," sofern in ihnen irgendetwas erlebt ist' (Ms. C 3 26a).

14. Brough 1987, 23.

15. It is noteworthy that in the beginning of *Sein und Zeit* Heidegger makes a similar claim. As he writes: 'With regard to the awkwardness and "inelegance" of expression in the following analyses, we may remark that it is one thing to report narratively about *beings* and another to grasp beings in their *being*. For the latter task not only most of the words are lacking but above all the 'grammar" (Heidegger 1986, 38–39).

16. Held 1966, 77, 160.

17. As will become clear through my presentation of Husserl's theory of intersubjectivity, Husserl also claims that objectivity and reality cannot be defined in terms of an optimal presence to a self-sufficient subject. On the contrary, we are dealing with forms of validity that are always mediated through the alterity of the Other (cf. p. 115).

18. Brough 1972, 319.

19. For a more extensive treatment of Husserl's philosophy of time, see Brand 1955; Held 1966; Derrida 1967a; Brough 1972, 1993; Sokolowski 1974; Bernet 1983; Zahavi 1999b, 63–90.

20. For this happy phrasing, cf. Prufer 1988; Sokolowski 1978, 128; and Hart 1992, 162.

21. Although it is true that the horizonal appearance of my perceptual object (and the implied differentiation between present and absent profiles) is correlated with my being situated in a central 'here' (Hua 4/158); and although it is also true that the object is only given horizonally, because it is in principle impossible for any perceiving subject to be situated 'here' and 'there' simultanously, it would be wrong to conclude that the horizonal givenness of the object merely manifests the finiteness or corporeality of the observer. Husserl is known for his rejection of any anthropological interpretation of the horizonal structure. Ultimately, it is the ontological structure of the object (its transcendence and worldliness) that necessitates that it can only be given for a subject situated in a 'here.' As Husserl declares in *Ideen I*, even God (as the ideal representative of absolute knowledge) would have to perceive the object through its adumbrations (Hua 3/351).

22. Gibson 1979, 53, 205.

23. These analyses of the importance of *kinaesthesis* for the constitution of spatial objects can be found scattered around in Husserl's works, but two of the central places are Part 4 of *Ding und Raum* (with the subtitle 'Die Bedeutung der kinästhetischen Systeme für die Konstitution des Wahrnehmungsgegenstandes'), and Part 1, Chapter 3 of *Ideen II* (with the subtitle 'Die Aistheta in bezug auf den aisthetischen Leib'). Husserl's reflections on these issues in many ways anticipate the work of not only Gibson, but also of Merleau-Ponty and Lakoff.

24. Cf. Merleau-Ponty 1964, 284.

25. As Husserl writes, apropos the relation between the kinaesthetic and the hyletic sensations: 'The system of kinaestheses, however, is not constituted in advance; rather, its constitution takes place along with the constitution of the hyletic objects that it is aiming toward in each case.' 'Das System der Kinästhesen ist aber nicht im voraus konstituiert, sondern seine Konstitution erfolgt in eins mit der Konstitution hyletischer Objekte, auf die es jeweils hinauswill . . .' (Ms. D 10 11a).

26. 'Das Ich ist nicht etwas für sich und das Ichfremde ein vom Ich Getrenntes und zwischen beiden ist kein Raum für ein Hinwenden. Sondern untrennbar ist Ich und sein Ichfremdes' (Ms. C 16 68a).

27. Merleau-Ponty 1945, 344, 431–432, 467, 485, 487, 492.

28. Cf. Tugendhat 1970, 73; Melle 1983, 40–52; Gallagher 1986; Adorno 1981, 152–164; and especially Mohanty 1972, 108–13, where Sartre's, Merleau-Ponty's, and Gurwitsch's classical criticism are summarized.

29. Sokolowski 1974, 91. Cf. Hua 5/10–11, 16/148.

30. Thus, Husserl can write that it is an abstraction to speak of a purely passive world of sensations. They can only be understood in their correlation to active kinaestheses (Hua 11/185). Cf. Claesges 1964, 71, 123, 131, 134–135, and Landgrebe 1963, 120.

31. For some remarks on Husserl's phenomenological analysis of sleep, cf. Zahavi 1999b, 209–210.

32. For a more extensive analysis of Husserl's concept of the body, cf. Claesges 1964; Franck 1981; Gallagher 1986; and Zahavi 1999b.

33. On several occasions, Husserl called attention to the lecture-course *Grund-probleme der Phänomenologie* from 1910/11 (now in Hua 13/111–194) as the place where intersubjectivity was assigned a decisive role for the first time (Hua 17/250, 5/150, 13/245, 8/433, 14/307). Although his reflections in *Ideen I* (from 1913) appear strictly egological, Husserl was already at that time aware of the significance of intersubjectivity, and, as he later wrote (Hua 5/150), he had originally planned for his presentation in *Ideen I* to be complemented by the reflections on intersubjectivity to be found in *Ideen II*. However, these reflections were only published posthumously.

34. Cf., for instance, Apel 1973, I/60, II/315, and Habermas 1985, 178.

35. This formulation, which is from Husserl's London lectures in 1922, can be found in Schuhmann 1988, 56.

36. See for instance Theunissen 1977, § 19–28; Schütz 1957, 107; Ricoeur 1981, 124–25; Rohr-Dietschi 1974, 144–150.

37. This is also true of Schütz 1957, 81–107.

38. The most extensive analyses can be found in Yamaguchi 1982 and Depraz 1995.

39. Cf. Waldenfels 1989; Boehm 1969; and Zahavi 1996/2001. As Levinas writes: 'The absence of the Other is exactly his presence as Other' (Levinas 1983, 89).

40. Cf. Derrida 1967b, 181.

41. That every experience of an Other implies the validity of the Other's experience should not be misunderstood. Of course, Husserl is neither claiming that it is no longer possible to speak of disagreement or dissent (but only that all disagreement presupposes a common world), nor that our experience of an Other is always accompanied by a thematic re-presentation of the Other's experiential content. Husserl's claim is merely that the *validity* of the Other's experience is implicitly accepted when we experience him, and that our own object of experience is consequently apprehended as something that can also be experienced by other subjects, for which reason it must be transcendent (Hua 6/308, 13/469). When experiencing my tennis partner returning the ball, I implicitly assume that he is perceiving the same ball as I am.

42. Theunissen 1977, 84.

43. This is a finitude (and mortality) that Husserl claims remains hidden until the co-being of the Other is taken into account: 'Here is the place for the possibility of death—which, however, cannot be objectivated in egological self-observation; it cannot have any lived experiential intuitability, for it can only obtain a sense for me by way of an understanding of others' (Hua 15/452. Cf. Ms. C 17 32a.).

44. A similar kind of argumentation can be found in Carr 1973, 14–35. Carr claims that Husserl's incorporation of transcendental intersubjectivity led to a radical revision of his earlier concept of philosophy, insofar as the *nos cogitamus* does not possess the same kind of infallible apodictical certainty as the *ego cogito* (Carr 1973, 32–35). That this is only partially true will become clear in a moment.

45. For a more extensive discussion, see Zahavi 1996/2001 and 1997.

46. See also Dorion Cairns's account of a conversation he had with Husserl, June 4, 1932 (Cairns 1976, 82–83).

47. 'Meine Erfahrung als Welterfahrung (also jede meiner Wahrnehmungen schon) schließt nicht nur Andere als Weltobjekte ein, sondern beständig in seinsmäßiger Mitgeltung als Mitsubjekte, als Mitkonstituierende, und beides ist untrennbar verflochten' (Ms. C 17 36a).

48. 'Wenn Einfühlung eintritt—ist etwa auch schon die Gemeinschaft, die Intersubjektivität da und Einfühlung dann bloß enthüllendes Leisten?' (Ms. C 17 84b).

49. It must be emphasized that the relation between the three kinds of intersubjectivity is a relationship of founding. In other words: The three types are hierarchically structured but are different and irreducible kinds of transcendental intersubjectivity, each with its own special constitutive function and performance.

50. For a more detailed account of Husserl's use of Leibniz, see Cristin 1990, 163–174.

51. Schütz 1962, 167.

52. Marbach (1974, chap. 5) argues that it was exactly Husserl's insight into the necessity of construing a transcendental theory of intersubjectivity that made him abandon the nonegological theory of consciousness, which he had been advocating in *Logische Untersuchungen* (cf. Zahavi 1999b, 138–156). In a related way, Gurwitsch has claimed that his own nonegological theory of consciousness made the problem of transcendental intersubjectivity superfluous. If there is no transcendental ego, but merely an empirical one, then the relation between ego and Other must be an empirical-mundane problem (Schütz and Gurwitsch 1985, 369).

53. 'Das einzige Ich—das transzendentale. In seiner Einzigkeit setzt es "andere" einzige transzendentale Ich—als "andere", die selbst wieder in Einzigkeit Andere setzen' (Ms. B I 14 138b).

54. This proposal has been made by Fink in a number of his otherwise very knowledgeable articles about Husserl. Cf., for instance, Fink 1976, 223, as well as Fink's remarks to the English version of Schütz's article 'Das Problem der transzendentalen Intersubjektivität bei Husserl' in Schütz 1975, 86. For a more extensive criticism, see Zahavi 1994c.

55. This is also true for Heidegger (1989, 360, 377, 426) and Merleau-Ponty (1945, 428). For further investigations of Husserl's theory of intersubjectivity, see Schütz 1957; Waldenfels 1971; Held 1972; Theunissen 1977; Yamaguchi 1982; Hart 1992; Depraz 1995; Steinbock 1995; and Zahavi 1996/2001.

56. Cf. Habermas 1981, II/171–293 and Schütz and Luckmann 1979.

57. Cf. for instance Hua 4/375, 9/56.

58. Galileo 1957, 237–238.

59. Cf. Descartes 1984, II/56–57.

60. As Merleau-Ponty remarks apropos Husserl's idea concerning the inter-subjective structure of transcendental subjectivity: 'Now if the transcendental is intersubjectivity, how can the borders of the transcendental and the empirical help becoming indistinct? For along with the other person, all the other person sees of me—all my facticity—is reintegrated into subjectivity, or at least posited as an indispensable element of its definition. Thus the transcendental descends into history. Or as we might put it, the historical is no longer an external relation between two or more absolutely autonomous subjects but has an interior and is an inherent aspect of their very definition. They no longer know themselves to be subjects simply in relation to their individual selves, but in relation to one another as well' (Merleau-Ponty 1960, 134 [1964, 107]). There are many similarities between Husserl and Merleau-Ponty, and it is worth noticing that Merleau-Ponty, who already before World War II gained access to Husserl's unpublished manuscripts (cf. Van Breda 1962, 410–430), often interpreted Husserl in a way that was not in accordance with the prevailing view, as, for instance, when he claimed that Husserl took the problem of historicity more seriously than Heidegger (Merleau-Ponty 1988, 421–422). Cf. Zahavi 2002a.

61. Cf. Brand 1979, 118.

62. To give a concrete example: Our constitution of colors is not impeded by the fact that there are blind people who are unable to perceive them (Hua 1/154, 15/48). For a more extended treatment of this problem, see, for instance, the text in *Zur Phänomenologie der Intersubjektivität I*, which carries the title 'Solipsistische und intersubjektive Normalität und Konstitution von Objektivität' (Hua 13/360–385), and the two texts in *Zur Phänomenologie der Intersubjektivität III*, which are called respectively 'Die Welt der Normalen und das Problem der Beteiligung der Anomalen an der Weltkonstitution' (Hua 15/13–142) and 'Apodiktische Struktur der transzendentalen Subjektivität. Problem der transzendentalen Konstitution der Welt von der Normalität aus' (Hua 15/148–170).

63. Cf. Held 1991; Lohmar 1994; and Steinbock 1995.

64. To a certain extent Husserl's analysis resembles Heidegger's observations regarding Dasein's *being lost* in the publicness of the 'they.' Cf. Heidegger's analysis of idle talk in *Sein und Zeit* (§ 35).

65. Husserl's most well-known account of this process can be found in the third appendix to *Krisis*. Cf. Derrida's extensive commentaries to this appendix (1989).

66. Cf. Wittgenstein 1984, 290–291.

67. This does not imply that there are no apodictic truths at all, but only that everything that can be corrected are in principle open for further corrections.

68. For more extensive discussions of Husserl's concept of the lifeworld, see Derrida 1989; Claesges 1972; Aguirre 1982, 86–149; Soffer 1991; Held 1997; Bernet 1994, 93–118; and Steinbock 1995.

CONCLUSION

1. Cf. Strasser 1975, 33.
2. In Depraz and Zahavi 1998 one can find a number of contributions exemplifying this change of paradigm.

Bibliography

THE HUSSERLIANA EDITION*

The Husserliana edition is cited in the text and notes with the abbreviation 'Hua.'

Husserliana 1. *Cartesianische Meditationen und Pariser Vorträge.* Ed. Stephan Strasser. Den Haag: Martinus Nijhoff, 1950, rpt. 1973; *The Paris Lectures.* Trans. Peter Koestenbaum. The Hague: Martinus Nijhoff, 1964 (1/3–39); *Cartesian Meditations: An Introduction to Phenomenology.* Trans. Dorion Cairns. The Hague: Martinus Nijhoff, 1960 (1/43–183).

Husserliana 2. *Die Idee der Phänomenologie. Fünf Vorlesungen.* Ed. Walter Biemel. Den Haag: Martinus Nijhoff, 1950, rpt. 1973; *The Idea of Phenomenology.* Trans. William P. Alston and George Nakhnikian. The Hague: Martinus Nijhoff, 1964.

Husserliana 3, 1–2. *Ideen zu einer reinen Phänomenologie und phänomenologischen Philosophie. Erstes Buch. Allgemeine Einführung in die reine Phänomenologie.* Ed. Karl Schuhmann. Den Haag: Martinus Nijhoff, 1976; *Ideas Pertaining to a Pure Phenomenology and to a Phenomenological Philosophy. First Book. General Introduction to a Pure Phenomenology.* Trans. Fred Kersten. The Hague: Martinus Nijhoff, 1982.

Husserliana 4. *Ideen zu einer reinen Phänomenologie und phänomenologischen Philosophie. Zweites Buch. Phänomenologische Untersuchungen zur Konstitution.* Ed. Marly Biemel. The Hague: Martinus Nijhoff, 1952; *Ideas Pertaining to a Pure Phenomenology and to a Phenomenological Philosophy. Second Book. Studies in the Phenomenology of Constitution.* Trans. Richard Rojcewicz and André Schuwer. Dordrecht: Kluwer Academic Publishers, 1989.

Husserliana 5. *Ideen zu einer reinen Phänomenologie und phänomenologischen Philosophie. Drittes Buch: Die Phänomenologie und die Fundamente der Wissenschaften.*

*This list includes bibliographical information about some of the existing English translations of Husserl's writing, namely those that I have made use of in the text itself. (Thanks to Elizabeth Behnke for compiling these references.) For a full list of English Husserl translations see Steven Spileers, ed., *Husserl Bibliography.* Husserliana Dokumente 4. Dordrecht: Kluwer Academic Publishers, 1999.

Ed. Marly Biemel. The Hague: Martinus Nijhoff, 1952, rpt. 1971; *Ideas Pertaining to a Pure Phenomenology and to a Phenomenological Philosophy. Third Book. Phenomenology and the Foundations of the Sciences.* Trans. Ted E. Klein and William E. Pohl. The Hague: Martinus Nijhoff, 1980 (5/1–137); *Ideas Pertaining to a Pure Phenomenology and to a Phenomenological Philosophy. Second Book. Studies in the Phenomenology of Constitution.* Trans. Richard Rojcewicz and André Schuwer. Dordrecht: Kluwer Academic Publishers, 1989, 405–430 (5/138–162).

Husserliana 6. *Die Krisis der europäischen Wissenschaften und die transzendentale Phänomenologie. Eine Einleitung in die phänomenologische Philosophie.* Ed. Walter Biemel. The Hague: Martinus Nijhoff, 1954, rpt. 1962; *The Crisis of European Sciences and Transcendental Phenomenology: An Introduction to Phenomenological Philosophy.* Trans. David Carr. Evanston, IL: Northwestern University Press, 1970 (6/1–348, 357–386, 459–462, 473–475, 508–516).

Husserliana 7. *Erste Philosophie (1923/24). Erster Teil. Kritische Ideengeschichte.* Ed. Rudolf Boehm. The Hague: Martinus Nijhoff, 1956.

Husserliana 8. *Erste Philosophie (1923/24). Zweiter Teil. Theorie der phänomenologischen Reduktion.* Ed. Rudolf Boehm. The Hague: Martinus Nijhoff, 1959.

Husserliana 9. *Phänomenologische Psychologie. Vorlesungen Sommersemester 1925.* Ed. Walter Biemel. The Hague: Martinus Nijhoff, 1962; *Phenomenological Psychology: Lectures, Summer Semester, 1925.* Trans. John Scanlon. The Hague: Martinus Nijhoff, 1977 (9/3–234); *Psychological and Transcendental Phenomenology and the Confrontation with Heidegger (1927–1931).* Ed. and trans. Thomas Sheehan and Richard E. Palmer. Dordrecht: Kluwer Academic Publishers, 1997 (9/237–349, 517–526).

Husserliana 10. *Zur Phänomenologie des inneren Zeitbewusstseins (1893–1917).* Ed. Rudolf Boehm. The Hague: Martinus Nijhoff, 1966; *On the Phenomenology of the Consciousness of Internal Time (1893–1917).* Trans. John Barnett Brough. Dordrecht: Kluwer Academic Publishers, 1991.

Husserliana 11. *Analysen zur passiven Synthesis. Aus Vorlesungs- und Forschungsmanuskripten 1918–1926.* Ed. Margot Fleischer. The Hague: Martinus Nijhoff, 1966.

Husserliana 12. *Philosophie der Arithmetik.* Ed. Lothar Eley. The Hague: Martinus Nijhoff, 1970.

Husserliana 13. *Zur Phänomenologie der Intersubjektivität. Texte aus dem Nachlass. Erster Teil: 1905–1920.* Ed. Iso Kern. The Hague: Martinus Nijhoff, 1973.

Husserliana 14. *Zur Phänomenologie der Intersubjektivität. Texte aus dem Nachlass. Zweiter Teil: 1921–1928.* Ed. Iso Kern. The Hague: Martinus Nijhoff, 1973.

Husserliana 15. *Zur Phänomenologie der Intersubjektivität. Texte aus dem Nachlass. Dritter Teil: 1929–1935.* Ed. Iso Kern. The Hague: Martinus Nijhoff, 1973.

Husserliana 16. *Ding und Raum. Vorlesungen 1907.* Ed. Ulrich Claesges. Den Haag: Martinus Nijhoff, 1973; *Thing and Space: Lectures of 1907.* Trans. Richard Rojcewicz. Dordrecht: Kluwer Academic Publishers, 1997.

Husserliana 17. *Formale und transzendentale Logik. Versuch einer Kritik der logischen Vernunft.* Ed. Paul Janssen. The Hague: Martinus Nijhoff, 1974; *Formal and Transcendental Logic.* Trans. Dorion Cairns. The Hague: Martinus Nijhoff, 1969 (17/5–335).

Husserliana 18. *Logische Untersuchungen. Erster Band. Prolegomena zur reinen Logik.* Ed. Elmar Holenstein. The Hague: Martinus Nijhoff, 1975; *Logical Investigations.* 2 vols. Trans. J. N. Findlay. London: Routledge & Kegan Paul, 1970, 41–247.

Husserliana 19, 1–2. *Logische Untersuchungen. Zweiter Band. Untersuchungen zur Phänomenologie und Theorie der Erkenntnis.* Ed. Ursula Panzer. The Hague: Martinus Nijhoff, 1984; *Logical Investigations.* 2 vols. Trans. J. N. Findlay. London: Routledge & Kegan Paul, 1970, 248–869.

Husserliana 20. *Logische Untersuchungen. Ergänzungsband. Erster Teil.* Ed. Ullrich Melle. Dordrecht: Kluwer Academic Publishers, 2002.

Husserliana 21. *Studien zur Arithmetik und Geometrie.* Ed. Ingeborg Strohmeyer. The Hague: Martinus Nijhoff, 1983.

Husserliana 22. *Aufsätze und Rezensionen (1890–1910).* Ed. Bernhard Rang. The Hague: Martinus Nijhoff, 1979.

Husserliana 23. *Phantasie, Bildbewußtsein, Erinnerung.* Ed. Eduard Marbach. Dordrecht: Kluwer Academic Publishers, 1980.

Husserliana 24. *Einleitung in die Logik und Erkenntnistheorie. Vorlesungen 1906/07.* Ed. Ullrich Melle. Dordrecht: Martinus Nijhoff, 1984.

Husserliana 25. *Aufsätze und Vorträge (1911–1921).* Ed. Thomas Nenon and Hans Rainer Sepp. Dordrecht: Martinus Nijhoff, 1987.

Husserliana 26. *Vorlesungen über Bedeutungslehre. Sommersemester 1908.* Ed. Ursula Panzer. Dordrecht: Martinus Nijhoff, 1987.

Husserliana 27. *Aufsätze und Vorträge (1922–1937).* Ed. Thomas Nenon and Hans Rainer Sepp. Dordrecht: Kluwer Academic Publishers, 1989.

Husserliana 28. *Vorlesungen über Ethik und Wertlehre (1908–1914).* Ed. Ullrich Melle. Dordrecht: Kluwer Academic Publishers, 1988.

Husserliana 29. *Die Krisis der europäischen Wissenschaften und die transzendentale Phänomenologie. Ergänzungsband. Texte aus dem Nachlass 1934–1937.* Ed. Reinhold N. Smid. Dordrecht: Kluwer Academic Publishers, 1993.

Husserliana 30. *Logik und allgemeine Wissenschaftstheorie.* Ed. Ursula Panzer. Dordrecht: Kluwer Academic Publishers, 1996.

Husserliana 31. *Aktive Synthesen: Aus der Vorlesung 'Transzendentale Logik' 1920–21. Ergänzungsband zu 'Analysen zur passiven Synthesis.'* Ed. Roland Breeur. Dordrecht: Kluwer Academic Publishers, 2000.

Husserliana 32. *Natur und Geist. Vorlesungen Sommersemester 1927.* Ed. Michael Weiler. Dordrecht: Kluwer Academic Publishers, 2001.

Husserliana 33. *Die 'Bernauer Manuskripte' über das Zeitbewußtsein 1917/18.* Ed. Rudolf Bernet and Dieter Lohmar. Dordrecht: Kluwer Academic Publishers, 2001.

Husserliana 34. *Zur phänomenologischen Reduktion. Texte aus dem Nachlass (1926–1935).* Ed. Sebastian Luft. Dordrecht: Kluwer Academic Publishers, 2002.

In 1994 Husserl's correspondence was published:

Husserl, E. *Briefwechsel.* Husserliana Dokumente III/1–10. Ed. Karl Schuhmann and Elisabeth Schuhmann. Dordrecht: Kluwer Academic Publishers, 1994.

In 2001, Kluwer started publishing a new series of carefully edited volumes which, unlike the Husserliana edition, lack a critical apparatus and a historical and systematical introduction. So far, four volumes have appeared:

Husserliana Materialienbände 1. *Logik. Vorlesung 1896.* Ed. Elisabeth Schuhmann. Dordrecht: Kluwer Academic Publishers, 2001.
Husserliana Materialienbände 2. *Logik. Vorlesung 1902/03.* Ed. Elisabeth Schuhmann. Dordrecht: Kluwer Academic Publishers, 2001.
Husserliana Materialienbände 3. *Allgemeine Erkenntnistheorie. Vorlesung 1902/03.* Ed. Elisabeth Schuhmann. Dordrecht: Kluwer Academic Publishers, 2001.
Husserliana Materialienbände 4. *Natur und Geist. Vorlesungen Sommersemester 1919.* Ed. Michael Weiler. Dordrecht: Kluwer Academic Publishers, 2002.

The most important work by Husserl not published in the Husserliana is:

Husserl, E. *Erfahrung und Urteil.* Ed. Ludwig Landgrebe. Hamburg: Felix Meiner, 1985.

The references to the research manuscripts that are found throughout this book are all marked with the signature Ms. together with the respective designation of the manuscript, which refer to the shorthand original that can be found in the Husserl-Archives in Leuven, Belgium. (A substantial part of these manuscripts have also been transcribed, and copies of these transcriptions can be found in archives situated at the University of Cologne and the University of Freiburg im Breisgau in Germany, the New School for Social Research in New York City, Duquesne University in Pittsburgh, Pennsylvania, and Ecole Normale Supérieure in Paris.) Husserl's manuscripts have been divided into the following different categories:

A. Mundane Phenomenology
B. The Reduction
C. Time-Constitution as Formal Constitution
D. Primordial Constitution (*Urkonstitution*)
E. Intersubjective Constitution
F. Lecture Courses and Public Lectures
K. Autographs, Not Included in the Critical Inventory of 1935.
L. The Bernau Manuscripts
M. Copies of Husserl's Manuscripts in Running Hand or Typescript, Carried Out by Husserl's Assistants Earlier than 1938
N. Transcriptions

P. Manuscripts by other Authors
Q. Husserl's Notes from Lecture Courses by His Teachers
R. Letters
X. Archival Material

In this book I have made use of the following manuscripts:

A III 9 (1920–1921)	C 17 (1930–1932)
A V 5 (1933)	
	D 12 (1931)
B I 14 (1934)	D 13 (1921)
B III 12 IV (1922)	
	E III 2 (1920–1921, 1934–1936)
C 2 (1931–1932)	E III 4 (1930)
C 3 (1930–1931)	
C 7 (1932)	L I 15 (1917)
C 10 (1931)	L I 19 (1917–1918)
C 12 (no date)	L I 20 (no date, but presumably 1918)
C 16 (1931–1933)	

As general introductions to Husserl's philosophy, I can recommend:

Bernet, R.; Kern, I.; and Marbach, E. *An Introduction to Husserlian Phenomenology.* Evanston, IL: Northwestern University Press, 1993.
Dastur, F. *Husserl. Des mathématiques à l'histoire.* Paris: PUF, 1995.
Held, K. "Einleitung." In Husserl, E. *Die phänomenologische Methode: Ausgewählte Texte I*, s.5–51. Stuttgart: Reclam, 1985.
———. "Einleitung." In Husserl, E. *Phänomenologie der Lebenswelt: Ausgewählte Texte II*, s.5–53. Stuttgart: Reclam, 1986.
Sokolowski, R. *Husserlian Meditations.* Evanston, IL: Northwestern University Press, 1974.
———. *Introduction to Phenomenology.* Cambridge: Cambridge University Press, 2000.

Apart from works that have been referred to in the text, the following list also contains other classical and significant contributions to Husserl research.

Adorno, T.W. *Zur Metakritik der Erkenntnistheorie.* Frankfurt am Main: Suhrkamp, 1981.
Aguirre, A. *Genetische Phänomenologie und Reduktion.* The Hague: Martinus Nijhoff, 1970.
———. *Die Phänomenologie Husserls im Licht ihrer gegenwärtigen Interpretation und Kritik.* Darmstadt: Wissenschaftliche Buchgesellschaft, 1982.

Apel, K.-O. *Transformation der Philosophie I–II*. Frankfurt am Main: Suhrkamp, 1973.

Augustine. *The Confessions of St. Augustine*. London: Thomas Nelson and Sons, 1937.

Becker, O. *Beiträge zur phänomenologischen Begründung der Geometrie und ihrer physikalischen Anwendung*. Tübingen: Max Niemeyer, 1973.

Benoist, J. *Autour de Husserl*. Paris: Vrin, 1994.

Benoist, J. *Phénoménologie, sémantique, ontologie. Husserl et la tradition logique autrichienne*. Paris: PUF, 1997.

Bernet, R. "Bedeutung und intentionales Bewußtsein. Husserls Begriff des Bedeutungsphänomens." *Phänomenologische Forschungen* 8, 1979, 31–63.

———. "Die ungegenwärtige Gegenwart. Anwesenheit und Abwesenheit in Husserls Analyse des Zeitbewußtseins." *Phänomenologische Forschungen* 14 (1983): 16–57.

———. "Husserls Begriff des Noema." In S. IJsseling, ed., *Husserl-Ausgabe und Husserl-Forschung*. Dordrecht: Kluwer Academic Publishers, 1990, 61–80.

———. *La vie du sujet*. Paris: PUF, 1994.

Bernet, R., Kern, I., and Marbach, E. *Edmund Husserl. Darstellung seines Denkens*. Hamburg: Felix Meiner, 1989.

Biemel, W. "Die entscheidenden Phasen der Entfaltung von Husserls Philosophie." *Zeitschrift für philosophische Forschung* 13 (1959): 187–213.

Boehm, R. *Vom Gesichtspunkt der Phänomenologie*. The Hague: Martinus Nijhoff, 1968.

———. "Zur Phänomenologie der Gemeinschaft. Edmund Husserls Grundgedanken." In T. Würtenberger, ed., *Phänomenologie, Rechtsphilosophie, Jurisprudenz*, Frankfurt am Main: Suhrkamp, 1969, 1–26.

Brand, G. *Welt, Ich und Zeit. Nach unveröffentlichten Manuskripten Edmund Husserls*. The Hague: Martinus Nijhoff, 1955.

———. "Die Normalität des und der Anderen und die Anomalität einer Erfahrungs-gemeinschaft bei Edmund Husserl." In W. M. Sprondel and R. Grathoff, eds., *Alfred Schütz und die Idee des Alltags in den Sozialwissenschaften*. Stuttgart: Ferdinand Enke, 1979, 108–124.

Brentano, F. *Psychologie vom empirischen Standpunkt I–II*. Hamburg: Felix Meiner, 1924–1925.

Brough, J.B. "The Emergence of an Absolute Consciousness in Husserl's Early Writings on Time-Consciousness." *Man and World* 5 (1972): 298–326.

———. "Temporality and the Presence of Language: Reflections on Husserl's Phenomenology of Time-consciousness." In A. Schuwer, eds., *Phenomenology of Temporality: Time and Language*. Pittsburgh, PA: Duquesne University Press, 1987, 1–31.

———. "Husserl and the Deconstruction of Time." *Review of Metaphysics* 46 (1993): 503–536.

Bruzina, R. "Solitude and Community in the Work of Philosophy: Husserl and Fink." *Man and World* 22 (1989): 287–314.

Cairns, D. *Conversations with Husserl and Fink.* The Hague: Martinus Nijhoff, 1976.

Carr, D. "The 'Fifth Meditation' and Husserl's Cartesianism." *Philosophy and Phenomenological Research* 34 (1973): 14–35.

————. *The Paradox of Subjectivity. The Self in the Transcendental Tradition.* Oxford: Oxford University Press, 1999.

Claesges, U. *Edmund Husserls Theorie der Raumkonstitution.* The Hague: Martinus Nijhoff, 1964.

————. "Zweideutigkeiten in Husserls Lebenswelt-Begriff." In U. Claesges and K. Held, eds., *Perspektiven transzendentalphänomenologischer Forschung.* The Hague: Martinus Nijhoff, 1972, 85–101.

Cobb-Stevens, R. *Husserl and Analytical Philosophy.* Dordrecht: Kluwer, 1990.

Cristin, R. "Phänomenologie und Monadologie. Husserl und Leibniz." *Studia Leibnitiana* XXII/2 (1990): 163–174.

Dastur, F. *Husserl. Des mathématiques à l'histoire.* Paris: PUF, 1995.

De Boer, T. *The Development of Husserl's Thought.* The Hague: Martinus Nijhoff, 1978.

Depraz, N. *Transcendance et incarnation. Le statut de l'intersubjectivité comme altérité à soi chez Husserl.* Paris: Vrin, 1995.

Depraz, N., and Zahavi, D., eds., *Alterity and Facticity. New Perspectives on Husserl.* Dordrecht: Kluwer, 1998.

Derrida, J. *La voix et le phénomène. Introduction au problème du signe dans la phénoménologie de Husserl.* Paris: PUF, 1967a.

————. *L'écriture et la différence.* Paris: Éditions du Seuil, 1967b.

————. *Edmund Husserl's 'Origin of Geometry'—An Introduction.* Lincoln: University of Nebraska Press, 1989.

Descartes, R. *The Philosophical Writings of Descartes I–II.* J. Cottingham, R. Stoothoff and D. Murdoch, eds., Cambridge: Cambridge University Press, 1984.

Diemer, A. *Edmund Husserl—Versuch einer systematischen Darstellung seiner Phänomenologie.* Meisenheim am Glan: Anton Hain, 1965.

Dreyfus, H.L., and Hall, H., eds., *Husserl, Intentionality and Cognitive Science.* Cambridge, MA: MIT Press, 1982.

Dreyfus, H.L. "Introduction." In H.L. Dreyfus and H. Hall, eds., *Husserl, Intentionality and Cognitive Science.* Cambridge, MA: MIT Press, 1982, 1–27.

————. "Husserl's Perceptual *Noema.*" In H.L. Dreyfus, and H. Hall, eds., *Husserl, Intentionality and Cognitive Science.* Cambridge, MA: MIT Press, 1982, 97–123.

————. "Husserl's Epiphenomenology." In H.R. Otto and J.A. Tuedio, eds., *Perspectives on Mind.* Dordrecht: D. Reidel, 1988, 85–104.

————. *Being-in-the-World.* Cambridge, MA: MIT Press, 1991.

Drummond, J.J. "Husserl on the Ways to the Performance of the Reduction." *Man and World* 8 (1975): 47–69.

————. *Husserlian Intentionality and Non-Foundational Realism.* Dordrecht: Kluwer, 1990.

————. "An Abstract Consideration: De-ontologizing the Noema." In J.J. Drummond and L. Embree, eds., *The Phenomenology of the Noema*, 89–109. Dordrecht: Kluwer Academic Publishers, 1992.

Duval, R. *Temps et vigilance.* Paris: Vrin, 1990.

Fink, E. "Die phänomenologische Philosophie Edmund Husserls in der gegenwärtigen Kritik." *Kantstudien* 38 (1933): 319–383; "The Phenomenological Philosophy of Edmund Husserl and Contemporary Criticism." In R.O. Elveton, ed., *The Phenomenology of Husserl: Selected Critical Readings.* Chicago: Quadrangle Books, 1970, 74–147; 2nd ed., Seattle: Noesis Press, 2000, 70–139.

————. "Das Problem der Phänomenologie Edmund Husserls." *Revue Internationale de Philosophie 1* (1939): 226–270.

————. "Operative Begriffe in Husserls Phänomenologie." *Zeitschrift für philosophische Forschung* 11 (1957): 321–337.

————. *Studien zur Phänomenologie. 1930–1939.* The Hague: Martinus Nijhoff, 1966.

————. *Nähe und Distanz.* Munich: Karl Alber, 1976.

————. *VI. Cartesianische Meditation I–II.* Dordrecht: Kluwer, 1988a&b.

Fisette, D. *Lecture frégéenne de la phénoménologie.* Combas: L'éclat, 1994.

Franck, D. *Chair et Corps. Sur la phénoménologie de Husserl.* Paris: Les Éditions de Minuit, 1981.

Føllesdal, D. "Husserl's Notion of Noema." *Journal of Philosophy* 66 (1969): 680–687.

Gadamer, H.-G. "Die phänomenologische Bewegung." *Kleine Schriften III.* Tübingen: J.C.B. Mohr, 1972, 150–189.

Galileo. *Discoveries and Opinions of Galileo.* Transl. by S. Drake. New York: Anchor House, 1957.

Gallagher, S. "Hyletic Experience and the Lived Body." *Husserl Studies* 3 (1986): 131–166.

Gibson, H.J.J. *The Ecological Approach to Visual Perception.* Hillsdale, N.J.: Lawrence Erlbaum Associates, 1979.

Gorner, P. "Husserl's 'Logische Untersuchungen.'" *Journal of the British Society for Phenomenology* III/2 (1972): 187–194.

Gurwitsch, A. *Studies in Phenomenology and Psychology.* Evanston, IL: Northwestern University Press, 1966.

Habermas, J. *Theorie des kommunikativen Handelns I–II.* Frankfurt am Main: Suhrkamp, 1981.

————. *Der philosophische Diskurs der Moderne.* Frankfurt am Main: Suhrkamp, 1985.

Hall, H. "Was Husserl a Realist or an Idealist?" In H.L. Dreyfus and H. Hall, eds., *Husserl, Intentionality and Cognitive Science.* Cambridge, MA: MIT Press, 1982, 169–190.

Hart, J.G. "Constitution and Reference in Husserl's Phenomenology of Phenomenology." *Husserl Studies* 6 (1989): 43–72.

————. *The Person and the Common Life*. Dordrecht Kluwer, 1992.

————. "A Precis of an Husserlian Philosophical Theology." In S. Laycock and J.G. Hart, eds., *Essays in Philosophical Theology*. Albany: State University of New York Press, 1986, 89–168.

Heidegger, M. *Logik*. Frankfurt am Main: Vittorio Klostermann, 1976.

————. *Prolegomena zur Geschichte des Zeitbegriffs*. Frankfurt am Main: Vittorio Klostermann, 1979; *History of the Concept of Time: Prolegomena*. Trans. Theodore Kisiel. Bloomington, IN: Indiana University Press, 1985.

————. *Sein und Zeit*. Tübingen: Max Niemeyer, 1986; *Being and Time*. Trans. Joan Stambaugh. Albany: State University of New York Press, 1996.

————. *Die Grundprobleme der Phänomenologie*. Frankfurt am Main: Vittorio Klostermann, 1989; *The Basic Problems of Phenomenology*. Trans. Albert Hofstadter. Bloomington, IN: Indiana University Press, 1982.

Held, K. *Lebendige Gegenwart*. The Hague: Martinus Nijhoff, 1966.

————. "Das Problem der Intersubjektivität und die Idee einer phänomenologischen Transzendentalphilosophie." In U. Claesges and K. Held, eds., *Perspektiven transzendentalphänomenologischer Forschung*. The Hague: Martinus Nijhoff, 1972, 3–60.

————. "Einleitung." In E. Husserl, *Die phänomenologische Methode: Ausgewählte Texte I*. Stuttgart: Reclam, 1985, 5–51.

————. "Einleitung." In E. Husserl, *Phänomenologie der Lebenswelt: Ausgewählte Texte II*. Stuttgart: Reclam, 1986, 5–53.

————. "Heimwelt, Fremdwelt, die eine Welt." *Phänomenologische Forschungen* 24/25 (1991): 305–337.

Henry, M. *Phénoménologie matérielle*. Paris: PUF, 1990.

Holenstein, E. "Passive Genesis: Eine begriffsanalytische Studie." *Tijdskrift voor Filosofie* 33 (1971): 112–153.

————. *Phänomenologie der Assoziation: Zu Struktur und Funktion eines Grundprinzips der passiven Genesis bei E. Husserl*. The Hague: Martinus Nijhoff, 1972.

Hutcheson, P. "Husserl's Problem of Intersubjectivity." *Journal of the British Society for Phenomenology* 11 (1980): 144–162.

Kant, I. *Kritik der reinen Vernunft*. Hamburg: Felix Meiner, 1956.

Kern, I. "Die drei Wege zur transzendentalphänomenologischen Reduktion in der Philosophie Edmund Husserls." *Tijdskrift voor Filosofie* 24 (1962): 303–349.

————. *Husserl und Kant*. The Hague: Martinus Nijhoff, 1964.

————. *Idee und Methode der Philosophie*. Berlin: De Gruyter, 1975.

————. "Selbstbewußtsein und Ich bei Husserl." In G. Funke, ed., *Husserl-Symposion Mainz 1988*. Mainz: Akademie der Wissenschaften und der Literatur, 1989, 51–63.

Klausen, S.H. "Husserl og den moderne sprogfilosofi." In D. Zahavi, ed., *Subjektivitet og Livsverden i Husserls Fænomenologi.* Aarhus: Modtryk, 1994, 31–52.

Lakoff, G. *Women, Fire, and Dangerous Things.* Chicago: University of Chicago Press, 1987.

Landgrebe, L. *Der Weg der Phänomenologie. Das Problem der ursprünglichen Erfahrung.* Gütersloh: Gerd Mohn, 1963.

————. *Phänomenologie und Geschichte.* Gütersloh: Gerd Mohn, 1968.

————. *Faktizität und Individuation.* Hamburg: Felix Meiner, 1982.

Lee, N. *Edmund Husserls Phänomenologie der Instinkte.* Dordrecht: Kluwer, 1993.

Lenkowski, W.J. "What Is Husserl's Epoche?: The Problem of Beginning of Philosophy in a Husserlian Context." *Man and World* 11 (1978): 299–323.

Lévinas, E. *Le temps et l'autre.* Paris: PUF, 1983.

————. *Théorie de l'intuition dans la phénoménologie de Husserl.* Paris: Vrin, 1989.

Lohmar, D. "Hjemverdenens ethos og den overnationale etik." In D. Zahavi, eds., *Subjektivitet og Livsverden i Husserls Fænomenologi.* Aarhus: Modtryk, 1994, 123–144.

Marbach, E. *Das Problem des Ich in der Phänomenologie Husserls.* The Hague: Nijhoff, 1974.

Meist, K.R. "Monadologische Intersubjektivität. Zum Konstitutionsproblem von Welt und Geschichte bei Husserl." *Zeitschrift für philosophische Forschung* 34 (1980): 561–589.

————. "Die Zeit der Geschichte. Probleme in Husserls transzendentaler Begründung einer Theorie der Geschichte." *Phänomenologische Forschungen* 14 (1983): 58–110.

————. "Intersubjektivität zwischen Natur und Geschichte. Einige Anmerkungen über Probleme einer transzendentalen Letztbegründung." *Phänomenologische Forschungen* 24/25 (1991): 265–304.

Melle, U. *Das Wahrnehmungsproblem und seine Verwandlung in phänomenologischer Einstellung.* The Hague: Martinus Nijhoff, 1983.

————. "Objektivierende und nicht-Objektivierende Akte." In S. IJsseling, ed., *Husserl-Ausgabe und Husserl-Forschung.* Dordrecht: Kluwer, 1990, 35–49.

Merleau-Ponty, M. *Phénoménologie de la perception.* Paris: Gallimard, 1945; *Phenomenology of Perception.* Trans. Colin Smith. London: Routledge & Kegan Paul, 1962.

————. *Signes.* Gallimard, Paris 1960; *Signs.* Trans. Richard C. McCleary. Evanston, IL: Northwestern University Press, 1964.

————. *Le visible et l'invisible.* Paris: Tel Gallimard, 1964.

————. *Merleau-Ponty à la Sorbonne.* Paris: Cynara, 1988.

Mishara, A. "Husserl and Freud: Time, Memory and the Unconscious." *Husserl Studies* 7 (1990): 29–58.

Mohanty, J.N. *Edmund Husserl's Theory of Meaning.* The Hague: Martinus Nijhoff, 1964.

———. *The Concept of Intentionality*. St. Louis, MO: Warren H. Green, 1972.

———. "Husserl and Frege: A New Look at Their Relationship." In J.N. Mohanty, ed., *Readings on Edmund Husserl's Logical Investigations*. The Hague: Martinus Nijhoff, 1977, 22–32.

Montavont, A. "Passivité et non-donation." *Alter* 1 (1993): 131–148.

———. "Le phénomène de l'affection dans les *Analysen zur passiven Synthesis* (1918–1926) de Husserl." *Alter* 2 (1994): 119–140.

Olesen, S.G. "Variation." *Analecta Husserliana* 34 (1991): 129–138.

Prufer, T. "Heidegger, Early and Late, and Aquinas." In R. Sokolowski, ed., *Edmund Husserl and the Phenomenological Tradition*. Washington, DC: Catholic University of America Press, 1988, 197–215.

Putnam, H. *Meaning and the Moral Sciences*. Oxford: Routledge & Kegan Paul, 1978.

———. *Representation and Reality*. Cambridge, MA: MIT Press, 1988.

Rabanaque, L.R. "Passives Noema und die analytische Interpretation," *Husserl Studies* 10 (1993): 65–80.

Rang, B. *Kausalität und Motivation*. The Hague: Martinus Nijhoff, 1973.

———. "Repräsentation und Selbstgegebenheit." *Phänomenologische Forschungen* 1 (1975): 105–137.

Ricoeur, P. *Temps et récit. 3. Le temps raconté*. Paris: Éditions du Seuil, 1985.

———. "Phenomenology and Hermeneutics." In J.B. Thompson, ed., *Hermeneutics and the Human Sciences*. Cambridge: Cambridge University Press, 1981.

Rohr-Dietschi, U. *Zur Genese des Selbstbewußtseins*. Berlin: De Gruyter, 1974.

Rorty, R. *Philosophy and the Mirror of Nature*. Oxford: Blackwell, 1980.

Rosen, K. *Evidenz in Husserls deskriptiver Transzendentalphilosophie*. Meisenheim am Glan: Anton Hain, 1977.

Sartre, J.-P. *L'être et le néant*. Paris: Gallimard, 1943.

Schuhmann, K. *Husserl-Chronik. Denk- und Lebensweg Edmund Husserls*. The Hague: Martinus Nijhoff, 1977.

———. *Husserls Staatsphilosophie*. Freiburg: Karl Alber, 1988.

Schütz, A. "Das Problem der transzendentalen Intersubjektivität bei Husserl." *Philosophische Rundschau* 5 (1957): 81–107.

———. *Collected Papers I*. The Hague: Martinus Nijhoff, 1962.

———. *Collected Papers III*. The Hague: Martinus Nijhoff, 1975.

Schütz, A., and Gurwitsch, A. *Briefwechsel 1939–1959*. Munich: Wilhelm Fink, 1985.

Schütz, A., and Luckmann, T. *Strukturen der Lebenswelt*. Frankfurt am Main: Suhrkamp, 1979.

Seebohm, T. *Die Bedingungen der Möglichkeit der Transzendentalphilosophie*. Bonn: Bouvier, 1962.

Smith, D.W., and McIntyre, R. "Husserl's Identification of Meaning and Noema." *Monist* 59 (1975): 115–132.

————. "Indexical Sense and Reference." *Synthese* 49 (1981): 101–127.

Smith, D.W., and McIntyre, R. *Husserl and Intentionality*. Dordrecht: D. Reidel, 1982.

Smith, D.W. "Husserl on Demonstrative Reference and Perception." In H.L. Dreyfus and H. Hall, eds., *Husserl, Intentionality and Cognitive Science*. Cambridge, MA: MIT Press, 1982a, 193–213.

————. "What's the Meaning of 'This'?" *Nous* XVI/2 (1982b): 181–208.

————. "Content and Context of Perception." *Synthese* 61 (1984): 61–87.

————. *The Circle of Acquaintance*. Dordrecht: Kluwer, 1989.

Soffer, G. *Husserl and the Question of Relativism*. Dordrecht: Kluwer, 1991.

Sokolowski, R. "The Logic of Parts and Wholes in Husserl's 'Investigations.'" *Philosophy and Phenomenological Research* 28 (1967–1968): 537–553.

————. *The Formation of Husserl's Concept of Constitution*. The Hague: Martinus Nijhoff, 1970.

————. "The Structure and Content of Husserl's Logical Investigations." *Inquiry* 12 (1971): 318–347.

————. *Husserlian Meditations*. Evanston, IL: Northwestern University Press, 1974.

————. *Presence and Absence*. Bloomington: Indiana University Press, 1978.

————. "Intentional Analysis and the Noema." *Dialectica* 38 (1984): 113–129.

————. "Husserl and Frege." *The Journal of Philosophy* 84 (1987): 521–528.

————. *Pictures, Quotations, and Distinctions*. Notre Dame, IN: University of Notre Dame Press, 1992.

————. *Introduction to Phenomenology*. Cambridge: Cambridge University Press, 2000.

Steinbock, A. *Home and Beyond. Generative Phenomenology after Husserl*. Evanston, IL: Northwestern University Press, 1995.

Stern, D. *The Interpersonal World of the Infant*. New York: Basic Books, 1985.

Stevenson, L. *Seven Theories of Human Nature*. Oxford: Clarendon Press, 1974.

Strasser, S. "Grundgedanken der Sozialontologie Edmund Husserls." *Zeitschrift für philosophische Forschung* 29 (1975): 3–33.

————. "Monadologie und Teleologie in der Philosophie Edmund Husserls." *Phänomenologische Forschungen* 22 (1989): 217–235.

Ströker, E. "Husserls Evidenzprinzip. Sinn und Grenzen einer methodischen Norm der Phänomenologie als Wissenschaft." *Zeitschrift für philosophische Forschung* 32 (1978): 3–30.

————. *Husserls transzendentale Phänomenologie*. Frankfurt am Main: Vittorio Klostermann, 1987.

Theunissen, M. *Der Andere*. Berlin: Walter de Gruyter, 1977.

Toulemont, R. *L'Essence de la Sociéte selon Husserl*. Paris: PUF, 1962.

Towarnicki, F.D. *À la rencontre de Heidegger. Souvenirs d'un messager de la Forêt-Noire*. Paris: Éditions Gallimard, 1993.

Tugendhat, E. *Der Wahrheitsbegriff bei Husserl und Heidegger*. Berlin: Walter de Gruyter, 1970.

Twardowski, K. *Zur Lehre vom Inhalt und Gegenstand der Vorstellungen*. Vienna: Philosophia Verlag, 1982.

Van Breda, H.L. "Die Rettung von Husserls Nachlaß und die Gründung des Husserl-Archivs." In H.L. Van Breda and J. Taminiaux, eds., *Husserl und das Denken der Neuzeit*. The Hague: Martinus Nijhoff, 1959, 1–41.

Van Breda, H.L. "Maurice Merleau-Ponty et les Archives-Husserl à Louvain." *Revue de métaphysique et de morale* 67 (1962): 410–430.

Waldenfels, B. *Das Zwischenreich des Dialogs: Sozialphilosophische Untersuchungen in Anschluss an Edmund Husserl*. The Hague: Martinus Nijhoff, 1971.

———. "Erfahrung des Fremden in Husserls Phänomenologie." *Phänomenologische Forschungen* 22 (1989): 39–62.

Wittgenstein, L. *Werkausgabe I*. Frankfurt am Main: Suhrkamp, 1984.

Yamaguchi, I. *Passive Synthesis und Intersubjektivität bei Edmund Husserl*. The Hague: Martinus Nijhoff, 1982.

Zahavi, D. *Intentionalität und Konstitution. Eine Einführung in Husserls Logische Untersuchungen*. Copenhagen: Museum Tusculanum Press, 1992a.

———. "Constitution and Ontology. Some Remarks on Husserl's Ontological Position in the *Logical Investigations*." *Husserl Studies* 9 (1992b): 111–124.

———. "Intentionality and the Representative Theory of Perception." *Man and World* 27 (1994a): 37–47.

———, ed., *Subjektivitet og Livsverden i Husserls Fænomenologi*. Aarhus: Modtryk, 1994b.

———. "The Self-Pluralisation of the Primal Life. A Problem in Fink's Husserl-interpretation." *Recherches husserliennes* 2 (1994c): 3–18.

———. *Husserl und die transzendentale Intersubjektivität. Eine Antwort auf die sprachpragmatische Kritik*. Dordrecht: Kluwer, 1996.

———. "Horizontal Intentionality and Transcendental Intersubjectivity." *Tijdschrift voor Filosofie* 59/2 (1997): 304–321.

———. "Self-awareness and Affection." In N. Depraz and D. Zahavi, eds., *Alterity and Facticity. New Perspectives on Husserl*. Dordrecht: Kluwer, 1998a, 205–228.

———. "The Fracture in Self-awareness." In D. Zahavi, ed., *Self-awareness, Temporality and Alterity*. Dordrecht: Kluwer, 1998b, 21–40.

Zahavi, D. and Parnas, J. "Phenomenal Consciousness and Self-awareness. A Phenomenological Critique of Representational Theory." *Journal of Consciousness Studie* 5/5–6 (1998c): 687–705.

Zahavi, D. "Brentano and Husserl on Self-awareness." *Études Phénoménologiques* 27–28 (1998d): 127–168.

———. "Michel Henry and the Phenomenology of the Invisible," *Continental Philosophy Review* 32/3 (1999a): 223–240.

————. *Self-awareness and Alterity. A Phenomenological Investigation.* Evanston, IL: Northwestern University Press, 1999b.

————. "Self and Consciousness." In D. Zahavi, ed., *Exploring the Self.* Amsterdam, Philadelphia: John Benjamins, 2000, 55–74.

————. *Husserl and Transcendental Intersubjectivity. A response to the Linguistic-Pragmatic Critique.* Trans. Elizabeth A. Behnke. Athens: Ohio University Press, 2001.

————. "Merleau-Ponty on Husserl. A Reappraisal." In L. Embree and T. Toadvine, eds., *Merleau-Ponty's Reading of Husserl.* Dordrecht: Kluwer Academic Publishers, 2002a, 3–29.

————. "Husserl's Metaphysical Neutrality in Logische Untersuchungen." In D. Zahavi and F. Stjernfelt, eds., *One Hundred Years of Phenomenology. Husserl's Logical Investigations Revisited.* Dordrecht: Kluwer Academic Publishers, 2002b, 93–108.

Zahavi, D., and Stjernfelt, F., eds. *One Hundred Years of Phenomenology. Husserl's Logical Investigations Revisited.* Dordrecht: Kluwer Academic Publishers, 2002c.

Index

Cultural Memory | *in the Present*

Martin Stokhof, *World and Life as One: Ethics and Ontology in Wittgenstein's Early Thought*

Gianni Vattimo, *Nietzsche: An Introduction*

Jacques Derrida, *Negotiations: Interventions and Interviews, 1971-1998*, ed. Elizabeth Rottenberg

Brett Levinson, *The Ends of Literature: Post-transition and Neoliberalism in the Wake of the "Boom"*

Timothy J. Reiss, *Against Autonomy: Global Dialectics of Cultural Exchange*

Hent de Vries and Samuel Weber, eds., *Religion and Media*

Niklas Luhmann, *Theories of Distinction: Re-Describing the Descriptions of Modernity*, ed. and introd. William Rasch

Johannes Fabian, *Anthropology with an Attitude: Critical Essays*

Michel Henry, *I am the Truth: Toward a Philosophy of Christianity*

Gil Anidjar, *"Our Place in Al-Andalus": Kabbalah, Philosophy, Literature in Arab-Jewish Letters*

Hélène Cixous and Jacques Derrida, *Veils*

F. R. Ankersmit, *Historical Representation*

F. R. Ankersmit, *Political Representation*

Elissa Marder, *Dead Time: Temporal Disorders in the Wake of Modernity (Baudelaire and Flaubert)*

Reinhart Koselleck, *The Practice of Conceptual History: Timing History, Spacing Concepts*

Niklas Luhmann, *The Reality of the Mass Media*

Hubert Damisch, *A Childhood Memory by Piero della Francesca*

Hubert Damisch, *A Theory of /Cloud/: Toward a History of Painting*

Jean-Luc Nancy, *The Speculative Remark (One of Hegel's bon mots)*

Jean-François Lyotard, *Soundproof Room: Malraux's Anti-Aesthetics*

Andrew Baruch Wachtel, *Making a Nation, Breaking a Nation: Literature and Cultural Politics in Yugoslavia*

Niklas Luhmann, *Love as Passion: The Codification of Intimacy*

Mieke Bal, ed., *The Practice of Cultural Analysis: Exposing Interdisciplinary Interpretation*

Jacques Derrida and Gianni Vattimo, eds., *Religion*